The Floating
Pool Lady

For Larry—
the wind in my sails,
the rudder to steer me, and
the keel to keep me centered

The Floating Pool Lady

A Quest to Bring a Public Pool to New York City's Waterfront

ANN L. BUTTENWIESER

THREE HILLS

an imprint of Cornell University Press

ITHACA AND LONDON

First published 2021 by Cornell University Press
Printed in the United States of America

Library of Congress Cataloging-in-Publication Data
Names: Buttenwieser, Ann L., 1935- author.
Title: The Floating Pool Lady : a quest to bring a public pool to New York
    City's waterfront / Ann L. Buttenwieser.
Description: Ithaca [New York] : Three Hills, an imprint of Cornell
    University Press, 2021. | Includes bibliographical references and index.
Identifiers: LCCN 2020040005 (print) | LCCN 2020040006 (ebook) | ISBN
    9781501716010 (hardcover) | ISBN 9781501716027 (epub) | ISBN
    9781501716034 (pdf)
Subjects: LCSH: Floating Pool Lady (Barge)--History. | Swimming
    pools--Social aspects--New York (State)--New York. | Public baths--New
    York (State)--New York--History.
Classification: LCC GV838.53.S85 B87 2021 (print) | LCC GV838.53.S85
    (ebook) | DDC 797.2009747/1--dc23
LC record available at https://lccn.loc.gov/2020040005
LC ebook record available at https://lccn.loc.gov/2020040006

Cover and interior design by Michael J. Walsh

Contents

Acronyms and Abbreviations

ABS	American Bureau of Shipping
ACOE	United States Army Corps of Engineers
BB Park Conservancy	Brooklyn Bridge Park Conservancy (originally Brooklyn Bridge Park Coalition)
BB Park Corporation	Brooklyn Bridge Park Development Corporation
BOE	New York City Board of Estimate and Apportionment
CB	community board
CBC	Citizens Budget Commission
CGL	commercial general liability
CSO	combined sewer outfall
Coast Guard	United States Coast Guard
DCP	New York City Department of City Planning
DD	New York City Department of Docks

DEC	New York State Department of Environmental Conservation
DEP	New York City Department of Environmental Protection
DOH	New York City Department of Health
DOT	New York City Department of Transportation
DPW	New York City Department of Public Works
EDC	New York City Economic Development Corporation
ESDC	Empire State Development Corporation
FEMA	Federal Emergency Management Agency
LDC	Brooklyn Waterfront Local Development Corporation
MBP	Manhattan borough president
MTA	Metropolitan Transportation Authority
MWA	Metropolitan Waterfront Alliance
NJDEP	New Jersey State Department of Environmental Protection
P&I	protection and indemnity
Parks Department	New York City Department of Parks and Recreation
PDC	Public Development Corporation
Port Authority	Port Authority of New York and New Jersey
RFEI	request for expressions of interest
RFP	request for proposals
UDC	New York State Urban Development Corporation

Members of the Floating Pool Crew

NYC CREW

Adrian Benepe, Commissioner, New York City Department of Parks, 2002–12

Michael Bloomberg, Mayor of New York City, 2002–14

Bill de Blasio, Mayor of New York City, 2014–present*

Daniel Doctoroff, Deputy Mayor for Economic Development and Rebuilding, 2002–8

Liam Kavanagh, First Deputy Commissioner, New York City Department of Parks, 2002–present*

Joshua Laird, Director of Planning; Assistant Commissioner for Planning and Parklands, New York City Department of Parks, 1997–2013

Robert Moses, Commissioner, New York City Department of Parks, 1934–60

* Office held as of the writing of this book.

Mitchell Silver, Commissioner, New York City Department of Parks, 2014–present*

Henry J. Stern, Commissioner, New York City Department of Parks, 1983–90, 1994–2000

David Yassky, Member, New York City Council, 2002–9

NYS CREW

Richard Dorado, Senior Counsel, Empire State Development Corporation

Udo Drescher, Assistant Regional Attorney for New York State Department of Environmental Conservation, Region 2

Pat Foye, Downstate Chairman, Empire State Development Corporation, 2007–8

Pete Grannis, Commissioner, New York State Department of Environmental Conservation, 2007–10

Stuart Gruskin, Executive Deputy Commissioner, New York State Department of Environmental Conservation, 2007–10; Staff of New York State Department of Environmental Conservation, Region 2, 2000–2007

Rose Keville, Consultant to the Empire State Development Corporation and the Brooklyn Bridge Park Development Corporation, 2007

Marianna Koval, Executive Director, Brooklyn Bridge Park Coalition (renamed Brooklyn Bridge Park Conservancy), 1998–2009

Wendy Leventer, President, Brooklyn Bridge Park Development Corporation, 2004–7

Suzanne Mattei, Director, New York State Department of Environmental Conservation, Region 2, 2007–10

* Office held as of the writing of this book.

Regina Myer, President, Brooklyn Bridge Park Development Corporation (renamed Brooklyn Bridge Park Corporation), 2007–16

Jennifer Rimmer, Vice President for Subsidiary Development, Brooklyn Bridge Park Development Corporation, 2007–9

Avi Schick, President and Chief Operating Officer, Empire State Development Corporation, 2007–9

Eliot Spitzer, Governor of New York State, 2007–8

HOBOKEN CREW

Jack Carbone, Attorney

Robert Drasheff, Director, Waterfront Development

L. Michael Krieger, Port Authority of New York and New Jersey: Manager, Hoboken Waterfront Development, and General Manager, Regional and Economic Development; Hoboken: Special Waterfront Counsel

David Roberts, Mayor of Hoboken, 2001–9

Anthony Russo, Mayor of Hoboken, 1993–2001

Cassandra Wilday, Landscape Architect

TEAM NEPTUNE

Kent Barwick, Neptune Board Member

Lawrence B. Buttenwieser, Neptune Board Member

Svein Christofferson, Maritime Attorney, Holland & Knight

Carter Craft, Metropolitan Waterfront Alliance

Steven Crainer, Attorney, Rosenman & Colin; Seyfarth Shaw

Charles Cushing, Naval Engineer, C. R. Cushing & Company

John Keenan, Insurance Agent, Keenan Marine Insurance Agency

Jonathan Kirschenfeld, Architect, Jonathan Kirschenfeld Architect, PC

Malcolm McLaren, Maritime Engineer, McLaren Engineering Group

Kent Merrill, Naval Architect and Marine Engineer, Project Manager, C. R. Cushing & Company

Johann Mordhorst, Associate, Jonathan Kirschenfeld Consultants

Steven Sivak, Construction Manager

Brian Starer, Attorney, Holland & Knight

Tillett Lighting, Lighting Consultants

Joe Tortorella, Engineer, Robert Sillman Associates, Structural Engineers

Joel Trace, Architect, Swimming Pool Consultant

Truax & Company, Translucent Murals

OTHERS

Eric Bernholz, Chief, United States Coast Guard Inspections Division

Edith K. Ehrman, Benefactor

Stephen Kass, Senior Environmental Counsel, Carter Ledyard & Milburn

Steve Kass, President, American Leisure Corp.

Lillian Liburdi (Borrone), Director of Port Commerce, Port Authority of New York and New Jersey

Joe Mizzi, President, Sciame Construction Company

Frank Sciame, Chairman/CEO, Sciame Construction Company

Paul Seck, Landscape Architect, Michael Van Valkenburgh Associates

The Floating
Pool Lady

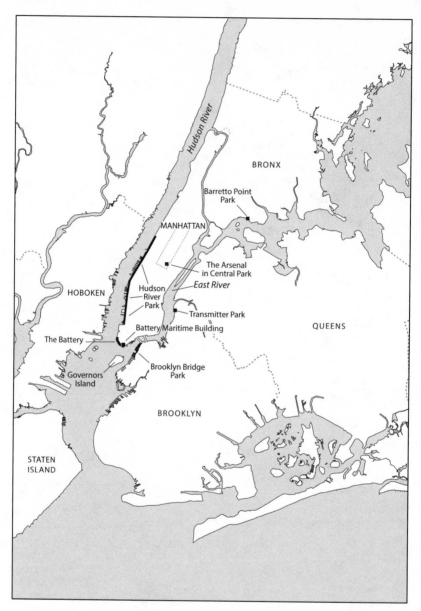

MAP 1. New York City and New Jersey's Hudson River Waterfront. Courtesy of William Nelson.

Prologue

SWIM, ANNIE, SWIM!

THE LATE AUTUMN DAY was brisk. A wind off the Chesapeake Bay ruffled the sparse hairs on the balding heads of a group of middle-aged men who were comfortably ensconced on the yacht *Daniel*, out for a relaxing day of fishing. Clad in windbreakers and with Cuban cigars dangling from their lips, each one had a whiskey neat in one hand and in the other a rod with a worm-baited hook that bobbed in the salty, tidal waters below. The men paid scant heed to the motherless little girl on board.

Huddled against the cold in the open cabin, I—a seven-year-old girl my father's friends and colleagues knew as Annie—was totally bored. The "crew" consisted of my father, Isador Lubin, then a special adviser to President Franklin D. Roosevelt; Leon Henderson, head of the federal Office of Price Administration; and various hangers-on. Missing were women. Myrlie Henderson, Leon's wife, was at home on the upper bank of the river caring for their four-year-old son. Ann Shumaker Lubin, my mother, had died giving birth to me.

I rose from the hard, wooden bench that formed a horseshoe around the floor of the sunken, open cabin and decided to absent myself from discussions of perch, eels, and the Consumer Price Index. Climbing onto the gunwale, I didn't see the fishing rod leaning against the step that gave access to the *Daniel's* bow. I tripped and fell fully clothed into the South River.

My socks and sneakers quickly became waterlogged, and their sodden weight pulled me down into the chilly water. I expected speedy salvation in the form of one of the men diving overboard and swimming over to save me, but instead they just tossed me a small, white life preserver, which fell just out of the reach of my thrashing arms. "Swim, Annie, swim!" the chorus of observers shouted through cupped hands.

And swim I did.

SIXTY-FOUR YEARS LATER, on July 3, 2007, the *Floating Pool Lady*—length 250 feet, width 76 feet, and weighing 2,540 tons—opened to the public on Brooklyn's East River Waterfront. Sunken into her deck was a seven-lane, half-Olympic-size swimming pool filled with water clear enough to see multiple dents on her bright blue metal bottom from her former career as an industrial barge. A few dozen children lined the concrete-paver edge, waiting excitedly for the speeches to be over and the signal to jump in. I stood at a microphone surrounded by the parks commissioner, local politicians, community activists, and a reporter and spoke: "Normally it takes nine months to gestate and give birth. My baby took twenty-seven years."

This book is the story of those twenty-seven years, an adventure that began with my love of the waterfront and my singular passion: to build a floating pool and donate it to the city for use by recreationally underserved New Yorkers. A team of professionals, many of whom worked long hours without extra recompense, helped me turn my passion into a physical reality. City, state, and federal officials and countless other individuals gave the political, financial, and moral support that led to the July opening. The path from dream to reality was far from linear. Yet I was compulsively engaged and could not turn away.

Several themes emerge as I trace the steps from my discovery of the Progressive Era's nineteenth-century floating baths and my first nearly adversarial meeting with a community board to securing a barge to contain the pool; financing the project and designing and refitting the vessel; and finally, finding a berth, a willing operator, and an insurer. These themes—the long time it can take from conception to implementation of an individual citizen's idea; the lack of receptiveness on the part of agents from the city and state to a perceived "outsider"; the labyrinth of jurisdictions and parties whose approval must be secured, and prioritizing those approvals; the importance of having a dedicated, loyal team and personal contacts; and the number of built-in unknowns, particularly for innovative projects—all reveal both the pleasant and unpleasant details of the sausage-making process called public engagement.

The story of the decline of and attempts to revitalize the New York and New Jersey waterfronts in the 1980s and 1990s illustrates both the problems and benefits of projects that take a long time to realize. In the case of the floating pool, periodic rises in the real estate market and a previous oil spill had a direct negative impact on locating a barge to house the pool. The political currents were uncontrollable and fluctuating. The election of a new mayor in Hoboken, New Jersey, stalled the project, but this had the unexpected advantage of allowing me more time to put a team together, find a barge, fundraise, and eventually return to my original dream of opening the floating pool in New York City. A new governor in New York State and mayor in New York City put the floating pool back on track, leading to the opening.

We knew from the beginning that various agencies would have their say in the project. Some, such as the US Coast Guard, would accept me as a known individual who had worked in and out of city agencies for years to effect change along the New York City shoreline. Others knew me but had their own agenda, and a floating pool was not on their list of priorities. It took time to determine who the friends and foes of the project were, and then what we needed to do to gain the approval of the naysayers. The New York State Department of Environmental Conservation had decades-old legislative rules to follow and were understandably adversarial. The staff of the Empire State Development Corporation in charge of insurance were mandated by law to make sure that all of the i's were dotted and t's crossed before the pool could land in Brooklyn.

Innovative, quirky, and hybrid projects entail many unknowns, both mundane and esoteric. Insurance and weather were the most difficult problems we faced during implementation. Two days before the *Floating Pool Lady* was due to open, underwriters—who seemed to view the floating pool as an alien spacecraft—refused to issue crucial insurance. They found risk difficult to assess. A person could slip and fall at any pool on land, but on a barge, they could slip under the railings into a dark, deep river and be swept out to sea by tidal currents. They feared someone might jump over the railing just for fun. And, to add to the insurance conundrum, marine insurers bonded boats, not pools, while nonmarine insurers bonded pools, not boats.

Climate change was not actively on the public's radar (nor on mine) when we began the reconstruction of the barge that was to become the Floating Pool Lady, although hurricanes were hardly unknown to the Louisiana bayous where the work was in progress. Not one but two major hurricanes occurred on our watch. This meant extreme risk and caused broken communication, anxiety, and weeks of delays. There was terrible damage elsewhere, but fortuitously none to our project.

Throughout this history of the *Floating Pool Lady*, the reader will find that I was fortunate to have many personal contacts. From an academic mentor to a parks commissioner and many others in between, all were crucial to getting the job done. In the 1970s my PhD adviser, Kenneth Jackson, opened the door for me to the floating bath archives. When the project was still just my personal passion, a chance meeting at a waterfront conference with a Port Authority of New York and New Jersey official, L. Michael Krieger, Esq., started the pool's exploratory voyage to Hoboken. A decade later, New York governor Eliot Spitzer answered my personal appeal to help the *Floating Pool Lady* open in Brooklyn. And in 2008 my good friend, New York City parks commissioner Adrian Benepe, accepted my gift of the pool to the city and, with Mayor Bloomberg, opened her at Barretto Park, a recreationally underserved community in the Bronx.

My intention when donating the *Floating Pool Lady* to the New York City Department of Parks and Recreation in 2008 was to reintroduce a popular late nineteenth- and early twentieth-century resource—free to the public—to the twenty-first-century waterfront. What follows are the dos and don'ts as well as the potential pitfalls that can face any citizen who wants to follow in my footsteps and use her own resources and grit to realize a public project to improve the quality of life for urban residents.

The bottom line is simple: you gotta fight like hell!

CHAPTER 1

Fire and Water

ON JULY 29, 2004, I stood before the storefront entrance to the office of Brooklyn's Community Board 1 (CB1) at the corner of Frost Street and Graham Avenue, across from Anthony and Son's grocery, quaking in my sandals with fear. "What have I gotten myself into?" I murmured to myself. Holding my breath, I stepped into the office and heard several voices in the adjacent meeting room. I peeked in and saw that the room where I would soon have to present my proposal was filled to capacity with a colorless sea of rumpled, sweating men and women who shifted uncomfortably on hard folding chairs.

Since childhood I had been congenitally shy in front of strangers, and having to present myself, albeit as an adult with a history of community activism, to this sweltering, stuffy roomful of people from this Greenpoint community and offer them my project, my obsession, was terrifying. What if they turned down my idea to bring them a new swimming facility?

I had heard about Julie Lawrence, the chair of the Waterfront Committee, and her fiery red hair and matching temperament. Seated a few steps from the door, she noticed my arrival and said to one of her board members, "Oh, here comes the Floating Pool Lady!"

Her voice sounded vexed, as if my presence was unwelcome. I smiled in her direction, nervously examined the audience again, and sat down. I wished for obscurity but knew that I had to be front and center to make a strong pitch for the project that would become my namesake. What I did not realize was that all of the issues I would face here, and those I would continue to face on my journey, were on display that evening.

In retrospect my presentation at CB1 was good practice. I had met with a recalcitrant audience at the regional office of the New York State Department of Environmental Conservation (DEC) back in 1998. I had needed to convince those regulators that a floating pool was a "water-dependent use." Perhaps if I handled myself well at CB1's Waterfront Committee meeting, future encounters with political officials—council members, congressmen, a mayor, and even a governor—would go smoothly.

My appearance at this community board subcommittee was partly fortuitous, as would be many future meetings. In the fall of 2001 I had presented the concept of a floating pool to a panel at a Waterfront Center Conference discussing methods to open up urban riverfronts for recreation. At the time I had researched the history of floating pools in New York City, secured a grant for a feasibility study, created the not-for-profit Neptune Foundation to raise money for the project, and hired an architect to design the "houses" or pavilions for changing, offices, concessions, and storage. We planned to place these normally land-based architectural elements on a second level at the stern of a barge. At the break after the panel, I was approached by a young attorney, Adam Perlmutter. Adam was a Greenpoint resident interested in local environmental and legal issues along the northwestern Brooklyn waterfront. When he asked me where my floating pool would be located, I remember indicating that I was looking for an area in the New York/New Jersey region where the population had few recreational facilities and limited access to the waterfront. Then I asked him if he had a specific site in mind. He did, and thus began my foray to the CB1 committee meeting in Greenpoint, Brooklyn.

One can safely say that New York City community boards are the legacy of author and activist Jane Jacobs. The idea of local groups having a voice in the making of public policy stems from Jacobs's effort to save Washington Square Park in the 1950s. Jacobs and her Greenwich Village neighbors fought an eight-year battle against the famously imperious Robert Moses, who sought to construct a four-lane highway that would intersect the park, remove play space, and cut off the eastern swath of the park from its Greenwich Village environs. At the time a grassroots group, made up largely of local mothers and their children, met in Washington Square Park, put up posters, gathered signatures on petitions, and held rallies, all activities that effectively enlarged the constituency opposed to the highway. Ultimately, politicians running for office, Congressman John Lindsay (who in 1966 became mayor) and the leader of Manhattan's Democratic Party known as Tammany Hall, Carmine de Sapio, helped the group secure a temporary closure of the park. Lesson learned: once closed to development by intense public pressure, no official would again dare to destroy the park to build a highway.

In her influential book *The Death and Life of Great American Cities*, Jacobs argued that municipal governments were no longer able to govern effectively. The layers of bureaucracy were too vast and complicated, and the decision makers at the top had no knowledge of "what the citizens of [local neighborhoods] consider[ed] of value in their lives." Her descriptions of the 1950s are vivid. Mothers with "fidgeting" children in their laps waited for hours to speak before the board of estimate (the precursor to the city council, today's next-to-last stop for approvals) on issues of local importance in the city, such as allocating money into the annual budget for playground safety surfacing. Their efforts were for naught because the board had already made its decision, behind closed doors, well in advance of public comment.

Jacobs recommended more inclusiveness in the political and administrative processes by creating a subdivision within every public agency whose portfolio affected a locality, agencies such as police, sanitation, and parks. "District administrators" would receive budgets for staff and would supervise and provide service to each "administrative district." It was important to Jacobs that the functioning of the districts give residents and businesses sufficient clout to fight city hall. The voice of these bodies, in other words, should not be merely advisory.

In her book, published in 1961, Jacobs does not mention the city's twelve community planning councils that then Manhattan borough president Robert F. Wagner, Jr., had created a decade earlier to advise him on budgetary and planning matters. Probably influenced by Jacobs's book, in the early 1960s Wagner added "community planning boards" to the city charter. These boards gave neighborhood governance a start in all five boroughs. Today, these meetings are still the first step in building local support for any new project. The boards have strictly advisory roles in four areas: placement of municipal facilities such as jails, changes in zoning, assessing neighborhood needs such as new schools, and other community concerns such as garbage transfer stations or new parks. It was local concern about a new park that brought me to CB1's Waterfront Committee meeting at the district office on July 29, 2004.

THE VERY IDEA OF a park along the waterfront in this part of Brooklyn would have been deemed ridiculously dangerous in the latter half of the nineteenth century. Greenpoint is the northernmost neighborhood of Brooklyn. It is bordered by the East River to the west, and to the north and east by its tributary, Newtown Creek, which separates Brooklyn from Queens. The East River's changing tides and currents back up preponderantly stagnant and polluted water into Newtown Creek. Beginning in 1872, blocks of land along the south of the creek were developed by Standard Oil into refineries. Related industrial plants followed: tank construction factories; paint and varnish companies that used oil in their products; chemical plants to make sulfuric acid used in processing the less odorous kerosene; and fertilizer plants that added the tar from the kerosene refinement to flesh, bones, fish scraps, and other animal parts to produce glue, animal feed, and superphosphate fertilizer. In this era before environmental awareness, waste from these industries and fertilizer plants, as well as from copper ore production, were dumped on the ground and into Newtown Creek. Waste fumes were emitted directly into the surrounding airways.

The twentieth-century history of Newtown Creek and Greenpoint is one of oil spills and sewer overflows. Between 1940 and 1950, leaks from the oil facilities created what two researchers have called "the largest pool of underground oil spills in the country." (According to the Hudson River Riverkeeper, New York's clean water advocate, the amount was 17 to 30 million gallons, at least 50 percent bigger than the infamous 1989 Exxon Valdez oil spill.) A sewer explosion and fire in 1950 were the first indications of the oil spill. The damage was not recognized until 1978 when the Coast Guard noticed a large plume of oil flowing in the creek. A rudimentary cleanup began in 1990, but since then, and despite lawsuits by Riverkeeper and local and state political leaders, the leaks continue.

While oil was spreading on land and into the waterway, Greenpoint's environmental issues were compounded. Manhattan's sewage problem was brought to Greenpoint to be solved. In 1967 the City Department of Environmental Protection (DEP) opened the city's largest wastewater treatment plant adjacent to Newtown Creek. Rather than deal with Manhattan's East Side waste in situ (an impossibility due to lack of space and well-organized, powerful neighbors who would surely contest such a move), all of the liquid waste from that area's sewers was piped away to vats at Newtown for storage and treatment. Beyond using land in Greenpoint to resolve Manhattan's problems, there was a built-in structural problem that would contaminate the Greenpoint waterfront: a large proportion of the city's sewer system was originally designed with combined sewer outfalls (CSOs). Instead of sending sewage in one pipe to the vats at the waste treatment plant and rainwater to river outflows in another, a single CSO pipe carried rainwater and all the debris from Manhattan to Newtown. As a result, during periods of power outages and heavy rainfall, when the system temporarily stopped working, the capacity of the Newtown facility was overwhelmed. Rather than being stored safely, all of the residential and business toilet, sink, and bath wastes, plus the muck that the rain washed into the street gutters, emptied untreated into the East River along the Greenpoint waterfront. This is what happened during the extreme rainy weather and snow melt of 2004, and the problem still exists today.

OILY RIVER WATER and pipes emitting sewage during rainfalls were hardly amenable to recreation in Greenpoint. Roads and streets, not parks, were the norm along Brooklyn's waterfront. A pool floating in sewage would never be acceptable to the Greenpoint community. Yet people like me kept dreaming and planning.

In 1974 some non-Greenpoint open-space activists—I among them—saw the possibility of adding a small park to the Williamsburg waterfront a mile south of Greenpoint. The Parks Council, an advocacy group fighting to improve parks and open space citywide, turned its attention to the lack of public access to the city's waterfront. As a board member of the Parks Council who was soon to pursue a degree in urban planning, I was intrigued.

Historically the exclusion of recreational space on the city's waterfronts was deliberate. The Randall Commission of 1811 laid out Manhattan's streets primarily to accommodate commerce, not public recreation. The defense for designating "so few vacant spaces . . . for the benefit of fresh air and the benefit of health" was that because the rivers were wide, they would always be available for "the convenience of commerce" and for "health and pleasure." The commission's rationale was false. By 1974 the Williamsburg/Greenpoint waterfront was just one indication that the public's health and enjoyment of fresh air had been totally imperiled by commerce and industry. Sulphur dioxide as well as dust, pollen, soot, smoke, and liquid droplets known as "suspended matter" in the area were 50 percent higher than citywide averages.

After touring several street ends in Manhattan, the Parks Council director, several interns, and I approached the western end of Grand Street in Williamsburg, which terminated at the East River. Under the jurisdiction of the Department of Transportation (DOT), the street was open, and it was a perfect site to try adding green space. Here was both a place for "health and pleasure," and a reminder of the commercial past. Ahead of us, a rather perilous, rocky outcrop led down to the East River, with a view across to Manhattan's Lower East Side. On the left was the huge, triangular bow of a ship from which stevedores were unloading sugar cane into the Domino sugar refinery. The air was redolent with the sweet, slightly burnt aroma of the sugar being processed. With the approval of DOT, and the temporary support of community residents—who also volunteered to maintain the oasis—the Parks Council opened an "unofficial park" on the site in 1994 using recycled materials. We added handmade wooden benches and tires for seating, and waste cans for picnic and cigarette debris. We placed large boulders at the river's edge to prevent entry into the polluted water. Initially, the trial was a success, and the Parks Council began to negotiate with the relevant city agencies to make it an official city park. But DOT policy prohibited street-end waterfront access due to fears that instead of creating a space for residents to reach the heretofore-closed-off waterfront, access would encourage unsafe entry into the river.

It took time to make the Grand Street Park an official city park. Two decades later, in the early 1990s, I was working at the New York City Economic Development Corporation (EDC) and assigned to work with the Department of City Planning on the "Public Waterfront" section of a Comprehensive Waterfront Plan. This was the city's first attempt to guide land use along the waterfront. The plan, which the department published for comment in 1992, included the following: "An overriding principle of this waterfront plan is to re-establish the public's connection to the waterfront by creating new opportunities for visual, physical and recreational access. This goal can be realized in various ways: by extending and improving a network of public spaces through parks, street ends and numerous publicly owned properties along the shoreline." On page 65 is a picture with the caption: "Waterfront Cleanup on an East River Street End." I don't remember if this was due to my participation in the writing of this document, but finally—a quarter century after its opening—we had the opportunity to formalize and permanently maintain the Grand Street street end. In 1997 DOT transferred the 1.55 acres of what is now known as Grand Ferry Park to the New York

City Department of Parks and Recreation (Parks Department), which has maintained it ever since.

By 1974 the public's perception of the desirability to be near the East River to swim had begun to change. The Federal Clean Water Act (amended in 1974) was a start. The act forbade the discharge of pollutants into US navigable waters without a permit. In addition, the act posited a timeline: the nation's rivers should be swimmable and fishable by 2016. Begun as the Hudson River Fishermen's Association, Riverkeeper began work toward meeting the federal government's timetable to clean up one of these rivers. Along with getting the public on board to fight water pollution, the not-for-profit tested the waters of the Hudson and issued monthly reports on the river's condition from Albany to New York City. The estuaries around Manhattan, in particular the East River fronting Greenpoint, which registered high amounts of fecal matter, would not be swimmable in the near future. Despite the objective conditions, beginning in 1993 hundreds of people dove into the river under the Brooklyn Bridge to take part in NYC Swim's first Manhattan-to-Brooklyn swim. Perhaps the time was right for a floating pool.

GROWING OUTRAGE OVER an additional type of industrial contamination around Newtown Creek—the huge garbage and dump trucks that hauled household and construction wastes through Greenpoint to fifteen private waste transfer stations—helped precipitate in 1997 the creation of another larger park in Greenpoint. The mechanism for creating the park was a 197-a plan, an expansion of the community planning process begun by Jacobs. Since their codification in the city charter in the 1950s, the role of community boards was only to advise and react to private and public development proposals that affected their community. By 1975 Section 197-a of the revised city charter gave communities a new power: to prepare and produce their own plans. But it took a while for them to learn how to use this planning capability.

Community activism was new to Greenpoint. Traditionally, the residents were resigned to living with the garbage transfer stations, the soot, and the "Greenpoint stink," a potent combination of refuse, sewage, oil, and brine. In 1997 a more diverse coalition of Greenpoint residents—traditional populations and new arrivals such as Polish and Hispanic ethnic groups, property owners, artists and students who could no longer afford Manhattan, environmental advocates, fishermen, kayakers, elected officials, and CB1—joined together to articulate a vision for the Greenpoint community and to create a plan for the future of this district. In this 1997 document, which the City Planning Commission and the City Council approved in 2002, the Greenpoint community sought "higher and better uses" for their waterfront. Instead of new, stinky, and toxic gasworks, the community wanted a tree-lined esplanade and public parks along an undisturbed East River in Greenpoint. Work on Transmitter Park, one of the areas selected in the plan, began quickly.

The Transmitter site, located on the East River between Greenpoint Avenue and Kent and Java Streets, had been in limbo since 1990 when radio station WNYC moved its AM station to a radio tower in the New Jersey Meadowlands. Two disused metal structures loomed over the plot, rusting to the point of imminent collapse until the Parks Department was given emergency funds to remove the dangerous and unsightly towers, but nothing more was allocated or planned. Until 2010, when the Parks Department broke ground for the WNYC Transmitter Park, all the site boasted was a small, art deco building storing Parks Department monuments in need of repair, a splendid fig tree with abundant fruit, and a spectacular view of Manhattan from Stuyvesant Town in the 20s, north to the United Nations in the 40s. The Greenpoint Community plan lacked funds and the political will to do more.

Both of these necessary elements, however, arrived in 2002. When Michael Bloomberg became mayor one of his stated goals was to expand public access to the waterfront. To speed up the process, Bloomberg put the EDC in charge of building Transmitter Park. EDC is a not-for-profit organization contracted annually by the City of New York to promote and implement economic development. The EDC is an independent entity with in-house construction expertise to work on administration priorities and, more importantly, the ability to procure services quickly to start projects. The languishing community plan was suddenly alive and active.

The EDC has always had a waterfront development component. The enterprise is run by a chairperson who is appointed and serves at the pleasure of the mayor, and a board of directors nominated by a group of elected officials and the chair. The mentor-to-be of my professional life, Carl Weisbrod, was appointed the first chair by Mayor Dinkins. Shortly thereafter Carl asked me to join his staff as vice president for waterfront planning.

During this period, as a result of the closure of the Department of Ports and Terminals (originally the Dock Department, lessor of dock space to many of the floating baths of the nineteenth and early twentieth centuries), EDC acquired a portfolio of city-owned, working waterfront property. I encouraged Carl to include public access in these redevelopment projects. With the Parks Department, EDC helped reconstruct and reopen a historic recreation pier in Manhattan located at East 107th Street. On the other side of the East River, to improve the quality of life for Asian and Latin American immigrants who were moving into Sunset Park in Brooklyn, I led the work on a preliminary plan for a public open space on a portion of a former port complex. The plan lingered unimplemented, waiting for demand from a redeveloped business community and more residents. Long after my departure from EDC, in 2014 the Parks Department and EDC opened Bush Terminal Park. Also while at EDC, I worked to fashion a public connection along the waterfront between the closed-off South Street Seaport and the Battery Maritime Building at the tip of Manhattan. I worked with DOT to hang huge, plywood fish under the East River Drive and to paint a directional pathway of colorful, swimming fish. Today, the team of EDC, DOT, and the Department of Parks have turned that pathway into a two-mile esplanade running from the Battery Maritime Building to just beyond the Manhattan Bridge.

THE COMMUNITY ACTIVISM in Greenpoint that had begun with a 197-a plan in 1997 was missing a crucial element. No funds had been attached for its implementation. At the beginning of the Bloomberg administration the political will was in place to increase public access to the city's waterfront. In addition, the greening of the Brooklyn waterfront had tax implications. It would create an atmosphere to encourage the development of private, high-rise housing and increase the city's tax base. It might also lead to the cleanup of Newtown Creek (but that would be decades away). By fall of 2003, two years after Mayor Bloomberg had astutely assigned EDC to take on a piece of Greenpoint, the corporation had applied for a state grant for public access improvements and hired landscape architect Donna Walcavage to design a waterfront park that the Greenpoint community had recommended in its 197-a plan back in 1997.

The plan included two proposals that would make Transmitter Park worth pursuing for a home for my floating pool. Reconstruction of the demolished Kent Street pier at the north end of the Transmitter site could include a berth for the pool. Development of the site itself, for both passive recreation and an adjoining ferry or water taxi slip, could also provide access by water for people using the pool, as well as by land from Greenpoint Avenue. But these were only idealized assumptions on my part in 2003. First, I needed to ascertain that there was city and local political interest in a pool. I needed support before I even had a chance to make a pitch for a floating pool to Community Board 2 (CB2). Thus began sometimes serendipitous, but more often planned, encounters with administrators and politicians, professionals, and local not-for-profits, many helpful and some less obliging, which over many years would form the complex context establishing the viability of the floating pool.

The most important of these early contacts was parks commissioner Adrian Benepe, an unflagging supporter of the floating pool. We were longtime friends, having worked together at the agency under Henry Stern, the preceding commissioner of parks. When Adrian rose to that position in 2002, preliminary work on the design and fundraising for the pool were already under way, and I asked him if he would host and maintain the first pool at a park site. Adrian liked the idea, calling it "innovative and forward looking." He thought the pool could be the way to add to the city's land-based outdoor pool inventory.

His June 6, 2002, memo to the special assistant to the mayor, Nanette Smith, sought support from City Hall and described my work: "Ann has championed the idea of re-introducing floating pools to New York for many years . . . and she has raised sufficient funds to construct a first pool next year." The memo contained a list of possible park sites, among them the East River Waterfront adjacent to the WNYC Transmitters, Pier 1 in Brooklyn Bridge Park, and Tiffany Street in the Bronx.

A meeting with Donna Walcavage came next on my agenda. She was working with EDC to prepare a scope of work statement for the design of Transmitter Park and its adjacent Kent Street pier. Now was the time for me to insert a floating pool into her plan for the park. In September 2003 I arranged a meeting to take Donna to the office of my architect, Jonathan Kirschenfeld, to see the model and drawings for the floating pool. Three months later I received a spreadsheet prepared by the McLaren Engineering Group, also hired by EDC, titled "Floating Swimming Pool." The sheet listed the following tasks: McLaren to handle the waterfront engineering work; the Walcavage Team, the lead on the project, to design the piles to which the pool barge would be attached and the attachment to land of a platform (eventually a pier) leading from the barge into the park; and the floating pool team to submit the barge design, the depth of water needed—pool empty and full—and soundings (measurement of the water depth) in the East River along the Transmitter property. Here was confirmation that we were "in"! I called Jonathan Kirschenfeld on my landline, and seated in our offices, we each raised a glass of water in celebration.

That same month I had an unplanned meeting with another key contact, city council member David Yassky, who represented a large area of Brooklyn's waterfront. I met him in late 2003 at a conference run by the Citizens Budget Commission (CBC). At the time, my husband Lawrence chaired this research and advocacy nonprofit that pushed for New York City and State government reform. Larry introduced me to Yassky, whose wife was president of CBC, and he sat down next to me in the audience. We chatted between speakers and presentations, and I learned that he knew of my past positions in charge of waterfront planning and development at the Parks Department and EDC. He asked what I was doing now. I told him that I was in the process of retrofitting a barge to contain a floating pool that would offer free access to all. I also mentioned that I might have a landing site in Brooklyn. I recall that Yassky was intrigued. He had procured money from the city council for sinkhole repairs at the Transmitter site, and he quickly assessed that the floating pool was not only a perfect complement to the project but also a boon to his Brooklyn constituency. I presumed he also saw some advantage to him politically in supporting the project.

In the following six months the three teams were at their drawing boards. Walcavage worked on the seawall that separated the East River from the Transmitter site, where the water depth, which ranged from seven feet at the shore to nine feet at the river's deepest point, could accommodate the pool. The floating pool team awaited bids from shipyards for the work to transform a barge into a floating pool. The trends of more public interest and mayoral support were cascading into the micro matters of project planning and support.

ON JUNE 23, 2004, Adam Perlmutter reappeared in my life. He suggested that we ask for a spot at a public hearing of the Waterfront Committee in July to make a presentation on the pool. (He loved the idea.) I immediately sent the information about the public hearing on to the two city agencies working on the park and pier project—the Parks Department and EDC—saying: "Are you ready to begin the process?? We're ready." Both agencies said they were in.

I had a last stop to make before taking my proposal to CB1's Waterfront Committee: EDC, the lead partner in the plan for the park. Looking for advice and moral support, I chose to speak with a friend, Jeannette Rausch. She had been my intern at the corporation in the early 1990s and was now a staff member. We met on June 28 in a conference space at 110 William Street in Manhattan, near the glassed-in, interior office where I had sat as an EDC vice president. Jeannette stated that the agency was ready to present initial concepts for the park and pier. We discussed the how-tos of my presentation. She advised that I should let the group know that mine was not an off-the-wall project and that I was working with the Parks Department and EDC to see how the pool could be accommodated at the site. Jeannette informed me that EDC wanted to achieve two of the community's goals: a place for fishing and a ferry or water taxi stop. She also assured me that she had added to these EDC comments my goal of a floating pool for Greenpoint. I left Jeannette's office with advice to contact Julie Lawrence, head of the Waterfront Committee of CB1, and affirmation that EDC had joined the pro-pool team.

SO IT WAS THAT I came to be, on a beastly hot July evening in 2004, in a crowded, airless room, dreading the public presentation I was about to make arguing for the pool.

The agenda read as follows:

A: The Java/Kent/Greenpoint Avenue Waterfront (EDC and Parks):
> *Background*
> *Project team*
> *Discussion of community and stakeholder outreach*
> *Schedule*

B: The proposal for a Floating Pool at the waterfront (Ann Buttenwieser)

The community was anxious to meet Walcavage, and she presented the EDC program for the park. Task 7A of the draft schedule read: "Floating Pool Work/Conceptual" to be complete December 2004. Architect Jonathan Kirschenfeld stood at his projector in a back corner of the room and, sweating heavily, showed his slides. The audience was polite, occasionally leaning into one another to whisper comments. Then abruptly the redhead, Julie Lawrence, chair of the Waterfront Committee of CB1, was on her feet and firing questions.

How will the pool fit with a ferry landing?

Won't it rock with the waves?

How much will it cost to get in?

Where will people line up, and how will they get on and off?

Will it negatively affect fishing?

Will it be noisy at night?

Given the sewer outfalls at local street ends, will it use river water? Wouldn't that be a bad thing?

Isn't this just eye candy distracting attention and money from the restoration of the only neighborhood pool, McCarren Park, that's been closed since 1983?

Have you done something like this before? No? Then are we to be your guinea pigs?

The crowded room had no stage, and, since I had no slides to show, I stood at my seat hoping people could see me, thinking: "I should have worn heels." I answered the chair's questions calmly, but inwardly I was shaking. My face burned with the heat and my discomfort at being put on the spot in public. Julie Lawrence, agitated, walked toward me. "And what will YOU get out of this?" she asked, pointing her finger accusingly at me.

Still standing, knees shaking, I wondered how I was going to get through this do-or-die moment. I took a deep breath to compose myself and answered: "I have swum in rivers and on school teams since my childhood and have for over twenty years dreamed of bringing land-bound New Yorkers, who ironically live on islands, back to the water. We cannot yet safely swim in the East River. It is for you and all New Yorkers that I am building a floating pool." Suddenly, Lawrence was right next to me. She embraced me and whispered, "Thank you."

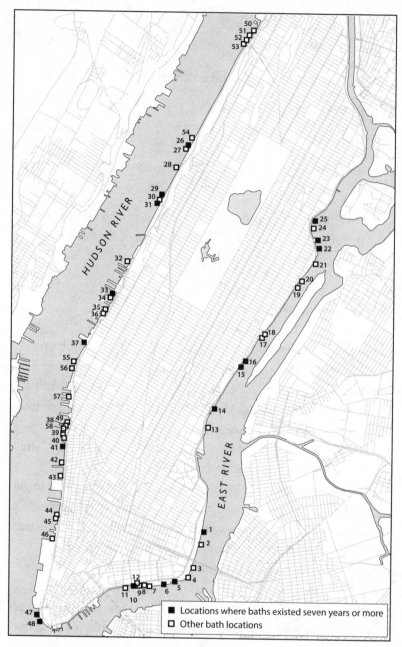

MAP 2. The floating baths. Courtesy of William Nelson.
For map key, see page 280.

CHAPTER 2

The Eureka Moment

IN THE LATE 1970S I entered a tiny, doorless room in the basement of the historic Battery Maritime Building. The sooty gray-green of the once-multicolored Beaux Arts former municipal ferry pier, which presides over the Upper Bay at the tip of lower Manhattan, presaged the condition of the interior space allotted to me to conduct research for my PhD. The cast- and wrought-iron columns and ceramic tile vaults were in a state of decay, all covered in the same gray-green paint that was supposed to match the color of the patina on the Statue of Liberty. I also noticed a visual echo of the battleship-gray color painted on the Robert Moses–era playground facilities where I had spent many hours with my sons and daughters.

My study spot was alongside the lower level of the ferry terminal that at the turn of the twentieth century was the loading area for wagons and motor vehicles on their way to and from Brooklyn. A few feet away was the former waiting room, a vast, damp, dark space through which echoed the long horn blasts of ferries on their way to the US Coast Guard base on Governors Island, or to some other destination in New Jersey. I heard slapping waves, tinkling piano notes, the radio voice of Don Imus, and the *bomp, bomp* of someone dribbling a basketball somewhere in the cavernous building. I sat down at a broken-down desk layered in over a century's worth of dust and sneezed.

I had gotten access to this inner sanctum through my PhD adviser and academic mentor at Columbia University, Professor Kenneth Jackson. Ken had recently explored what was described to him as the "useless stacks" of archives that the Department of Ports and Terminals, the city agency with offices on the top floor, would soon discard. He told me there might be some useful material there for my study of the planning of Manhattan's waterfront. Ken's recommendation that I get down to the Battery as soon as possible would be crucial to the next chapter of my life.

In the shadows of the dimly lit waiting room, amid mounds of assorted debris, cat excrement, and the evidence of the daily visits of curious waterfront rats—conditions not unlike those in New York City's late nineteenth-century tenements—stood an acre of long-closed wooden and metal file cabinets containing the archives of the New York City Department of Docks (DD); they dated back to 1880. I was seeking documents to confirm my theory that recreational facilities played a role in the primarily industrial New York City waterfront. Printed and elegantly handwritten documents were pressed in folders labeled with the numbers of every pier, and the names and numbers of every street terminating on the Hudson and East Rivers. Carefully, I positioned my flashlight and, with white-gloved hands that were quickly covered in dust and dirt, pulled a brittle piece of paper from one of the drawers. I read the following command: "Open the floating baths!" Eureka! I had found proof of my theory. Furthermore, right then and there, the idea of floating baths captured my imagination. I knew at this moment that I wanted to introduce them to late twentieth-century readers in magazine articles and in my book, *Manhattan Water-Bound*. This find was also the beginning of my twenty-seven-year-long campaign to reintroduce the floating baths to New York City and to give the recreationally underserved urban public a place to swim on the city's riverfront.

To convince others of the historical appropriateness and modern-day desirability of creating a twenty-first-century "Floating Pool Lady"—and, moreover, to understand what I was getting into—I needed to learn the history. What policies encouraged or hindered the creation of New York City's floating pools? Where did politics intervene? How were they constructed? How much did they cost and what were the financial constraints? Whom did they serve, and was the public happy to use them?

FLOATING POOLS, OR BATHS, as they were once called, were in use in the northern cities of the United States beginning in the mid-nineteenth century. They resembled giant houseboats with an enormous hole in their centers that was filled with polluted river water. The baths, like improved housing and small parks, were intended by mid-nineteenth-century sanitary and late nineteenth-century progressive reformers as a means to improve the health, decorum, and morality of the mostly immigrant poor and working-class population. They were also a way to protect middle- and upper-class New Yorkers from the perceived threats of disease and crime accompanying the arrival of vast numbers of Americans. The pools were good for the immigrant poor and kept them in separate recreational spaces.

Between 1820 and 1870 New York City's population grew to over 942,000, a ninefold increase in fifty years. These numbers would swell again with the influx of over 478,000 immigrants by 1880, and over 600,000 more until the turn of the century. In a city unprepared for such rapid population growth, a significant proportion of the new arrivals were relegated to the tenements, where they were forced to live packed into substandard housing that lacked bathing or sanitary facilities. Infectious diseases such as cholera, yellow fever, and tuberculosis were rampant. Misbehavior and disorder in the form of violence, thievery, drunkenness, gambling, prostitution, and vagrancy were also typical under these stressful living conditions.

The middle- and upper-class New Yorkers living in better circumstances in larger single-family homes feared that their lifestyles might be in jeopardy. And with good reason: the cause of disease in that period was thought to be a miasma that accompanied the foul air emanating from dirty streets and building yards, back alleys, and basements. In 1845, with this belief prevalent, Dr. John Griscom, one of the original New York City sanitary reformers, published his *Report on the Sanitary Condition of the Laboring Population of New York.* In the report he frightened well-heeled citizens with his dire prognosis that the disease and disorder that he and his associates observed among the lower-class working people of the city would eventually contaminate citizens of the wealthier classes as well. With disease literally in the air, the better classes of New York necessarily constrained their social and business lives to healthier environs.

An 1853 study by the New York Association for Improving the Conditions of the Poor examined the issue of squalor. "Among the conditions favorable to disease," they wrote, "uncleanliness holds high rank." Delving deeper, later authors found that 39 percent of the tenement population surveyed were "very dirty" or "dirty." They placed the greatest blame for uncleanliness on three ethnic groups: Germans, who arrived in great numbers before the Civil War; the postwar flow of Italians from southern Italy; and Russian and other Eastern European Jews (most often lumped together as "Hebrews"). The question asked by the middle-class white reformers was whether tenement living perpetuated the bad habits that the immigrants brought with them or vice versa. In other words, was the city getting filthier because of the immigrants, or were the immigrants living in squalor because of the failure of the city to provide a proper environment for them?

In the case of the Italians, reformers concluded that both assertions were true. At home in southern Italy, they claimed (without accompanying proof), Italians simply washed infrequently. Once in New York, they worked as ragpickers and were labeled "the scum of New York Ragpickers" because their appearance tended to reflect the inherent filthiness of their profession. The Jews, packed in what activist Jacob Riis termed "Jew Town," were assumed to be dirty because according to Riis, they had "strange customs, an unintelligible language and were clannish." The sanitarian reformers

worried that the filth and odors emanating from the Jewish ped-
dlers' pushcarts would convey health problems to surrounding districts.

Some Progressives called for environmental reform and focused
on the well-being of immigrant children. They posited that if tenement dwellers had places to go where they could enjoy sunlight and
fresh air, and where their children could safely play and even get
clean, they would be uplifted both morally and physically. While
the parents were thought to be unimprovable, they believed that
given the right environment, their offspring could be made into civ-
ilized members of the community.

Jacob Riis was a strong and successful proponent of the child-cen-
tered approach to the social problems of the late nineteenth century. Instead of dry facts in the form of data and diagrams, Riis
added the new dimension of vivid illustration to the city's sanitary
and tenement studies. Through his speeches, writings, and photographs, he brought to life for the wider public the desperate living
conditions in the slums.

Riis was an activist and a realist. For many years he worked to
bring environmental change to the slums by advocating for local
playgrounds. Tenement children seeking light, fresh air, and an
outlet for their energy played baseball, enjoyed hopping games, and
drove makeshift go-karts in the city streets for lack of any other
place to go. This annoyed residents, storekeepers, and passersby
when the children's balls broke windows and street lamps, and
when they got in the way of the throngs of pushcarts that were a
commonplace component of street commerce. Health advocates
also became alarmed about the rising death rates among street children, who were often run over by horse-drawn trucks, which tech-
nically always had the right of way. The spread of teenage civic
unrest—in the form of interethnic gang fights—into upper-class
neighborhoods was another fear.

Riis shared those fears, and so his joy was palpable when, in 1897,
after ten years of writing, taking photographs, and sitting on committees, he arrived at the newly opened Mulberry Bend Park. "The
sun shone upon flowers and the tender leaves of young shrubs, and

the smell of new-mown hay was in the air. Crowds of little Italian children shouted with delight over the garden." There were sunlight and air, but there was also control. In his delight, Riis could barely wait to place his feet on the grass. But his walk was short-lived. A policeman accosted Riis right in front of a group of "wide-eyed children," striking him with his bully stick, and commanding: "Hey! Come off the grass! D'ye think it is made to walk on?"

The city's waterfront was just another venue of conflict between poor immigrants seeking relief and those who were intolerant of their presence there. Tenement residents gravitated to Manhattan's prime natural resource: its rivers. In 1868, according to the *New York Times*, without the benefit of official facilities, it was common for "multitudes" of naked men and unruly boys to push their way through the crowded wharves to jump into the city's rivers. Perhaps they became cleaner and enjoyed themselves, but their naked bodies also offended those who used the rivers daily for commerce and travel. The New York City Common Council reacted to this social affront and possible health risk by passing laws against swimming in the rivers.

New York City's population explosion; the packed tenement districts that lacked light and air and basic sanitation; the resulting upper-class fears of contagion and the spread of crime; and the growing pressure of the sanitary reformers and Progressives on the government to intervene ultimately all led the city to build its free, floating baths.

But the process to establish the baths in the nineteenth century was a convoluted one. The People's Bathing and Washing Association, a subsidiary of the Association for Improving the Condition of the Poor, was incorporated in 1849 "for the purpose of supplying facilities to the people of the city in regard to bathing and washing." As a result of the powers granted to it, the association used state-allocated funds to construct and run the city's first bathhouse. Although seventy-five thousand people a year used the facility initially, declining patronage soon caused it to close. Among the rationalizations for the failure were the inability of patrons to pay the small entry fee, the insufficient return on the investment to cover maintenance, and the fact that the immigrants' bathing habits, or lack thereof, were so ingrained that they were not ready to properly appreciate and use the convenience offered by this private reform group. So the problem of the unbathed masses persisted. It took another twenty-one years for the first free bath to open. And when it did, it floated.

In 1866, one year after the end of the Civil War, the city's board of health, made wiser by lessons from the battlefield as to the role of cleanliness in the preservation of life, issued a new plea for the creation of free public baths "as a sanitary measure." But there remained the recurring question of the role of government in providing services for the poor: How could the city achieve the goal of bathing the people most in need without reallocating funds from other more politically popular and well-funded causes?

Whether it was in the spirit of competition to bring New York City in line with Boston's already well-established floating pool system, Tammany elected officials' desire for votes, or the growing fear of epidemics and chaos, in 1868 the state legislature finally succumbed. It authorized the mayor to retain a slip to the west of Castle Clinton at the Battery and lease it for a "public salt-water floating bath." The state also authorized the city to erect two floating baths, one on the East River and another on the Hudson. The original bath at the Battery slip, which had been run by a private company since 1832, remained, paid rent to the city, and charged a nominal entry fee. It took two more years for the city to construct the two new public pools and hire attending and security staff, and for the common council to approve the rules governing the use of the facilities.

IN MY DARK and dirty study spot in the Battery Maritime Building, my research was often disturbed by the loud toot of a ferry horn and the sound of slapping waves. I would hold my breath at the loud surprise. In these moments of forced reflection, I considered that the floating baths were built as a result of the Progressives' good deeds and sometimes dubious motivations. If my plan worked, a twenty-first-century floating pool might hopefully not be considered a philanthropist's good deed. But my motivation was not to provide a resource for the poor that would protect the rich or to keep the upper classes from illness. As clearly written in Neptune's charter, I hoped "to promote floating swimming pools to be operated on a not-for-profit basis along the waterfront areas of the New York City/New Jersey metropolitan region for the use and recreational benefit of the population of the New York City/New Jersey metropolitan region." The linchpin was a free pool to be installed in areas where residents had few recreational opportunities and had no idea that they lived in a city of islands.

In reviewing the history, I was also struck by the fact that it took twenty-one years for bath advocates to convince the state to legislate, and then the city to build and open the nineteenth-century floating pools. What politics and unexpected events might delay and otherwise negatively affect the construction and financial support of a new floating pool in the twenty-first century? If I really wanted to even consider proceeding with the idea, a proposal that was growing on me in my dark study quarters, I needed to describe how these original floating pools looked and worked. In the mold-ridden file drawers that held the secrets of the past of New York's waterfront, I started searching for photos, drawings—anything that would give me an architectural link to their history and a template for a floating pool.

The baths I discovered were novel constructions. Viewed from the outside, the facilities, with their second-story turrets, some with decorative roofs, resembled floating houseboats or entertainment venues. A primarily single-story rectangular wood structure, 95 feet long and 60 feet wide, surrounded an open-air swimming pool that typically measured 93 by 34 feet, or roughly one-third of today's Olympic standard. The building sat on eight pontoons, four on each side, which kept it afloat. Attached outside of the pontoons were large planks and slats that were six to eight feet deep in the water and acted as a huge sieve, keeping large pieces of floating debris out of the pools. Initially, additional wooden slats formed the floor of the swimming well, which was usually around 4.5 feet deep, subject to the amount of air in the pontoons and the depth of the riverbed. The openings between the floorboards allowed a constant flow of river water through the well and were useful for keeping the bathers from being swept away by the swift tidal currents.

A small clapboard-roofed second-story apartment located above the entrance provided year-round office space and living quarters for one guard. To allow their use at the end of the workday, the baths had to be lit. For this, they were initially connected to on-land gas lines in locations where possible. Patrons boarded the bath from a portable gangway connected to a pier or bulkhead and then were ushered to one of the sixty-eight to eighty-one (depending on the bath) tiny tin-roofed dressing cubicles that lined the inside of the rectangular structure. These doorless spaces could hold two to four people each, but more bodies, big and small, were often crammed into them. Once outside the dressing room, patrons stepped onto a narrow platform that hung over and around the pool. Here bathers either sat, dangling their legs into the water, or climbed over the railing and jumped in.

William Marcy Tweed opened the first public floating bath in 1870 at the foot of East Fifth Street on the East River, and the second at the foot of Charles Street (in today's West Village) on the Hudson River, where it shared space with the Washington Ice Company. Their immediate popularity was a combination of men and boys trying something new with juvenile misbehavior. The *New York Times* described one of the first Sundays from the Progressives' point of view. A wide variety of workers, from truck drivers to skilled tradesmen, were on their way to the baths on their one day off. But their entry was prevented by rowdy boys who had come early, skirted the police, and bought out all of the sessions. To keep tenement children under control in this contained environment, and in addition to station policemen, Tweed appointed Charles Krack, a former assembly member from Ulster County and the owner/operator of several private floating baths on the East River, to be the superintendent of both facilities.

If the baths were meant to serve the immigrants of the tenements, one might ask why there, rather than closer to where they lived? The walk to the foot of East Fifth Street from the nearest tenement, for example, was a half mile at minimum. The most logical reason for their placement was financial. They couldn't interfere with shipping or other economically viable uses—such as the ice company—that had priority on the waterfront. The East Fifth Street site might also have been chosen because poor children were already accustomed to risking life and limb by diving into the East River from nearby waterfront lots and unused piers. Using that location, in other words, would formalize and bring order to a spot that was already familiar to the poor. One might also conjecture that given the power base that Tweed had built as head of Tammany Hall, the thirty-nine jobs for opening and managing each pool may have enlarged his sphere of political patronage.

Each floating bath, with a capacity of one hundred, could handle up to 4,500 bathers per day. In their first year, 1870, patronage approached the maximum allowable, totaling over 860,000 individuals. The yearly attendance figures after that were a relatively constant 3.3 million. How crowded the first pools must have been! The board of health was at once pleased and critical. The attendance figures meant that tenement house dwellers did, in fact, want to keep clean. Thus began more lobbying for year-round land-based bathhouses, but the financial panic of 1873 curtailed all municipal spending deemed unnecessary. Still, all was not lost. A sanitary inspector urged that more baths be opened all over the city. A year later, the state legislature authorized four more floating baths. The city was allowed to sell bonds totaling $80,000 ($1.9 million in 2020 dollars) for their construction under the auspices of the Department of Public Works (DPW), which used funds appropriated annually by the city to manage the facilities. The DD was ordered to assign "convenient" locations without charge. This assignment, over time, would increasingly pit the need for tenement dwellers to have easy access to the baths against the department's desire to attract rent-paying waterfront businesses.

The contractors who built the newer baths made changes to the design. They partitioned the bathing wells into two parts, one 90 feet long and 34 feet wide for adults, and a shallower section for children that was 2.5 feet deep, 70 feet long, and 8 feet wide. The girth of at least one bath was adjusted to fit into narrower slips. At the present-day Market Street, the pool portion was narrowed by nine feet to a width of twenty-five feet. To meet a yearly increase in demand, at least one of the new baths was doubled in size, allowing the placement of two wells that for the first time allowed simultaneous, but separate, use of the facility by men and women. The construction cost of a floating bath averaged from $9,500 to $12,500 ($228,000 to $300,000) in contrast to $95,000 ($2.9 million) for the first in-ground bathhouse. As would be expected, a bath floating on the water was millions of dollars cheaper than a land-based bath (an argument I would eventually use with environmentalists in favor of a floating pool). But in looking at these figures, I never thought of the money I would have to raise over a century later.

Once the floating baths opened in 1870, the superintendents in charge of them spent from $300 to $900 ($5,900–$17,700) per facility annually on maintenance and repairs. This amount fluctuated over time when the structures were either closed in certain locations or began to disintegrate from age. Included in the list of supplies to care for the facilities were ropes and hoses, a six-gallon cooler for drinking water, and badges and caps—initially emblazoned with a gold braid, a number, and the words "FREE BATH, DPW"—for the attendants. Pay for employees to staff the floating baths was fairly steady but unequal: during the summer, the male "keepers," as the attendants were known, were paid $2.50 ($49) per day, while matrons earned $2.00 ($39).

Between 1874 and 1888 the state legislature authorized the DPW to construct eleven more floating baths, bringing the total to fifteen. To achieve the public goals of cleanliness and control, the DD tried, where possible, to space one at every five blocks along the Manhattan waterfront. By 1877 the DPW operated six baths. Two served residents of the Lower East Side—one at Gouverneur Lane and the other at the original East Fifth Street location. Another bath was located at East Thirty-Seventh Street, where there was a growing German population, and another at East 114th Street, where nearby residents were still largely longtime New Yorkers. Only two baths were located on the Hudson River: one at Bethune Street in Lower Manhattan (replacing Charles Street), and the other at West Thirty-Fifth Street near the Tenderloin district.

It took ten years for the total number of floating baths to grow to fifteen. With a nearly 50 percent increase in the population of the Lower East Side, DPW added these public facilities to piers and street ends between Gouverneur Lane and East Nineteenth Street. On the West Side, the Battery replaced Bethune Street and became a permanent summer location, as a city bath joined the private floating pool that had been there for decades. In 1888, with the African American population growing and moving northward into Harlem, a landing opened at East 138th Street on the Harlem River. Finally, in 1890 DPW met the state mandate, and fifteen pools were open in Manhattan. In the next five years—due to the rise in immigration, occasional heat waves with temperatures soaring into the nineties, and the increase in the total number of floating baths—the annual attendance for the three months from July through September exploded to 4.5 million. Nevertheless, within a decade the usefulness of the floating baths as a place for the poor to become clean would be questioned.

THE RECORDS KEPT at the Battery Maritime Building provided pool data regarding design and administration, but I had to find out more about how the pools functioned, how they were used, and by whom. In a bunch of annual reports from the early twentieth century, I began to discover answers to those questions.

From the beginning, and throughout their sixty-seven years on the waterfront, the baths were extremely popular, and crowd control continued to be essential. In keeping with the morals of the age, the floating baths were sex-segregated. An insert in an engraving by Harry Ogden depicts the exclusion of men at a pool on opening day. A fully clothed man, mopping his brow with a handkerchief, stands at the entryway. To his left is a little girl wearing a striped dress and a wide-brimmed hat, with a bathing suit rolled up under her arm. The attendant is sitting, holding a bully stick in one hand, with the other hand raised to indicate "NOT TODAY."

One's gender was not the only deciding factor; it was also an issue of class and age. To ensure that working men were not hassled before or after work, after the first two pools had opened in disarray, unaccompanied boys under the age of fourteen were denied entry between 5:00 and 8:00 a.m. and after 6:00 p.m. Proper decorum was a concern from the outset, and the authorities posted rules—originally set by the common council and later by the superintendent of public buildings—in prominent places. There was to be no pushing, splashing, profanity, shouting, or loitering.

Most Sundays, depending on the weather, the baths were full to capacity. Working-class men on their days off—mechanics, truck drivers, ships' carpenters, shoemakers, tanners, oystermen, and milkmen among them—found their way to one of the facilities. Once in line, the men had to wait up to thirty minutes for the attendants to clear the pool. They boarded, packed their clothing in a dressing room, and, standing completely naked, knee-deep in the water, with rounded backs displaying bare bottoms, dove into the water.

As the baths became more crowded and their use more varied, rules became stricter and broader. A drawing of the Charles Street pool in its first year shows boys standing three to four deep on the platform in front of the dressing rooms. Others are climbing and somersaulting over the railings into the water. A keeper appears holding a stick over the head of a splashing boy as if to dissuade him from doing so. To improve order and avoid accidents, the list of forbidden practices at these "homes away from home" was eventually expanded to prohibit dogs, diving, drinking of liquor, running, lunching, and, curiously, bringing newspapers or other objectionable articles into the bathing area.

Among their many duties, attendants had to safeguard the clothes that patrons left at their own risk on hooks in the doorless cubicles. Boys were the primary culprits of garment theft. A letter to the author from then eighty-one-year-old Norman Katz in 1981 describes a scene of dressing compartments without latches that made it easy for anyone to take off with a swimmer's clothes. One day, Katz wrote, "A laddy's clothes were gone, and a few of us shielded him, stark naked until we got him home." Despite the fact that passersby were offended by the sight, men and boys could swim nude until 1889, at which point the DPW commissioner engaged with Mayor Hugh Grant over the Progressives' issues of public morals versus private rights and dirt versus cleanliness. The commissioner's plan would require men and adolescents to wear clothing in the baths. Grant was opposed, reasoning that the user population was too poor to buy proper bathing attire. "Let them wear old trousers," was the response. Ironically, most of these men and boys had only one pair of trousers and thus would have to forego bathing altogether. When the pools opened that June, boys over fifteen and men wore bathing attire, and the number of male attendees had declined by less than 10 percent.

Mondays, Wednesdays, and Fridays were reserved for women, who over the years made up one-quarter to one-third of the annual floating bath user population. Women caring for their families did not attend. Those who could not afford to buy or retrofit a dress to serve as a bathing suit stayed away, as did young women who were menstruating or who needed their hair dry for work. Others who did not know how to swim might even have feared the pool. Descriptions of attendees on "Ladies Day" in the *New York Times* include the wives and daughters of working men with babes in arms and toddlers in tow, along with a heavy-set, elderly woman, and another who sat with her rheumatic feet in the water. Some women were in the water for the first time, and others "swam like ducks." The shop girls used the facilities before work, beginning at 5:00 a.m., emerging wet-haired and clean. Others arrived after 6:00 p.m. Although the original mandate of the DPW commissioner was that the hours should be the same for all, closing time was an hour earlier for women than men, probably because during the season fewer of them actually used the facilities.

The women who could afford to come to the pools always wore bathing outfits. These frocks were no more than a dress or nightgown with cut-off sleeves and a modest neckline. A hand-sewn seam from hem to crotch assured propriety. Fabrics ranged from cotton to wool, and they were probably very heavy when wet. Eventually, matrons at the pools were allowed to rent out their hand-made bathing suits for a modest fee, which they pocketed. Their one-piece gingham suits had short sleeves and cut-out backs.

But cleanliness was now not the only goal for the baths, since swimming as exercise and sport had become part of the culture. Jacob Riis photographed the baths, perhaps to demonstrate the success of his social advocacy. One of his iconic images is of a women's swimming class at Bath Number 10 on West Fifty-First Street, Hudson River. With the use of early flash photography, Riis captured a fully focused scene of intense activity and laughter. The matron stands near the facility's entrance. She is wearing a long skirt and high-collared long-sleeved white blouse, and a straw bowler identical to those worn by attendants at the men's baths. Four wooden staircases lead from the gangway into the water. The steps are crowded with children watching the scene or standing, scared to move down and into the water. Two brave ones are on their bellies, holding onto a step and trying to kick. Several children, hair tied in topknots, wear cork belts that allow them to float awkwardly. A woman assigned by the board of education to give free swimming lessons—in the years the budget allowed—instructs a pigtailed girl who is holding a small child, perhaps a sibling, floating on his or her back. A rope at either end of the pool creates an area for more adventurous children to swim on their own. One girl, back to the camera, is holding onto the rope and kicking furiously. Perhaps a minute after the device clicks, she will let go and, with both hands and feet flailing, be off for her first swim.

THE CITY OPENED the floating baths as a result of the Progressives' concerns about the living conditions of the mass of immigrants who arrived in Manhattan in the fourth quarter of the nineteenth century. In *How the Other Half Lives*, Jacob Riis writes about tenements with separate ethnic enclaves of Irish, Germans, Italians, and Jews. Although there were political and economic reasons for the selection of earlier floating bath locations, in most cases in the early 1900s they also were placed where they might serve a specific group. For example, on the East Side, the bath at Pike Street catered to the Jewish population; the East Thirty-Seventh bath was for the Irish; at East 112th, the Italians bathed. On the West Side, Italians also frequented the Bethune Street pool, and the Irish the West Twenty-Seventh Street facility.

The pool managers recognized that the floating baths were also a means of assimilation. A sign at Corlears Hook listed regulations such as "NO DIVING" in Yiddish, Italian, and English, the languages of the immigrants who frequented the facility. According to the *New York Times*, "a congregation of every nation on earth" appeared at the Grand Street bath on the Lower East Side during a July heat wave, with Italians and Jews among the group. Other articles provide more detail: Jews, Germans, Irish, and so-called Americans frolicked at the Charles Street bath on the West Side in its second year of operation; Irish and German-Jewish working-class women patronized the baths at East Fifth and Nineteenth Streets, where they availed themselves of swimming lessons from Miss Bennett, one of the teachers hired by the board of education.

Although the baths were sex-segregated, all of them were open to the general public regardless of race. However, the engraving of the Charles Street bath in 1870 is the only evidence I found that African Americans used the baths. On the right side of the image, a single, apparently black figure is shown diving head first into the water in front of a large group of white boys.

Using information on where the poor African Americans lived and the dates and locations of the baths, it is possible to extrapolate that African Americans most likely used the West Fifty-First Street bath. In 1890 second-generation Irish and newly arrived African Americans lived in deplorable conditions in the Tenderloin district. A recent in-depth study of black neighborhoods in New York and Chicago points out that black and white people in the district met on the streets in their daily lives. Perhaps they were also comfortable swimming together; if so, they were quiet about it. Another study gives an opposing view. Forced by circumstance to live near each other in cheap rental housing and to compete for identical unskilled jobs, the Irish and African Americans in the Tenderloin district came to detest each other. This hatred resulted in at least one race riot between the two groups during a heat wave in August 1900. According to this view, the floating baths in this area could be assumed to have been racially self-segregated.

Despite the compatibility of some of the ethnic groups, there is evidence of prejudice through bullying, particularly toward the Jews. The same article on the Grand Street bath that praises the ethnic mix found the treatment of a young "Hebrew" newsworthy: the police allowed other bathers to taunt him, calling him a "goose." They also turned their backs when the boy showed that he was afraid to enter the water. He timidly set his feet into the water, "[withdrew] them quickly and [shuddered]." Another boy noticed this and snuck behind him to shove him into the pool. The article goes on to tell readers that the bullying was successful and that the boy now would come to the bath only on days of extreme heat.

Self-segregation by class was also not unusual. American wives of white-collar men took swimming lessons at East Twenty-Seventh Street, and other middle-class wives and women of various ethnicities came to the public Battery bath. An engraving in *Harper's Weekly* shows white, well-dressed ladies waiting in line with their daughters. They have come by elevated train from uptown Manhattan, Brooklyn, and New Jersey to be taught to swim by the aforementioned Miss Bennett, who had a full-time job making the rounds of the pools. Some women have brought their African American servants to mind their children while mother enjoys the saltwater bath. Also shown in the drawing is a poor white couple standing off to one side. The heavily bearded man is wearing workers' boots, and his white-haired companion is leaning on her cane with one hand and tightly clasping the hand of a small child with the other. Their heads turned, they gaze longingly at the well-dressed crowd, indicating that even though the pool was free to all, they, at the very least, felt themselves to be separated and possibly excluded, even if not officially so.

As I sat there, sifting through antique photos of its ancestors, I envisioned the twenty-first-century floating pool and the New York City residents who might use it. I studied these old, dusty images and, as if in a double exposure, envisioned men and women clad in flip-flops and bikinis. I saw the smiling faces of the Parks Department attendants greeting children at the entrance to the barge, pointing out the dressing rooms, and reminding them to shower before entering the pool. Two policemen, who during the winter worked at the local high school and knew all the kids, watched the fun in the pool below. The historical documents testifying to decades of awkward segregation and outright exclusion in public places show that a useful public amenity needs a supportive administrative and public culture.

NEW YORK'S ORIGINAL FLOATING baths were private, and upper-class men preferred these exclusive, pay-per-use facilities. As early as 1817, Edmund March Blunt's *Stranger's Guide to New York* advertised two marine baths, both located on Manhattan's Lower West Side. By 1830 chemist Jacob Rabinow and shipwright Isaac Hall had established elegant saltwater floating facilities on both sides of Castle Garden at the Battery. Fashionable New Yorkers from as far north as Greenwich (now Greenwich Village) paid a fee to enjoy these luxurious spas. In addition to their sheer novelty, the baths were attractive to the paying public because the notion existed at the time that saltwater swimming promoted physical well-being.

By 1874, my research showed, the popularity and overcrowding of the municipal floating baths led private entrepreneurs to invest in building more spacious pay facilities. At a capital cost of between $10,000 and $15,000 ($225,000–$340,000) measured against an income of $5 to $31 ($112–$700) a day per facility, owners believed that they would cover costs and start making a profit within two years. Indeed, they must have. Between 1870 and 1888 at least, entrepreneurs—among them Isaac Hall and Charles Krack, the first superintendent of the city's floating baths—ran private baths at the Battery and along the East and Hudson Rivers.

Kate Bennett, probably in the years when the board of education ceased funding swimming lessons at the public baths, was also in the mix. The owners' only complaint during the years of operation was the cost of renting waterfront space from the city. Unlike the city-run baths, which for many years received a free pass from the Dock Department, private owners paid from $150 per month to $1,700 per season ($3,400–$38,000). These fees brought the private baths in line with the amounts paid by other commercial users, but in some instances they stood in the way of expected annual profits, and the owners renegotiated the rentals. These private baths and goods coexisted with public goods uneasily. They drew off support and showed that "free association" and "public goods" came at a price.

The private facilities were more elaborate, somewhat liberal as to the sexes, and less crowded than the public floating baths. Hall repaired his historic Battery bath in 1874. The 150-by-80-foot river-fed pool could accommodate two hundred bathers at a time. The Hoeft and Ficken Company bath was located sufficiently distant from the foot of Grand Street to allow clean water to flow through the 110-by-70-foot pool. Instead of separating the sexes by day, this complex accommodated three hundred male and three hundred female patrons in two sex-segregated pools (similar to the public bath placed at the Battery beginning in 1879). A further accommodation to the propriety of the times was the provision of separate dressing rooms separated by thick partitions "to avoid any communications passing between them" (whatever that might imply). Patrons who paid twenty-five cents per visit or seven dollars per season could also avail themselves of warm salt baths or cold showers in the sixteen bathing rooms.

Public pools were thus passed to one side by private floating baths for the middling and elite people of New York. Documents also showed that the pressures of economic development had a negative impact on the siting and use of floating public pools. By the turn of the nineteenth century, because of commercial competition for the waterfront, it became increasingly problematic to find summer berths for the floating baths. One solution was to moor two baths at one location. Whether singly or doubly, the fifteen baths fought for recreational access among convoys of steamers, schooners, canal boats, and barges. They were moored chockablock at piers and wharves alongside ship repair yards, passenger and railroad terminals, ice depots, brickyards, oyster basins, and the garbage and open manure dumps of the growing urban center.

Floating bath placement had always depended on the availability of free or low-rent property near crowded residential districts. Boss Tweed located the first East Side bath in an area with minimal surrounding waterfront activity. Thirty years later, there was a paucity of berthing sites due to the understandable but inconvenient city policy of leasing property to the highest bidder. Many of the baths floated amid new uses and in pricier waters. The Duane Street free bath sat at a bulkhead adjacent to active railroad piers where the New York Lake Erie and Western Railroad held a ten-year, $100,000 ($3 million) renewable lease. The Horatio Street bath initially sat in an oyster basin, but later it was squeezed in between transatlantic steamers. The Cunard Line paid the city $80,000 ($2.4 million) to tie up at a new pier at Jane Street, one block to the south of the bath, while a new pier at Bank Street, four blocks away, commanded $84,000 ($2.6 million).

Another unwelcome competitor to the baths for space on the waterfront was the city sewer system. The putative purpose of the free floating baths was as a means for the public to get clean, but their proximity to raw sewage made them an oxymoron: the only source of water was rivers polluted by active commercial use and the waste matter produced by an ever-growing population. In 1868 a *New York Times* article pointed out that New York was remiss in not following Boston's example of creating facilities in the river for "bathing the masses." Ironically, the article also described the East and Hudson Rivers as "tainted with filth" from the sewers. By the turn of the century, civic reformers once again made their voices heard, this time questioning the utility of the baths. Riis wrote that the floating baths were a dying institution: "River baths were only for the summer, and their time is past. As the sewers that empty into the river multiply, it is getting less and less a place to bathe in, though the boys find no fault."

Riis and others were pressing the government to build more municipal in-ground, year-round bathhouses that would be protected from sewage and out of the fierce competition for tie-ups on Manhattan's shoreline. The city opened the first of these on Rivington Street in 1901. The 1902 annual report of Manhattan borough president Jacob Cantor, who now had jurisdiction over the floating baths in Manhattan, documented the city's desire for more of this type of facility. The report cited problems with finding wharf room for the facilities in the crowded commercial waterfront and noted that the board of health had condemned many of their locations due to their proximity to sewer outlets. But probably because it would take time for bathhouse reform to move through the political morass, the original baths remained open and floated in increasingly polluted waters. In 1902, because the season was shortened due to both berthing problems and inclement weather, Manhattan's floating baths had an attendance of 2.1 million men, women, and children, a major decline from their most successful season in 1892 of 4.8 million.

MY RESEARCH PROVIDED insight and access to a visible past. The physical layout of the floating baths on the Hudson and East Rivers over time was equitable in terms of sanitarian and progressive philosophy. The baths were there to protect the middle and upper classes from disease and crime, and to serve the poor, who had no sanitary facilities, in a contained venue. The early baths were placed on the East and West Side waterfronts as close to the tenement districts as the width of Manhattan Island allowed. As demand for their use increased, the baths reached a variety of ethnic communities. But, either in fear of interethnic or interracial strife, or because recently arrived immigrants preferred to bathe or recreate with their own kind, and due to moral strictures, women and men swam at separate hours. There was no assimilation.

The archives at the Battery Maritime Building held valuable lessons for me on the bureaucratic and political difficulties a single person will encounter in introducing a new enterprise to the powers that be. It took twenty-one years from the date that New York State authorized the city to build and maintain two floating baths to their opening day. Public policy initiatives do not come about immediately, and they do not die suddenly. A project is the result of many factors and a network of political wills. In the 1900s public floating baths survived, but the political will to maintain them was fading.

CHAPTER 3

Waterfront in Despair

AFTER I SORTED THROUGH the archives in the late 1990s, a twenty-first-century floating pool became an idée fixe for me. That commitment influenced the sort of history I was seeking and finding in the files. I knew that what was coming up in the records and historic newspaper articles was leading to the demise of the public and private floating baths, and that their closing was good policy. The Hudson and East Rivers were becoming toxic, and the outer banks were almost dead. I imagined what having a dip in that water did to people, especially children. But I could not help but feel some nostalgia, some sort of loss. The passing of the baths was, no matter the quality of the water, the loss of a public good.

By 1907 pollution had become the major topic for concern. The baths, founded to clean the great unwashed, were now a place of accumulating filth. The Merchants Association of the City of New York now added its voice to the chorus against polluted baths. This group of prominent businessmen, among them financier J. Pierpont Morgan, was bothered by any conditions at the commercial waterfront that might have deterred trade. Was theirs a hidden agenda? After an intensive pier-by-pier and street-end-by-street-end sanitary inspection of the waterfront, they published a report with the alarming title of "Pollution of New York Harbor as a Menace to Health by the Dissemination of Intestinal Diseases through the Agency of the Common Housefly."

The graphic details of this report provide one of the rare descriptions of what it must have been like to swim in the floating baths. There were flies in abundance, drawn by the sewage near the Corlears Hook and East Hundredth Street baths, and by piles of decayed fish at West Thirty-Fifth Street. At the East Third Street bath, flies congregated on an open manure dump. An appalling image in the report was of East Ninety-Sixth Street, where masses of raw sewage collected around the heads and shoulders of swimming children. Finally, there seemed to be ample evidence to compel change. However, as usual, change was not on the agenda. There was no scientific proof that either sewage or flies caused disease, and more studies would have to be made before the system of floating baths was reformed.

In the interim, probably due to pressure from earlier state legislation, the city constructed two additional year-round, municipal bathhouses on the land. As with the floating pools and the playgrounds, the city located these facilities in densely populated wards. The 232 West Sixtieth Street Municipal Bath opened in 1906 between an immigrant Irish and African American enclave. Manhattan borough president Jacob Cantor's office opened the second in-ground pool at the East Twenty-Third Street and Avenue A Municipal Bath in 1908. The belief was that tenement dwellers would rather "recreate" than bathe for improved hygiene, and perhaps to increase their use, both buildings included swimming pools. Patrons would have to shower before entering the pool, and thus they would ultimately get clean. The municipal mission remained the same, even as the new pool was located far from the rivers.

In its basement, the Sixtieth Street Bath contained a sixty-by-thirty-five-foot "plunge" pool with a cement bottom that sloped from three feet to seven feet to create a shallow and deep end. The pool was one-third shorter, but its width was equal to that of a floating pool. Although lit by an electric generator, a low, semi-arched ceiling made the room feel dark. Like the floating pools, these facilities were segregated by sex and were open to men and women on different days. They were also racially integrated. However, there were confrontations between the Irish and African Americans over the use of the West Sixtieth Street pool. In 1908, over a twelve-month period, nearly five million patrons availed themselves of the showers, tubs, pools, and hair-drying rooms available in the two indoor baths. Even so, the floating baths were still not defunct: their summer three-month user count remained steady at 2.3 million. The population requiring a cleansing bath, some physical recreation, or respite from the heat wanted to swim in the open air in the summer, preferred the larger pools, and were not drawn to the dark bathhouses in winter. Bath reformers began a public relations campaign to increase the use of these expensive on-land buildings.

The studies of the river baths also continued. Members of the Metropolitan Sewerage Commission were the next to voice their opinions. Appointed by the governor, this group of four engineers and a physician was mandated both to prove that pollution in New York Harbor was bad for the city and to recommend an improved sewerage plan. Although commerce was still a major concern of the sponsors of the study, a chapter from the commission's first report published in 1910 was devoted entirely to "the influence of the polluted waters on public health through bathing." The commission hypothesized that bacteria-laden sewage entered the waters above the Narrows, causing swimming in river water to endanger public health. However, admitting that it was still difficult to prove this theory, the authors postulated that swimmers inadvertently swallowed pool water containing bacilli that caused people to become ill.

One proof of this could be found in oysters. Locally inedible today—instead used by such educational institutions as the Harbor School on Governors Island as a method to clean up New York City's rivers—oysters for centuries had been a major, delicious food source for all. In 1909, a year before the commission's report, oyster beds sat near sewer outlets. A court in England that year ordered a New York City hotel to pay a fine to a British navy officer who had succumbed to cholera after eating raw oysters.

Oysters alone, however, were insufficient proof. If the commission wanted to change public policy, it had to prove that raw sewage did, in fact, enter the river baths in Manhattan. The experimenters injected red dye into the neighboring sewers and observed them, timing the speed of the dye's journey to the floating baths. Among the pools that turned a vivid red was the East Ninety-Sixth Street bath. These tests resulted in the strongest recommendation to date: close the floating baths as soon as possible. Even so, in 1911, with five pools located in the inland bathhouses, as many as eleven floating public baths remained open in the East and Hudson Rivers. However, their attendance declined to 1.8 million users, and that trend would prove to be irreversible.

THE ULTIMATE DEMISE of the floating baths was foretold in 1912 when the Health Department used its new permit powers to prohibit three of them from opening. Recommending any site for baths posed a dilemma. Officials acknowledged the polluted waters in the floating baths, yet the city still lacked sufficient alternative swimming and bathing facilities to make up for the closures. Underlying their decision was the old issue of public control: if the department closed all of the floating pools, the poor would just return to the age-old swimming hole, near sewer outlets in the dirty rivers. They would risk injury and drowning without the benefits of supervision and containment. Allowing eight baths, therefore, was a compromise. Here, even if they became ill specifically from the rivers' dirty water (the link still under debate), people could at least swim under controlled conditions at points along the waterfront chosen by city officials.

Despite the declining numbers, pressure to keep the existing floating baths continued, and in 1913 the Health Department tried a new approach. To obtain a permit, the borough presidents were forced to retrofit the floating baths. The pools were to be made watertight. Sealed, wooden tanks, their top layer open to the air, would replace the existing open-slat wells. A fire hydrant would fill the pool with filtered water from the Croton Aqueduct. In addition, similar to the inland bathhouses, there were now toilets, and patrons had to pass through newly installed showers located at each corner and at the steps before entering the pool. To assure its cleanliness, the water would be treated with large amounts of a bleach solution, hypochlorite of lime, the forerunner of chlorine. This enclosed arrangement with the scorching doses of bleach bore a strong resemblance to the pool that I had in mind for New York Harbor, but with appropriate amounts of chlorine.

The East Fifth Street floating pool was the first such facility to open in 1913, but it was a disappointment. The walls leaked, and in stormy weather the dirty salt water lapped over the edges of the pool. Bathers found the water too cold, and the bleach had a foul odor and stung their eyes; they preferred instead to jump directly into the putrid river. There was still a need to maintain control of the swimming population, and that same summer the Manhattan borough president's office opened six floating pools (five of them not retrofitted). Whether due to a shorter season, weather, or competition from in-ground pools, attendance declined to 1.5 million. This was an approximate average of 250,000 visits per pool compared with 333,000 in 1892, when there were fifteen pools.

Reading on in the files, I learned that in January 1915 the battle over keeping the floating pools open moved to another political body, the New York City Board of Estimate and Apportionment (BOE). Jane Jacobs would participate in hearings there in the late 1950s in her battle against Robert Moses as he sought to put a highway through Washington Square Park. Manhattan borough president Marcus Marks—who was now in charge of Manhattan's pools—required a unanimous affirmative vote to procure the appropriation needed to operate, maintain, and store the remaining six retrofitted floating pools for the coming summer. Board member and comptroller William Prendergast held the holdup vote. Just a year before, he had voted for the use of revenue bonds to enclose five baths, but he now argued the need for overall economy. He reasoned that the retrofitted pools were still unsanitary, as they could be contaminated when river water lapped over their sides, and he said the inland baths provided sufficient bathing facilities.

Why Prendergast—an elected official from the same political

party consisting of Republicans and a variety of other groups, among them liberals and independents, known as Fusion—was such a rabid opponent can only be surmised. The next election was not until 1917. It is likely that he was trying to reform the budgetary process after years of Democratic Party–led Tammany Hall mismanagement and overspending.

Marks's budgetary request came up on a bimonthly basis and was consistently denied by the Prendergast-led faction. Then, on May 29, at a public hearing at city hall a few days before the floating pools would have opened for the season, the battle over the appropriation came to a head. Marks came prepared. In a move similar to one that Jane Jacobs would use in her fight against Robert Moses, Marks arranged for a delegation of more than three hundred schoolchildren and their teachers to appear at city hall. A blind public school boy stood at the speaker's podium, joined by health and lifesaving advocates, members of a league of foreign-born citizens, the Moral and Hygienic Association, and a spokesman for a labor union to plead that the pools be kept open. Marks's effort was to no avail. Despite cries from the audience to impeach Prendergast, he once again prevailed, securing a week's postponement of the decision.

On June 8 Marks submitted one more request to the BOE: use funds that were already in his budget line of "Care of Public Buildings and Offices" to place Manhattan's floating baths in commission. Prendergast still had complaints and voted against the request on the grounds that this money would be taken out of the budget that included highway maintenance. Public baths for the poor now vied for money with the care of middle- and upper-class streets, as well as districts with Prendergast voters.

Because the money was in his budget, Marks no longer needed unanimous approval from the BOE or Prendergast's favorable vote. Therefore, in late July and August 1915 Marks opened six retrofitted baths. The attendance record of 1,408,942 men and women—84,600 more than in the prior year—is evidence of their continued popularity. In the tenement communities without bathtubs, the use of floating baths continued. Working men still needed a place to cleanse themselves of sweat and summer grime. Beyond pure functionality, however, a large number of people just found pleasure in swimming in water *on* water.

THE ARCHIVES CONTINUED to hold valuable lessons for me. Public policy initiatives do not care about immortality, and they do not die suddenly. A project is the result of many factors and a network of political wills. In the 1920s public floating baths survived, but the political will to maintain them was fading.

The number of Manhattan's free, floating baths remained at eight until 1927, but they were now more than fifty years old and required frequent and ever-costlier repairs. A storm severely damaged one of the structures; traffic in the harbor bumped into others. Still another, as if presaging its infelicitous ending, collided with a dumping board, a berth where garbage and manure scows picked up refuse to tote out of the city. A lack of funds to pay staff was a constant issue, sometimes forcing the pools to close before the end of the season. Accommodations for the automobile also affected their placement: the two remaining West Side baths were moved north of Seventy-Ninth Street to make way for the construction of the Miller Highway (now the West Side Highway). Winter storage was affected when the extension of the Grand Central Parkway forced a move from North Beach in Queens to Clason Point in the Bronx.

Several events in the 1930s caused the further decline of the floating baths. First, they were no longer needed as a place to become clean. All new or renovated low-income housing units now had bathtubs. The public's desire for multiple types of recreation also removed more patrons from the floating pools. To boost the attendance at Manhattan's land-bound municipal bathhouses, eight of them now contained swimming pools, six had gyms, and the Borough of Manhattan Department of Parks ran all of them. New Yorkers also gravitated to the beaches at Coney Island and the Rockaways, which were now made more easily accessible by public transit on the Brooklyn-Manhattan subway lines.

The floating pools were losing their public. In 1934, when the pools had been reduced to six, total attendance was less than three hundred thousand, or one-third the number of patrons at the six floating pools two decades earlier. The Health Department condemned two more of these six pools at the end of that summer, and there were no plans to replace them. That same year, Robert Moses unified the borough offices of what was then called the New York City Parks Department and became the agency's overall head. But the floating pools were not in his portfolio. Since New York City's consolidation in 1898, the borough president of Manhattan, now Samuel Levy, was still in control.

In the fall of 1935 the *New York Times* described the floating bath situation: "None has been built in 50 years, but the old ones have been brought down from Clason Point every June by the 85-year-old commodore of the fleet, Edwin T. Hyde, and probably will continue to be brought down until they fall to pieces."

The following year, the New Deal—now the center of progressive policy initiatives—offered cities grants to build outdoor, in-ground pools. Moses grabbed the opportunity. He could use Works Progress Administration funds to provide jobs during the Depression as well as create a means of keeping out-of-work New Yorkers and ragtag children from trouble. The Parks Department opened eleven in-ground pools from Upper Manhattan and Harlem to the Bronx, Queens, and Brooklyn. By Labor Day of that year 1.79 million city residents had used the pools.

In 1937, for the last time, the Manhattan borough president's budget was the source of funds for Edwin T. Hyde to lead his fleet of four from its winter headquarters to the pools' summer berths in Manhattan. Two pools were placed on the West Side at Gansevoort and Jefferson Streets, and two on the East Side at Twenty-First and Sixty-Second Streets, where there were no new WPA facilities nearby.

And then, with yet another bath no longer in usable condition, there were three. Early in 1938, Manhattan borough president Stanley M. Isaacs arranged with Moses to turn the remaining floating baths over to the Parks Department. Ever the politician, perhaps Moses thought he could use these remnants of the past to placate Upper West Side residents irritated by another one of his projects.

Construction of the West Side Highway now prohibited access to the Hudson River from Riverside Drive. So, to appease some well-heeled New Yorkers, he opened what he advertised as a "modern swimming hole" consisting of three reconstructed barges moored at Ninety-Sixth Street. Two outdoor pools floated on either side of a buoyant bathhouse. Already in their third incarnation, these floating pools once again became a public attraction. A period photograph shows a mass of white men, women, and children packed together at the edge of one of the pools, with others patiently waiting their turn in line on the banks of the Hudson River. But the novelty of this public floating bath was far from sustainable policy.

After a successful summer, Moses sought $4,921.50 ($89,000 in 2020 dollars) from the budget director, to continue to operate the new complex. A letter to me from Moses written a year before his death explained that the remaining barges were falling apart and that the city refused to appropriate funds for their repair. In fact, the floating baths were no longer needed. The Parks Department had federal funds to build in-ground pools.

The War Department wrote the epitaph for the floating baths. In June 1942 they sat in disuse at the mouth of Pugsley Creek in the Bronx. On their annual inspection, the department found three barges in a state of decay. Fearing that pieces of them might drift or flow down into the East River and cause hazardous conditions in the waterway, the department ordered their removal and disposal. The floating baths had allowed human access to a crowded, working waterfront for over a half century, and at the outset of World War II they were scuttled.

MY RESEARCH IN the musty documents detailing the administrative history of New York Harbor ended roughly with the demise of the floating public baths. These documents, which no one had seen or cared about for nearly a century, were about to be thrown out. I left the Battery Maritime Building, looking to the future, with a usable history and thoughts of the river baths floating through my mind.

Usable history has to be applied to the municipal reality. And since World War II swimming in the river, in any manner, became a risky and forbidden behavior. The story of the waterfront after 1942 is well known and part of my own historical memory. Beginning in the mid-1940s, little by little the edges of the island city began to decay both morally and physically. The 1954 movie *On the Waterfront*, filmed in Hoboken, New Jersey, exposed the corruption in the maritime industry. Prostitution along the docks on both sides of the river flourished, but even that most marginal and dangerous of work left as the longshoremen lost their jobs. In the 1960s a preponderance of New York City shipping moved to container ports in New Jersey, and the ascendance of airline travel dissipated the need for transatlantic passenger terminals. Left behind were empty piers, many of them merely skeletons of their former selves. Manhattan borough president Percy Sutton, speaking at a 1966 conference on the future of Manhattan's waterfront, described the situation: "It [the waterfront] has too long been regarded as marginal land, a dumping ground for industries, highways, rotting piers and raw sewage. The public has been and continues to be denied access to the waterfront."

Economic decline, which gripped the shoreline and had spread inland by the 1960s, did not cancel the desire on the part of citizens for aqueous recreation. The Parks Department under John Lindsay, who became mayor in 1966, began two programs to bring swimming facilities to underserved neighborhoods. Like the original floating baths, the pools were portable, but they were inland and land-based. Unlike the floating baths, the purpose of the pools was solely to keep residents cool during the hot summer. (In view of the riots that occurred in cities across the country that year, the pools were probably also a means to control tempers during a time of civil unrest.) The first of these facilities were small, prefabricated above-ground pools with a narrow, attached deck. They were installed in the street but could be moved as needed. In addition, several Swim-mobiles, "which resembled a semi-trailer filled with water," were hauled to various neighborhoods where Parks Department employees parked them, filled them from fire hydrants, and, at the end of each day, emptied and towed them away to a storage lot on Randalls Island.

Opening the river edges for public use was not ever on the agenda of the next mayor, Abraham Beame. The city had far more pressing problems. Homeless men slept on street corners, and crime and heroin addiction were rampant. Middle-class whites fled these real and perceived dangers, moving to the suburbs to follow the exodus of capital and jobs that was already under way and slashing the city's tax revenue. Severe budget cuts left streets dark, with lamp bulbs missing or shot out. Garbage abounded, either in its raw state or on fire. Access to the river, although it could have provided some relief to the population, was a nonpriority.

WHEN I DISCOVERED my interest in floating pools in the late 1970s, public awareness of the New York City waterfront had begun to return. Issues dear to the earlier Progressives (recreation and hygiene) were being addressed in various ways. People were bicycling, jogging, and even drawing with chalk on the now-collapsed and abandoned West Side Highway, a stone's throw from the Hudson. The 1972 Clean Water Act inspired hope that New York's rivers could one day be clean enough for swimming. Shelley Seccombe's photographs from the decade show a young man performing a backflip from a bulkhead into the Hudson. This risky jump was worth taking.

The nation's 1976 bicentennial celebrations brought thousands of New Yorkers—entrepreneurs and preservationists, tugboat captains and office workers, parents and children—to the waterfront. Lining the shore, they watched tall ships sail by, partied, and became conscious again that they lived in a city of islands. Three years later, the ideological momentum had been gathered, along with a more mundane need to improve the environment to keep business and high-income residents in the city. On January 18, 1979, Mayor Edward I. Koch announced that "if there is one thing I want my administration to be identified with, it is that . . . we opened the waters to the people of the city."

Awareness, however, did not yield easy or safe access to the city's waterways. As in the Progressive Era, the municipal and private entities needed population control. The government erected chain link fences to block access, not necessarily to avoid deaths from drowning or disease but to absolve its legal liability. In a 1992 photograph by Tom Fox, an elderly, white-haired man is trying to reach the Hudson River from West Street. Dressed in a white short-sleeved shirt that matches his hair and propped up by a brown cane in his left hand, he has just climbed over a waist-high concrete barrier. He is resting before attempting to break through a broken chain-link fence. To the west, he faces a disarray of decaying boards, the remnants of a once-active pier. One wonders if he ever reached his destination—the riverfront.

In 1981 I wanted to test the viability of my growing passion to reintroduce floating pools and submitted an op-ed piece to the *New York Times*. If it was published, how might the public and the municipality react? On Memorial Day weekend, accompanied by a Jacob Riis photograph, the article was published. In it, I asked: "Today, as our rivers are becoming cleaner, and water shortages prevalent, the idea of floating swimming pools is enticing. . . . Could we once again reserve space for a historically successful means of public access to the waterfront?"

As I formulated my early plans in the mid-1980s, I was no longer holed up in the Battery Maritime Building's bowels listening to Imus in the Morning on WABC or to ferry horns. I sat on top of the world, in an office with a floor-to-ceiling window listening to helicopters whir by. I had just secured my PhD, spent a few months working in the Waterfront Division of the Department of City Planning (DCP), and now, in a sparsely furnished office on the ninety-second floor of 2 World Trade Center, I worked as the deputy director of the West Side Task Force. On clear days, while peering over the verdigris, circular, and pyramidal roofs of Battery Park City's World Financial Center, I faced the grim sight of the Hudson River wholly absent of shipping traffic. Both shorelines within my sight were littered with empty, derelict piers. That decade's events, however, would bring signs of historic change to the waterfronts of New Jersey and New York City. As I wrote in the second edition of

Manhattan Water-Bound, my 1987 book that emerged from my graduate research in the Battery Maritime Building, "The waterfront is not dead. . . . The meaning of waterfront improvement merely changed and new activities have moved into spaces once reserved for shipping." In the postindustrial era that began in the 1970s, residential and recreational uses were already coming to the banks of the Hudson and East Rivers.

The new entries under way on the Manhattan waterfront were wide-ranging. On Lower Manhattan's West Side, thirteen apartment houses and the World Financial Center arose on the landfill that covered defunct piers in the southern half of Battery Park City. Thus, ninety-two acres of new parks and open public space, predominantly along the Hudson, became part of Lower Manhattan's landscape. The South Street Seaport's Festival Marketplace introduced a new kind of commercial venture, mixing leisure and tourism facilities with the working waterfront. A shopping mall, restaurants, and historic tall ships brought the public onto a reconstructed cargo pier extending out into the water. But the nineteenth-century fish stalls that received produce from boats landing nearby were smelly and dirty—not at all compatible with an elegant twentieth-century shopping and eating destination. The Fulton Fish Market was on line to close, ending another chapter in the working river.

I became interested in adapting old industrial sites and fascinated by new uses for outdated barges. The Waterfront Barge Museum opened on a covered cargo barge in Jersey City, New Jersey, in 1986 and moved to Red Hook in Brooklyn in 1994. Instead of carrying goods from ships to trains, as it did in the early twentieth century, this vessel now housed educational programs and exhibitions about the waterways. It also provided public access to once-closed piers. David Sharps, the museum's founder and owner, would be extremely helpful later by explaining to me the many layers of permits he had to procure to allow patrons onboard the Barge Museum.

I was also intrigued by the successful project of violinist Olga Bloom, whom I met at the Waterfront Center (where I also met

Adam Perlmutter). With the help of relatives, Olga had converted an 1899 steel coffee barge into a chamber music concert venue. Bargemusic, Ltd. opened at Fulton Landing in Brooklyn in 1977, at the foot of the Brooklyn Bridge. Notably, Olga's project offers the unique feeling of listening to music while floating on water, as the notes rise and fall with the gentle swells generated by passing vessels. This was the synchrony I hoped to capture with a floating pool: bodies rising and falling, swimming in water on water.

Also, in 1977, across Fulton Landing from Bargemusic, Michael O'Keefe opened the River Café below the Brooklyn Bridge. This floating restaurant opened on another converted coffee barge after a thirteen-year struggle with federal and state regulations and with city fire code inspectors who insisted on enforcing rules designed only for land-based buildings. Floating and eating with the rise and fall of waves doesn't sound attractive? Not a problem. O'Keefe foresaw your concern. The barge sits immobile atop the remains of a pier.

These attractive urban amenities notwithstanding, redeveloping the New York Harbor's waterfront was challenging. Derelict industrial lots were empty and also often brownfields. Street access could be established, but would people want to come? The water remained grossly polluted—the fish inedible, the water unswimmable, and the ebb tide odoriferous.

A spate of high-handed buyers and developers planned high-rise residential projects in the 1980s, responding to Mayor Koch's desire to open up the waterfront. The public-minded questions I asked in my *Times* op-ed were receiving privatized responses. The waterfront's river views of the 1980s would be available to renters and buyers of means as a semi-exclusive privilege. For Koch, "to open" meant allowing private interests to build financially viable projects that would transform the waterfront, improve residents' quality of life, and, most important to the recently bankrupt city, increase the tax base—all worthy goals in themselves. During this period, developers had plans for at least twenty-eight blocks of new structures along the Manhattan waterfront. The DCP required public access to the waterfront, but most of the proposed buildings' height and bulk would cast shadows where the public walked. Additionally, waterfront access would be at the mercy of residents complaining of "outsiders invading their space."

In June 1985 the Koch administration noted the demand for downtown office space and added my former "research library," the Battery Maritime Building, and the adjacent Staten Island Ferry Terminal to a list of city-owned properties available for private investment. Developers submitted eight plans for a multistory office building, for the restoration and modernization of the two ferry terminals, and for various new cultural activities. In 1985 Donald Trump also announced "his grandest plan yet." His Television City, as he called it, was to be constructed on the West Side waterfront between Fifty-Ninth and Seventy-Second Streets on land Trump acquired from the defunct Penn Central Transportation Company. Included in the mixed-use plan was a headquarters for the NBC network. Looming over the abandoned rail yards, but separated from the Hudson by an elevated highway, was to be the world's tallest edifice at forty-eight stories higher than the Empire State Building. It would be forty-six stories taller than the original World Trade Center.

By 1990, few shovels were in the ground to move these projects along. The 1987 stock market crash flattened the real estate market, and the ensuing recession challenged financing, leaving many projects on drawing boards. The Battery Park City apartments would eventually be on the auction block. The consortium that the city selected to construct the office tower at the Battery Maritime Building would soon return the unimproved property to the City of New York. To save Television City, Trump would ask Mayor Koch for a $700 million abatement. A verbal fight would ensue, and Trump's request was refused. He would also lose NBC when the city gave the company tax breaks to remain at Rockefeller Center. Years of community input would eventually yield a smaller residential waterfront park development known as Riverside South.

AS PRIVATE CAPITAL'S INTEREST regarding the waterfront waxed and waned with the economic cycle, a battle over a public project galvanized popular interest in access to New York's estuarial waters and in the water's health. Westway, a proposed 4.2-mile multibillion-dollar highway, development, and park project, was the first grand Manhattan plan of that era to be terminated. The cause of its failure was a new issue, one that would have been close to the hearts of Jacob Riis and to the early twentieth-century Health Department: waterway pollution. A six-lane interstate highway running from the Battery to Forty-Second Street had been planned, and the vision was even grander because, unlike the elevated West Side Highway the new roadway would replace, Westway would be constructed partially in a tunnel under the landfill pressing on the Hudson River's shore to the west. Above, it would consist of various residential and commercial developments.

First proposed in 1973, Westway's proponents had different objectives. The New York City DOT aimed to replace the elevated highway, now partially collapsed due to age and a lack of maintenance funds. City hall was interested in creating desirable real estate to encourage the middle class to return to the city, thus enlarging the tax base and encouraging the Lower West Side's redevelopment. David Rockefeller and the Downtown-Lower Manhattan Association he chaired believed the new roadway would speed up commutes from the suburbs and thus return business to downtown's declining financial center. Local community boards sought neighborhood traffic relief; organized labor and the New York Chamber of Commerce and Industry anticipated job creation for an area with high unemployment.

Perhaps to engage public support and to mitigate protest against the highway, the plan for the Westway landfill included ninety-three acres of parkland on Manhattan's West Side waterfront. I had studied the Progressives' swimming facilities and reform parks, and I had opened New York City's first riverfront street end to passive recreation, so I favored eking out a new, 2.6-mile stretch of waterfront with multiple types of recreation from the Hudson River landfill.

Likely because of my friendship with Claire Beckhardt (the New

York City regional director of the Department of State Parks) and my role as board member on the Parks Council, Governor Hugh Carey (one of three governors in office during the Westway fight) appointed me in 1980 to a committee to consult with architects Robert Venturi and Denise Scott Brown on a design for the Westway park-to-be. At a meeting in Claire's office with Venturi, Scott Brown, and Craig Whitaker (the state's in-house architect for the park) I showed the assembled a photograph of a nineteenth-century floating bath. I had also brought Rem Koolhaas's *delirious new york: A Retroactive Manifesto for Manhattan* and opened the book to "The Story of the Pool (1977)." On page 309 is a drawing showing an overhead view of a thin, rectangular-shaped pool—with dozens of people swimming in strict rows—making a tentative landing at Wall Street. In a ceremony for Russian architects who swam continuously to power the vessel from architectural purgatory in Moscow to freedom in New York City, the dapper American presenter reads the words on the medal: "THERE IS NO EASY WAY FROM THE EARTH TO THE STARS." I hoped that the Westway park, if it were actually built even though I had neither plans nor funds, could become the place for me to install a modern floating pool. But it would not be so. The architects submitted three drawings for a proposed park, but none with a floating pool. Soon, Westway itself disappeared from the drawing boards.

Why did Westway die? For fourteen years, the state and the city worked to secure this project backed by major business leaders, four US presidents, four New York governors, and various pro-Westway interest groups. But that formidable group was up against a broad coalition of opposition: "Citizens, their lawyers, and federal agency staff and scientists." Some, such as citizen opponent Marci Benstock, questioned whether federal dollars could adequately foot the bill. New Jersey officials feared that new residential development on the landfill would adversely affect the potential housing market on their side of the Hudson. In conversations with members of the DCP at the time, I found them loath to prepare a zoning or land-use plan for the landfill until Westway was assured. This planning vacuum created fear among the public about the possible types of development. Would it be high-rise buildings that blocked views and access to the waterfront? Crowded commercial venues? Noisy factories?

Environmental groups such as the NYC Clean Air Campaign (whose president was Benstock) fought against increased air and water pollution, the destruction of tidal wetlands, and the disturbance of the striped bass's habitat (it had only recently returned to the cleaner Hudson River waters). Their causes and concerted resistance would prove fatal to the highway project. Section 404 of the 1965 Federal Water Pollution Control Act, amended in 1980, required a water quality permit (which the floating pool would also require fifty years later under the New York State DEC) and gave opponents room to sue. As described by William Buzbee, "No filling in waters is allowed unless the underlying project is water-dependent" and even if it "is water dependent," it will not be allowed if it causes "'significant' degradation to important aquatic habitat." In other words, a project that was not water-dependent did not need to be in river waters; if it was water-dependent, it must not harm fish.

Of all the efforts and adversarial litigation, only one lawsuit succeeded. It was brought by a coalition of Westway opponents in 1985 asking to reverse a landfill permit issued by the Army Corps of Engineers. The legal claim was based on fish—indeed, a fish. Studies had revealed that there was "substantial" use of the Westway site by young striped bass. On the basis of this "adverse impact," federal judge Thomas Griesa denied the permit to begin the landfill. So, in September 1986 Mayor Koch and Governor Mario Cuomo announced a deal to reallocate the $1.725 billion the federal government had promised to the city fourteen years earlier to build Westway, to improve mass transit, and to conduct modest replacements of the West Side Highway.

THE ENVIRONMENTAL ISSUES that killed Westway and the reasonable suspicion toward private capital development created room to see water access as a public good for all New Yorkers. By the mid-1990s, New York City's parks and recreation had new meaning. Having changed little since the 1970s, when investment came to a standstill and open-space advocates had left the city, the new city officials were stimulated to think differently by a 9.4 percent population growth. Not unlike in the Progressive Era a century before, problems that needed attention included social, health, and environmental issues. And, as in the early twentieth-century reforms, parks with passive and active recreational facilities were one way to do this. This time, the newly arrived New Yorkers were Hispanic, African, and Asian. There was also an influx of white suburbanites who, despite Westway's failure, were returning to the city. The immigrants brought new customs, beliefs, social forms, and ways to recreate—from playing music and barbecuing outside to playing soccer. White suburbanites sought traditional activities, such as tennis, basketball, and sunbathing. How could these dissimilar population groups become a community, play together, and work together in new, diverse open spaces?

The lessons I learned in the Battery Maritime Building would only go so far. New projects for a new century would require traditional concepts and new planning strategies. While the earlier sanitarians equated the provision of places to become clean with improved health and morals, studies in the 1990s showed that most New Yorkers shared a different value system. Cleanliness was no longer the issue. With spaces and activities for exercise and for contemplation, parks addressed various concerns, including a growing epidemic of obesity and a desire for "increased life expectancy, and promotion of psychic well-being." By the end of the decade, waterfronts on both sides of the Hudson and on part of the East River evidenced this changing recreational philosophy. Sunbathing on the Battery Park City landfill and climbing over barriers to sit and view the water were replaced by grand plans for waterfront parks on the cusp of the twenty-first century.

As early as 1993, my close friend Warrie Price began implementing her dream to revitalize New York's birthplace, the Battery. Like me, Warrie had been mentored and motivated by people in high places. When she was in college, her roommate's mother was Lady Bird Johnson, the first lady. Warrie watched Johnson ensure that laws passed to make highways into garden-ways. Lady Bird's aspiration and the mantra of her dear friend, philanthropist Mary Lasker, was "to plant millions of flowers where the millions pass," and this drew Warrie toward revitalizing the Battery. Here was a manageable twenty-five acres that included the borrowed waterscape of 11,000 acres of historic New York Harbor. It was also the gateway to the Statue of Liberty and to Ellis Island, the figurative gates through which millions of people had passed to become Americans. After a failed political run for the New York City Council, Warrie decided to focus her civic drive on one project to thank New York for giving her, a Texan, such an adventure-filled life. Transforming the Battery from a dilapidated eyesore dominated by asphalt into a horticultural oasis became Warrie's passion.

Foreshadowing some of my adventures with the *Floating Pool Lady*, Warrie had to create partnerships with overlapping city, state, and federal government jurisdictions. Her first step was to design and rebuild the Battery Promenade that runs 1,500 feet along the seawall, which was then used for parking. She raised $200,000 (in mainly private funds), hired a landscape architect, and developed a plan for implementation. A major fight with National Park Service personnel and their ferry concessionaire over parking ensued. Warrie's plan required eliminating fifteen spaces to serve a greater public goal: better pedestrian access and the uninterrupted views of the historic harbor. Warrie won that battle but remembered every moment of the struggle. Warrie learned what I would also discover years later: few people like change, even if the public is better served. In the 1990s I would have benefited immensely from Warrie's example. As I embarked on my own quest to plan, design, and construct a floating public pool, however, she had imparted her hard-learned wisdom to me, and I was on a course for rough waters.

CHAPTER 4

Hoboken Ho

BY THE END OF the 1990s, with the history of floating pools in hand and the passion to build one growing, I was ready to act . . . in Hoboken, New Jersey! Ever since 1981, when my op-ed piece was published in the *New York Times*, I had become an evangelist for floating pools. I had proselytized for floating pools in my jobs at the New York City Department of Parks (Parks Department) and at the Economic Development Corporation (EDC). Whenever I spoke or wrote about it, I felt that my project should be a pretty easy sell. It's a gift! It is part of New York City history! Hey, it can be an attraction that draws people and other investment to the waterfront! However, the people to whom I pitched the pool were enthusiastic but reluctant to help me take action.

I would like to say that I had carefully considered the wisdom of changing the location of my floating pool from New York City, where my project's nineteenth-century progenitors were located and where parks commissioner Henry Stern had accepted the facility. However, Commissioner Stern had added a caveat that was not in my prospectus: I would have to provide the funds for the department to run the pool, and I had no ability to or intention of doing so.

Until a well-placed acquaintance invited me to Hoboken, where there was actually a constituency for a floating pool on my terms, there had been no serious suitors or partners.

For me, Hoboken was Frank Sinatra, the Stevens Institute of Technology, and a lawyer who would become a personal friend and ally, L. Michael Krieger, Esq., JD, MBA. I had listened to "Ol' Blue Eyes" as a teenager on a plug-in radio tucked under my pillow, while pretending to sleep and dreaming of romance. I knew Stevens for more down-to-earth reasons: the investigations that the institute's students conducted for me on tides, waves, and water depth in all the areas where I might locate the pool. I met Michael, an attorney and internationally known expert in the waterfront development field, at the first board meeting of the Waterfront Center in 1982. The founders of the center, Ann Breen and Dick Rigby, had invited interested parties to discuss how a nonprofit organization that they hoped to create could help communities open their waterfronts for public benefit. Michael and I became friends and stayed in touch over the years. My interest in promoting floating pools in urban areas and his experience with the politics of Hoboken's waterfront development would result in my first experience with the political impediments that would stand in the way of realizing my dream.

AS IN NEW YORK CITY in the 1980s, in Hoboken "to open" largely meant "privatizing." In 1986, according to the *New York Times*, plans for twenty-five major projects went before the New Jersey Waterfront Commission for approval. From Fort Lee on the north of Hoboken, to Bayonne eighteen miles to the south, private developers were planning or breaking ground on former railroad yards and abandoned piers for residences, offices, hotels, and shopping malls. Proposals also included parks, marinas, and a continuous waterfront walkway along the west side of the Hudson River. However, these ideas for public recreational facilities, as in the big city across the river, would be a long time coming.

In reality, the floating pool was as intangible as its presumptive home dock. All I had was an architect and a dream. I had the architect because, in 1998, two years before a Hoboken dock appeared on my horizon, I had won a $25,000 grant from the New York Community Trust to do a feasibility study for my floating project, and that had brought me to Jonathan Kirschenfeld's office to seek his professional help. At the time, Jonathan was struggling to open an independent practice centered on public work. He was forty-something and tall, with receding curly hair, and when we met he was wearing a navy-blue sweater with worn-out elbows. He was earnest, as the elbows of his sweater attested, and the very picture of a serious idealist. In the days before texting and FaceTime, I had met Jonathan only by phone in 1993 when I was working at the EDC. He had asked for my advice on securing the permits required for opening a floating theater on a barge in New York City. His calls had been so persistent that he became somewhat of an annoyance to me. By this time, during our first face-to-face meeting in 1998, he had procured the permits for the Theater Barge, but he still had no funds to build it.

"You were a godsend in so many ways," Jonathan wrote to me years later. "Not just because of the exciting nature of the floating pool project, but because this was a real-life demonstration that when one door closes another one opens. . . . The idea that you, as one of the strongest supporters of the Theater, would a few years later call me and ask if I would take on the Floating Pool was a reaffirmation that all that struggle and failure was not for naught."

Jonathan's desire to work with me on my project was more than money in the bank. Jonathan's unsinkable "fake it 'til you make it" attitude, along with his willingness to learn on his feet and improvise, would serve us well while handling the many crises we would later weather together. "I remember you asked on the phone before you came to the office if I was familiar with public pools and pool design, and I automatically answered, 'Of course!' even though I hadn't the faintest idea how I would learn all that I needed to know to put it together."

Had I known about this yawning gap in his knowledge then, I probably would have walked straight out of Jonathan's office. But I am so glad that I didn't. Unlike many state bureaucrats and insurance adjusters, when things looked bleak Jonathan never let me worry. Within an hour of our first in-person meeting, and with some money transferred to pay him to work on a once-in-a-lifetime public project, we had a deal. Jonathan would prepare a preliminary design for the changing rooms and offices, as well as a sunbathing area on two decks of a barge with a pool. It was slated to be afloat in an unknown location two years from then, in June 2000. I was excited. He was thrilled. How naive we were. However, perhaps Hoboken would give us that chance.

But we were also lucky, for we were directly in the path of a general atmosphere of rethinking people's relationships to the New York and New Jersey waterfronts. The public needed to use and interact with their riverine environment. It wasn't enough for the waterfront to be a pretty space to look at, and even though it was ecologically healthy, it also had to be a dynamic destination that offered publicly accessible activities. To achieve these ends, Kent Barwick, a tall, aristocratic, and patrician man with a gray receding hairline, as well as his younger, shorter, bespectacled, and dark-haired coconspirator, Carter Craft, were inventing the nonprofit Metropolitan Waterfront Alliance (MWA). Their first step was a regional campaign. They sought new, highly visible projects that could not only come about quickly but also make the waterfront paramount in the public's sensibility.

I had known Barwick for years in his leadership roles at the Municipal Arts Society, which incidentally had its offices in the Urban Center on Madison Avenue and Fifty-First Street, a floor above the Parks Council where I had worked. In passing on the staircase, we often talked about the floating pool. However, Barwick introduced me to Carter Craft, who became my first nonfamily cheerleader. It was the grant secured by the two of them from the New York Community Trust that allowed me to hire Jonathan Kirschenfeld and made the pool one of the MWA's first projects.

Jonathan immediately began to hold meetings with me, Barwick, and others to discuss what precisely this floating concept would be. One of our first decisions was to use as many financial and planning elements as possible of a template shown in the Floating Recreation

Center feasibility study conducted for the Parks Council in 1987. We would purchase a barge from southern waters where they were plentiful, at a cost of $350,000 to $400,000, and tow it to New York. A concern from day one was whether the facility should be self-contained, with its own energy source, waste removal, and freshwater supply. We debated the costs and benefits of solar and wind power, and, because of the expense entailed, we quickly decided to stick to standard technologies. The Clean Water Act clearly forbade emptying wastewater into rivers. We deemed that a triweekly pickup of the black waters stored in the tanks belowdecks would be too costly, and we decided that connecting utilities to city lines on land was preferable. We investigated using filtered river water in the showers and pool. However, Hoboken and New York City still used combined sewer outfalls that in heavy rainfalls allowed toilet waste to empty into the rivers. Psychologically, if not practically, this would be a huge problem for a health-conscious modern public that, unlike the early twentieth-century patrons of the floating baths, would refuse to swim in such waters.

I also asked Jonathan to describe to Barwick and the group the premise of the architecture that he would design and the basic specs. He answered as if he were talking to his architectural students in New York or Rome: "It's not the pool itself that's so critical but the structures around it that create an urban space. After all, the pool itself is really just a large tub filled with water (with lots of pumps and filters!), but making a vibrant space of public interaction is what we always aspire to in all of our work." I paused. "Hold on," I said, feeling the need to bring his vision down to earth. "We need dressing rooms, toilets, showers, an office, and items in the portfolio of you, the architect. Will these be on the same level as the pool? What will they look like?"

In response, Jonathan's imagination ran wild. (I was just learning how wild it could run.) "The design will be a gathering space on a level above the pool. I see a sun-court defined along its edges by steel cabanas or pavilions serving the various program needs." He paused a moment and added, "We need a snack bar as I remember from my childhood, with kids wolfing down spicy hot dogs and slightly melted ice cream sandwiches." Then, becoming a professor again, he proposed a design not like the nineteenth-century floating baths but in the style of "the very urban fifties beach clubs of Long Beach, Long Island" that he remembered from his childhood. "They were a collection of elements creating a shared communal space." And then his professorial mind returned to fun: "I envision whimsically painted roofs for the floating pool with open-air skylights as an homage to those casual beach structures, sometimes striped canvas, sometimes the wood that always evokes the summertime for me." I was learning that summer fun could be complicated and expensive.

I thought that agreement on the size of the pool would be easy. It should be twenty-five meters long (or, at that time, half Olympic length), with sufficient width for seven lanes. Depth was an issue. New York City public pools allow only a four-foot maximum. However, the newest competitive racing dives required a pike entry into the water and therefore deeper water. Should we include a movable floor? No, back to reality. Eventually, we would need to hire a pool architect to design gutters around the pool's edges to skim off unpleasant surface dirt, sun lotions and oils, and suspended materials, as well as capture the waves created by both the swimmers in the floating pool and the boats passing by outside. Things were going swimmingly, and then someone asked two crucial questions: What permits were required? What codes had to be met?

IN THE LATE 1990S, in addition to seeking unusual projects that would bring the public to the New York City and northern New Jersey waterfronts, the MWA also looked for problems that might hamper the achievement of these new projects. Permitting was an important topic to explore. And in the case of the floating pool—a hybrid structure—codes would also come into play. To open a floating pool in the region's waterways, permits were (and still are) a necessary stage as with every public project, with concomitant, unavoidable risks. But what permits? Although I knew there would be some, such as Health Department approvals, little did I know how many regulators would eventually stand in judgment of the floating pool project. How could we figure out which of the various city, state, and federal government agencies would insist on having a say in our project? Who was in charge? And how did we prioritize our applications? A floating pool was an odd and novel entity that in 1942, when the last three were scuttled, had disappeared from New York's regulatory world. There were no clear existing rules, and all precedents went back to an entirely different era.

Was it a ship? If so, we would have to meet US Coast Guard standards, but we were immune from landside codes. Did the onboard presence of pavilions containing dressing rooms make us a building/land structure? If so, approval of the US Army Corps of Engineers (ACOE) would be the first step, and jurisdiction of the Coast Guard would be limited to inspecting the barge for seaworthiness if and when it was moved from site to site and making sure it was properly lit. If the barge were to be permanently moored year-round, it would require the works: approvals from ACOE and all of the relevant city agencies such as the building, health, and fire departments. But that was not all. The Clean Water Act gave states jurisdiction over water-based facilities that might impact the waterway.

My experience working on waterfront projects for various New York City agencies had taught me that the state Department of Environmental Conservation (DEC) did not look kindly on waterfront structures that cast shadows over the river. Shadows, officers in the agency believed, killed fish. River Café and Bargemusic had both opened on the Brooklyn waterfront in 1977. But these types of water-based facilities, once built, came under closer government scrutiny and might not have been approved in 2000. Regional regulators often contested piers that were constructed on a new footprint and walkways that overlapped the water's edge. Only water-dependent uses such as floating piers for ferry landings or marinas were permitted. Before I could even consider building and bringing a floating pool to New York, I needed assurance that such a facility would be acceptable in principle. Would water floating on water be a use innocuous enough to convince regulators to accept it?

Past experience gave me good reason to be anxious. Two years before I began the 2000 foray into Hoboken, when I dreamed that my pool would be located in New York State, Joshua Laird, then director of planning at the Parks Department, suggested that I meet with several members of New York State DEC Region 2. This unit was responsible for any of the five New York City boroughs that might become home to my floating pool. Joshua was experienced in dealing with the DEC. With him holding my hand at that time, I faced the risk of an outright denial and went into the meeting in search of assurance from key regulators. However, I received more questions from them than answers.

The meeting was cordial. I was asked to justify why the pool had to be in the water. I explained that assuming that accessible and reasonably priced land could be found, the facility cost was higher and the building time frame longer. For example, an addition to the Gertrude Ederle pool in Queens would come in at over $70 million compared to the $2 million estimated in the floating pool budget. A floating pool could be available in a year, whereas an in-ground pool with a three-hundred-swimmer capacity would take at least five years to build. That seemed to be a winning response.

Then we discussed how the pool could be water-dependent. I had the feeling that several people in the group were trying to offer reasonable solutions: What about creating a safety barrier to protect swimmers from currents and letting them swim in the river? This possibility required shallow water and minimal currents. It was too risky in deeper waters with the stronger flows of New York Harbor. Use river water? Unlikely. Add an educational component to the barge where patrons could view fish that frequent the harbor? Possibly. We left the meeting with ideas to consider. More importantly, the door had been left open for a return visit. No one had said no.

MY FLOATING POOL was not going to be Hoboken's first. Historically, beginning in 1888, and for at least eighteen years, the German immigrants who worked in the German-owned shipyards and their families had access to a floating bath adjacent to a park (that would, in 1998, become Sinatra Park) at the foot of Fourth Street, a half block north of today's Pier C. The exact size of the bath is unknown. One might assume that with 150 dressing rooms on two floors at the turn of the century, it was less crowded than a comparable Manhattan facility.

After the turn of the century, Hoboken's blue-collar residents constructed and converted warships and serviced oil tankers in the Bethlehem Steel Yards. They processed coffee inside the factory with the famous Maxwell House Coffee sign perched on top. They packaged Lipton tea and turned out Wonder bread and Hostess cupcakes in two Continental Baking Company sites. However, by the 1970s factory jobs had shrunk, unemployment was high, and the population on welfare grew. In the 1950s and 1960s the new importance of air travel and the development of containerized cargo, necessitating deep-water ports, had increasingly undermined the Hoboken waterfront, which fell into a state of disrepair, and port jobs disappeared just as they had in Manhattan and Brooklyn.

To add to Hoboken's problems, the mainly nineteenth-century housing stock was in disrepair. In an effort to upgrade the face of the city, provide new jobs, and increase the tax base, in the mid-1970s city leaders hoped to attract middle-class residents from across the Hudson. First, the housing problem needed attention. Beginning in 1970 the private Applied Housing Company used the Federal Section 8 housing program to rehabilitate hundreds of handsome old one- and two-family brownstones in the blocks west of the waterfront. Under this program, the government granted subsidies to the developer to allow low-income and unemployed residents to pay a rent they could afford while the developer earned a market-rate income. During this period, homeowners who applied for and received federal low-interest loans also played a role in rehabilitating one-tenth of the city's residential buildings. Meanwhile, local construction companies, sensing the opportunity for profit, turned empty factories into expensive condominiums for more upscale buyers and renters.

The programs were a success in the sense that the majority of Hoboken's blue-collar wage earners and residents (i.e., those who had lost jobs in factories that had closed in the 1970s or in shipping activities that had moved to container ports in Port Elizabeth/Port Newark in the early 1980s) were able to remain in Hoboken. Also, the city could boast that only 15 percent of the renovated apartments had gone to "outsiders." However, in the 1980s Hoboken's residential facelift also led to gentrification and threatened housing affordability for blue-collar tenants, elderly pensioners, and retired seamen living in rooming houses. Socially mobile, middle-class New Yorkers seeking cheaper rents crossed the Hudson, thus creating the hip social and arts scene that drew more of their kind across the river. This group started to move into buildings originally renovated for low-income Hobokenites. Speculators bought out tenants and turned the now multiunit rental houses into more expensive condos.

The one-mile-square-shaped city that today sits between two Cross-Hudson tunnels, the Lincoln on the north and the Holland on the south, was thus in a state of flux in 1982 when I first met Michael Krieger. The residential real estate boom and changing demographics had encouraged plans for even more massive upscale development. Three Hudson River piers located south of Stevens Institute between First Street on the south (now Pier A) and Fourth Street on the north (now Pier C) were the lure for this renewal. That year, Congress had passed a bill requiring the federal government to sell back to Hoboken these three piers, along with the adjoining upland, all of which the government had confiscated from alien German shipping lines at the onset of World War I. Hoboken had no money in its budget to develop the newly returned waterfront, but the Port Authority had expanded its mandate from bistate transportation between New York City and New Jersey to a regional strategy.

Michael Krieger served then as general manager of regional and economic development for the Port Authority. He directed the agency's studies that informed its decision to add the redevelopment of urban waterfronts to its portfolio. He also helped secure the act of Congress mentioned above that returned the confiscated, old pier properties in Hoboken to allow for their redevelopment for mixed-use purposes. In 1982 the agency's board allocated $100 million in start-up funds for the South Waterfront project. The objective was to lease thirty-two waterfront acres from the City of Hoboken, clear the former maritime site—including demolishing the North German Lloyd piers and associated structures—commission plans, and solicit bids from developers to build a 370-slip marina, a 670-unit residential tower, a 400-room hotel, and a 6,000,000-square-foot office building. The boost to the economy that was projected would be dramatic: 10,000 construction jobs and 2,500–4,500 permanent jobs for a distressed city with a 19 percent unemployment rate.

The New Jersey legislature swiftly approved these plans, but their implementation would be held up by political bickering among leaders in New York City and New York State. Because the Port Authority was a bistate agency, New York City and State officials required their pound of flesh. Hoboken had thus been linked to Hunters Point, another Port Authority project planned for the Queens waterfront. Not until 1984 would the Hoboken plan have the legally required approvals of Mayor Ed Koch of New York City and the New York State legislatures. Having gone through the 1980s in Hoboken, Michael was a seasoned expert in the politics of the waterfront. He understood that effectuating changes to and on waterfronts is always complicated, for both small and large projects, since multiple political jurisdictions and regulatory agencies are involved.

By 1990, however, development was at a standstill on the New Jersey waterfront, as it was across the Hudson, where the Battery Maritime Building remained untouched, and Donald Trump had been forced first by a politically powerful community board to reduce the size of his project and then by Mayor Koch to lose NBC so that Trump's option lapsed on Television City. In Hoboken, like in Battery Park City, condos were auctioned off at a loss. The Port Authority 1984 South Waterfront development plans were on hold due to clashes between a very large number of political interests.

Had these pie-in-the-sky plans evinced hubris or just innocence? The reality was that neither government officials nor developers understood or were willing to spend the necessary time and money on the complicated steps involved in building nonshipping activities on the waterfront. Zoning had to be changed from industrial to commercial and residential. Absent or minimal infrastructure had to be put in place first, including sewage and water lines. New transportation lines had to be brought to the waterfront from the interior, where they had been located for nearly a century. All of these pieces had to be assembled for vision to become reality. However, a plethora of federal, state, city, borough, and community bodies had power over the shore, and within them were individuals who, many because of their own private interests, wished to and succeeded in stopping the necessary large-scale planning.

BY THE END OF the 1990s, I was keeping an eye on the New Jersey waterfront, especially Hoboken. There was evidence that parts of that waterfront were shifting from private to public use. And fortunately for my project, a park with a floating pool came into the picture. In Hoboken, the city-backed Port Authority mixed-use development project had undergone various changes on paper since 1984 but still lay fallow. In the early 1990s the Coalition for a Better Waterfront, a 150-member group of local residents from artists to truck drivers, lawyers, homemakers, and landscape architect and Hobokenite Cassandra Wilday, entered the scene. Instead of merely criticizing and fighting the original plan, the group—not unlike the Greenpoint residents who would come together in 1997 to create a 197-a plan for their Brooklyn waterfront—met to propose ideas for a replacement plan. They were helped by Mayor Patrick Pasculli, who had run for office in 1989 on a platform to open the waterfront to development. It was in his political interest not to let the waterfront return to a moribund state. Hoping to get the group to come up with an acceptable plan for voters in the next election, he simply asked the coalition, "What do you want?"

Several members of the coalition immediately began to research recreational waterfronts of the past, and they discovered images of the early twentieth-century sanitarians' floating baths. To put the community's varied ideas into a formal replacement plan that would appeal to Hoboken voters, the coalition hired Craig Whitaker, one of the architects of the ill-fated Westway park, who was in private practice at that time. He recommended a plan that was made into a model and a brochure that differed significantly from earlier ones. Included were passive and active recreational facilities (instead of high-rise residential and commercial structures) on the piers, and on the upland, housing and commercial structures were included that were to be no higher than eight stories. Everything would be connected by a continuous public walkway along the waterfront. A sign that the coalition's "Plan for the Hoboken Waterfront" reflected the group members' various voices is that a floating pool was attached to a pier near Castle Point, north of Stevens Institute, between Tenth and Eleventh Streets.

In 1999 a waterfront park with two recreational piers was finally in the works on the Hoboken waterfront. Pier A, the southernmost gem of the now-recreational waterfront, opened at 100 Sinatra Drive to great acclaim as a park. Hoboken also had a five-year-old plan for the redevelopment of Pier C between East Third and East Fourth Streets into an open space, but the project was still without funding, and political interest was waning.

So it was that in 1999, nearly two decades after we first met, Michael Krieger and I sat together in Washington, DC, at another meeting with members of the Waterfront Center and our missions converged again. I remembered Michael asking, "What are you doing these days?" "I am going to raise the money to build a floating pool," I had responded. By that time, Michael had retired from the Port Authority as general manager of regional and economic development. The City of Hoboken soon retained him as special waterfront counsel. He provided institutional memory and advice to city officials to help ensure that the new development on the South Waterfront would provide a maximum public benefit, and it was in that role that he suggested I visit him to discuss my project. The availability of a floating pool at no capital cost to the city could be a catalyst for inspiring the realization of the languishing five-year-old plan for Pier C.

Consequently, I grabbed this opportunity to implement my

dream, and I put myself in Michael's hands. We planned to approach two relevant members of the Hoboken community. My first step, at Michael's suggestion, was a call in January 2000 to Tom Costanzo, the manager of waterfront development capital projects for the Port Authority—another of my Waterfront Center acquaintances. Even though their residential and commercial plans had been voted down by Hobokenites, the Port Authority still had control of the waterfront property returned to Hoboken by the federal government in 1982. I wanted to ascertain whether the Hoboken Shipyards were a possible site for the floating pool. According to Costanzo, the pool could fit. I also needed assurance from city officials that it would be acceptable for me to proceed with the idea. Thus, with Michael's help, I prepared to make my case to Hoboken's mayor, Anthony Russo. However, the first of several adverse political situations interfered. Mayor Russo unfortunately was hospitalized with a brain tumor. Nonetheless, Michael kept things moving and asked that I send materials on the floating pool to Jack Carbone. Carbone, an attorney and confidante of the mayor, handled waterfront development issues for him. Michael also told me that I should prepare to present my materials at a meeting with other Hoboken city officials on March 31, although I had no idea who these officials might be.

ON MARCH 31, 2000, just two months before my originally planned date for New Yorkers to swim the first lap, with neither a pool in the water nor funds to pay for it, I ferried across the Hudson to Hoboken to test the waters as well as the administrative gatekeepers there. I hoped that word of the benefits of a floating pool would have reached Mayor Russo during his recovery, but again, the water gods intervened, and not in my favor on first glance. The ferry landed, and there stood Michael Krieger to inform me that the meeting had been canceled without explanation. My smile of greeting disappeared, and nervous anticipation transformed into a crescendo of anger. However, Michael had saved the day. When he discovered that I was already in transit, he arranged for Robert Drasheff, director of waterfront development, to meet with us in the mayor's office and to hold a hearing for the lady who was offering the City of Hoboken a free pool. The meeting went well, and I was impressed by both Drasheff and the potential of placing the pool at a still-to-be-designed open space called Pier C by July 1, 2001, if possible.

The meeting with Drasheff was also good practice for a hoped-for reprise with Mayor Russo. Representatives of both the mayor's office and the Port Authority were in attendance at that March 31 meeting: Carbone; Drasheff; business administrator George Crimmins; and Dwight Woodson, manager of the New Jersey Waterfront for the Port Authority (another of my contacts from Waterfront Center conferences). Calm now, and with Michael at my side for support, I quietly—yet ingenuously given the status of the project to that point—began to speak clearly and forcefully.

"I plan to retrofit a barge," I told the group, still wishing that Mayor Russo were present. I looked for their reactions when I added, "I will raise the capital funds for this facility privately." Did they smile and nod in agreement? Perhaps. Then came my kicker: "Connections to the upland and operational costs must be within the purview of others." Eyebrows raised.

I continued to tell the group about some work that was already under way in Hoboken. Students under the tutelage of Michael Bruno, director of the Center for Maritime Systems and Davidson Laboratory at Stevens Institute, had been conducting soundings of water depths in Hoboken, Manhattan, and Brooklyn. Then I made a four-point pitch for what the floating pool could do for a city hoping to make itself known "as the number one place to live. It could provide a much-needed recreational outlet for the young Wall Streeters who have moved into condos in the southern section of the city." My voice grew hoarse. "Similarly," I said, "it could benefit Hoboken's lower-income population crowded farther to the north, who have minimal open-space activities.

"The pool could be a draw for future residents and businesses that are expected to move into your planned waterfront structures," I continued, then paused to see their reactions. "Finally, the floating pool could be the linchpin for the reconstruction of Pier C." Straightening myself up to my full five feet, three inches, I added, "Am I not right in thinking it is now estimated to open in 2002?" The room was silent when I stopped speaking. I saw incredulousness in the faces of these men and wondered what they must be thinking: Who is this little blond lady with her crazy idea? What are her credentials? Has she ever raised money to realize a public project?

Yes, I had. In the 1950s I spent an inordinate amount of time in a playground on the East Side in Central Park with my (then) three children. Too often, I saw small kids topple from swings, slides, and seesaws onto the asphalt pavement, and mothers rushing them to the Lenox Hill Hospital emergency room for stitches. Much like Jacob Riis and the Progressives who pressed for and opened the city's first playgrounds, I worked for a change to the problem I saw. With two park friends, Adele Auchincloss—a member of the venerable Park Association formed in the 1880s with a goal similar to that of Riis: to acquire land for public parks—and author Barbara Goldsmith, I did my homework. We secured accident statistics from Lenox Hill and discovered that Minnesota Mining Company (now known as 3M) had recently invented a rubberized material called Safety Surf that could be placed under play equipment to protect children from the impact of falls. Together, we raised $50,000 from friends, family, and park users to purchase enough surfacing to underlay facilities in two Central Park playgrounds, one at East Eighty-Fifth Street that my family frequented, and the other near Barbara Goldsmith's home at East Sixty-Seventh Street. Now all the Parks Department had to do was accept our gift and agree to fund the installation.

The agency in those days was dominated by men. We knew there was no way that Commissioner Newbold Morris, successor to Robert Moses, would accept the word of three women. So we sent our husbands in our stead to argue for our project.

Two years later, black resilient material that fit together like puzzle pieces was in place in two Upper East Side playgrounds. Because these were only tests, after a festive opening I had to argue for the systemic adoption of the material in every playground. For the first time in my life, and following in the footsteps of Jane Jacobs, I faced my fear of public speaking and stood at the Board of Estimate and

Apportionment (BOE)—forerunner of the present city council—speakers' platform. With the strongest voice I could muster, I advocated for the installation of Safety Surf citywide. Money was in the budget the following year, but the asphalt surfaces remained for at least five more. The experience educated me about working with a municipal bureaucracy, gave me increased confidence, and prepared me to dare to speak to the small group of skeptical Hoboken officials about a twenty-first-century floating pool. The playground project also taught me that the wheels of the bureaucracy turn very slowly.

MY NEXT MEETING in Hoboken was scheduled for August 2, 2000. I knew from Krieger that Carbone had briefed Mayor Russo on the purpose of our meeting. Nonetheless, I was in limbo as to how seriously he took my proposal after having received neither a call nor written correspondence from the mayor. I wondered about entering the historic Beaux Arts city hall conference room on 94 Washington Street, five blocks from Pier A. Specifically, I wondered whether this meeting would be merely a recap or whether there would be evidence that the officials were looking to dock a pool in Hoboken. To my great surprise and pleasure, it was definitely the latter. In addition to the officials whom Michael had gathered to attend the meet and greet on March 31, two new faces were in the room: those of Timothy Calligy and Dean Marchetto.

Calligy, representing Hoboken's Department of Environmental Services, sat at the head of the table. His dominant presence indicated to me that city officials were already thinking ahead about the many state and local permits that must be procured. And indeed they were. Discussion ensued about the location of the pool. On the South Waterfront, it could complement the more recreationally passive Pier A with its greensward and views of Manhattan. Because I needed assurance that the pool would have access to land-based electric, freshwater, and sanitary pipes, one of the former maritime piers under Port Authority ownership would be perfect.

The second new person, Marchetto, sitting at the middle of the table, was a principal of Dean Marchetto and Associates, an architectural firm based in Hoboken. He proceeded to spread out on the conference table in front of him page A1 of the Hoboken Pier C Redevelopment Plan that he and both engineering and planning associates were working on for the city. My eyes widened, and I held my breath with excitement as Marchetto described the schematic drawing. His concept was in line with twenty-first-century recreational thought. Instead of a Robert Moses top-down-designed play and sitting area, Pier C would contain active recreation facilities to meet the year-round desires and needs of Hoboken residents: an ice rink in the winter, as well as a running track, tennis courts, kayak launch, community center, concession stand, and rental facilities. Many of the amenities would be open year-round, others just in warmer weather.

In answer to the Coalition for a Better Waterfront's plan eight years earlier—and likely also to accept my offer to provide such a facility at no cost to Hoboken—the plan showed a "pool barge" on the south side of Pier C. In parentheses, adjacent to the pool was a handwritten comment: "future." For the mayor and city officials, that word had several meanings. Pier C was still unfunded; therefore, the floating pool would have to open on the esplanade. In addition, that opening would not occur until July 1, 2002.

For me, the word "future" should have been a warning that there would be delays to come. (After all, 2002 was a year past the date I first mentioned to Drasheff, and two years past Jonathan's and my original goal for the completion of the floating pool.) In retrospect, I cannot today say why, with all of my experience in urban planning, I stayed in the Hoboken game despite that cautionary word. Perhaps it was because I still had neither money nor a pool. Or perhaps it was out of blind stubbornness to secure a location, any location, to realize my dream. There was a bit of a chicken-and-egg matter here— the actuality of the pool would make planning for mooring easier. But without a mooring secured, it was hard to fundraise for the pool itself.

I left the meeting promising to send to Drasheff more detailed descriptions of the pool as well as a photo of an architectural model. As I left, I laid out only one condition: I boldly informed the group that to accede to a sixteen-month deadline, I required the mayor's endorsement by August 2000, as well as a contractual agreement with the city by October 1. I was very hopeful, but my naivete was quickly disappearing.

Although coming out of that meeting I had no idea how or in what time frame Mayor Russo would react, it behooved me to get my act together. Fast. I needed financial projections to estimate the total expenditures for a pool in Hoboken. I needed an attorney to set up a not-for-profit foundation to accept donations, board members for that foundation to keep me honest, and a naval architect to find a barge for me. Contacts and chance encounters were my primary source of referrals. Steven Crainer, an associate in my husband's law office, was appointed as the pro bono attorney. He was young, patient, and easy to reach at times of stress. Plus, Steve could make me laugh.

Pro bono (or free) legal work is not unusual, but a case must be made to his or her firm by the attorney wishing to provide it. Eugene Vogel, the partner of my husband, Larry, presented the project in a tax meeting at their law firm, Rosenman & Colin. Crainer, the young attorney assigned to the project, recalls that there was a general atmosphere of amusement among those present. What is a floating pool? But amusement transformed into willingness to come on board, and that meeting began Crainer's eight years of pro bono work for Neptune. While at Rosenman, he spent approximately seventy-five hours attending pool design meetings and creating the not-for-profit Neptune Foundation. Crainer moved his practice to Seyfarth Shaw in 2002. There, he subsequently spent 610 hours on an aggregate of contracts, liability insurance policies, negotiations with the DEC, the transfer of barge documents to the Park Department, and, in 2018, the dissolution of the Neptune Foundation. The cost to his firm and the savings to Neptune was $242,102.50. The project would have been impossible without his skills and his firm's support of his donated work.

The initial directors were not hard to find. I, for one, was in my home office, set up in my younger daughter's former bedroom. My husband, chief morale booster, hand-holder, and twenty-four-hour supporter from the outset, signed on second. Next came Kent Barwick, a most reliable board member who not only attended every meeting and always cheered me on but also asked pertinent questions about matters that I hadn't considered. In so doing, he kept me on the right track.

Board in place, I needed to get a handle on what it might cost to accomplish my dream. I had met Professor Edward Rogoff, founder of the Field Center for Entrepreneurship at Baruch College, at an academic event in the fall of 2000. At no cost, and in record time, Rogoff and a graduate student crunched the numbers for me, the budget neophyte who needed a lesson on reading a spreadsheet. They figured that a used barge should cost $450,000 (or half of the capital cost of an in-ground bathhouse at the turn of the nineteenth century), and the bottom line for design and pool-related expenses was an approximate total of $2 million, a number that ended up falling short of actual needs.

Jonathan Kirschenfeld was creating an architecturally elegant plan. Now we needed other professionals to retrofit the barge and build the pool. I asked another of my contacts, Lillian Liburdi—now Borrone, the first female assistant executive director of the Port Authority and someone with whom I had worked on the West Side Task Force—for the name of the best naval architect. Kirschenfeld couldn't be my resource for this. Although he had learned a great deal about the technical sides of floating structures, including the issues of buoyancy and ballasting, while designing the Theater Barge, he was not conversant in either locating a suitable vessel or fashioning a pool in the deck of that vessel. We needed someone to engineer these tasks and others.

Lillian sent me to Charles Cushing, who is renowned worldwide for his design, conversion, and construction oversight of vessels from cargo ships to personal yachts. Charles, an ardent opera fan, remained elegant and on the case for free throughout his seven years as the floating pool's boatman. With Cushing on board, the marine team quickly grew. Cushing appointed Kent Merrill as project manager. A recent graduate of the University of Michigan with a degree in naval architecture and marine engineering, Merrill, with his youth, khakis, and polo shirts, resembled a preppy teenager. With a handshake, I immediately contracted Cushing and Merrill to begin the search for an appropriate barge within the $450,000 budgeted in Rogoff's financial pro forma. That initial and crucial summary amount was something I had not started to raise. There was no time to lose.

My most fortunate and rewarding experience in building the *Floating Pool Lady* was putting together this dedicated crew, one with a passion equal to mine. Mine was an energetic and patient team, focused and indefatigable in its commitment and loyalty to the project. Kirschenfeld, Crainer, and Merrill were the nucleus. Jonathan played the pied piper of what he described as a "somewhat unlikely and seemingly quixotic venture" with a crew of consultants that expanded as needed over time. Most of these team members had never worked together before. It took their collective imagination to knit together their various areas of expertise—land, marine, and pool architecture; naval and marine engineering; legal concerns and more—and their years of experience—from three years out of law school to thirty-three years founding and running a top-notch naval architecture/engineering firm. As Merrill recalled, "Each member was more interested in making sure the *Floating Pool Lady* successfully reached her grand opening . . . rather than ensure that their reputation or pride emerged unscathed from the project."

I FINALLY HEARD FROM Mayor Russo on September 25, 2000. A letter with a gold seal on the letterhead arrived at the door of our apartment. I tore open the letter and let out a whoop as I read the following: "After review of the proposal that you have submitted to the City of Hoboken, it has been recommended to me by my Directors that we enter into an agreement with you to move forward on the project. We consider this to be an exciting venture and a much-needed amenity for the City. . . . Please contact my office so that we can arrange whatever necessary steps in order to undertake your designation. . . . We also assume that you will wish to make a public announcement with us very shortly." The pool was finally in motion, having finally inspired an enthusiastic welcome from someone with the power to offer it a home. That late September afternoon, I blissfully assumed that with Russo's support, my project would sail forward without any more detours or delays.

Three weeks later, on October 18, I met with Hoboken's agency heads and attorney to lay out our respective roles to place "a floating swimming pool in Hoboken in the summer of 2002." According to my notes from that meeting, in two weeks I was supposed to deliver an outline of the terms of an agreement for a draft memorandum of understanding. The agreement was described in my notes as "will evolve."

On November 1 I wrote to Carbone that I had a team, we had begun the search for a barge, and Crainer had sent the necessary documents to the New York State attorney general to create a charitable entity. We needed a name, preferably something related to the sea. After finding that the Greek name Poseidon was already taken, Crainer reserved the name of the Roman god of the sea. In December I received a certificate of incorporation for the Neptune Foundation with its three initial board members, Barwick, Crainer, and my husband. Now I could legally start raising money for the feasibility studies as well as the design and construction of not one but "one or more" prototype floating swimming pools. To formalize my desire to put one of these prototypes in Hoboken, to my great relief the language Steve had supplied to the attorney general included the following: "To promote floating swimming pools to be operated on a not-for-profit basis along the waterfront areas of the New York City/New Jersey metropolitan region for the use and recreational benefit of the population of the New York City/New Jersey metropolitan region." The mission seemed less pie in the sky now that I had the mayor of Hoboken's gold-sealed letter on my desk.

Back in Hoboken, I then met with Krieger, Carbone, and a few New Jersey environmental officials. The issue of permits was on the table. To receive the necessary approvals from the New Jersey State Department of Environmental Protection (NJDEP), Hoboken would have to find ways to mitigate the shadow the pool was going to cast in the river. An abatement to this problem was suggested by another friend in government, Bill Nienhaus, a staff member in the department. Nienhaus was yet another of my contacts from Waterfront Center conferences. He mentioned that when a pier was removed, the law allowed a replacement in kind. Nienhaus suggested that the NJDEP might agree that the shadow cast by the floating pool would be the same, or even less, than the shadow of the pier currently there and slated to be removed to create Pier C. But there was a familiar, unspoken issue: as in New York State, this floating pool was clearly not a "water-dependent" use. And I had not yet figured out a way to define it as such.

On December 10 Mayor Russo took the lead to assure that the first contemporary floating pool would be berthed in Hoboken. That evening, with the help of my written descriptions and a photograph of Jonathan's model, the mayor presented the Hoboken City Council with plans for a new park on Pier C with its "crown jewel," a floating swimming pool. Paraphrasing some of the language that I used to woo city officials at our first meeting, Russo declared that "Hoboken is the number one place to live," and the plan "provides the largest access to the waterfront." At the termination of the mayor's presentation, the council, happy that no taxpayer funds were needed to purchase a pool, unanimously approved a resolution empowering the Neptune Foundation to start fundraising for the project.

On the following day, I was with the mayor at a press conference held on the South Waterfront. A blustery and bitter wind blew westward across the Hudson from New York City, ruffling the beautiful, hand-colored drawing by Marchetto Caulfield Associates that Mayor Russo held aloft to display our shared vision to the crowd of journalists there to report on the announcement. On the now-yellowed paper that I have saved in my archives was an illustration of a seven-lane floating pool attached to the south side of Pier C's Summer Pavilion.

Standing next to the mayor, I saw the New York City skyline across the river, with the World Trade Center towers pointing to what technology could accomplish, and I felt a pang. This floating pool could have been yours, I thought. But the Neptune Foundation's mission left the possibility open for other floating pools. Perhaps New York City would be next! I returned my mind to the moment and reveled in the first official announcement of a floating pool.

Three days later, without public relations assistance, but thanks to friends in high places, I talked my way onto the front page of the *New York Times*. In a "Public Lives" article by Joyce Wadler titled "Across the Hudson, a Dream Drops Anchor," I was described as a wealthy philanthropist with political connections through my husband, the great-nephew of Herbert Lehman. But Wadler's report was more sensitive and nuanced than that, telling her readers that I did not need to work but nonetheless had been involved in "serious projects" most of my life. Along with a brief description of my background, Wadler wrote of my then twenty-year-long passion to build a floating pool. Why was it slated to open in Hoboken and not New York? She reported that New York City had equivocated.

CHAPTER 5

Finding the
C500

IN MY STUDIES OF the floating baths, I had learned that the processes I would have to go through would be long, complicated, and buffeted by outside forces. In 1913, thirty-three years after their opening, pollution caused the design of the baths to change. To meet the public's demand over the years, there were locations, some better than others, for pools up and down the East and Hudson Rivers. But these free berths competed with activities necessary for the working life of the city, and those could afford to pay rent. The Battery public bath, located at the foot of a park, was the only one that remained in one place from the time it became public in the early 1880s until the tail end of the baths in 1930. Given this history, I could expect high waves ahead.

The Hoboken press conference and Joyce Wadler's article gave my pool project new impetus, but as usual, action depended on city officials and occurred at a slow pace. In January 2001 I heard from Lillian Liburdi Borrone that the Port Authority would soon begin to remove the pilings from Pier C. In March, in order to involve members of the public in the project, Mayor Russo appointed a "Swimming Pool Advisory Committee." The seven members of this group, with whom I met on April 26, represented a variety of interests that could help bring the community on board: An architectural lighting designer could speak about the pool's design and hours of operation. A parent and primary school principal knew that the children who lived so near the water required a learn-to-swim program. A lifelong Hoboken resident and parent was a member of the Hoboken River City Fair Committee. This group had, to my surprise, proposed a floating swimming pool in the 1980s, but without success.

With Hoboken apparently nailed down as a location, it was urgent to find a barge. Our first choice was a used steel cargo barge with a flat deck, a portion of which could be removed, allowing the pool to be constructed within the opening. However, after the Hoboken press conference, word of this unique project got out, and we were approached by Stolt Offshore Inc., a company that made concrete floating docks for open-sea oil and gas rigs. Why not place a pool on one of these structures, which required only minimal water depth?

I asked Stolt for a proposal, but I also asked Kent to pore over advertisements in maritime journals for the perfect used steel barge. To our dismay, he found that barges in good enough condition for our use were selling for over twice the $450,000 we had allotted in the Neptune budget. Undeterred, we discussed the merits of a brand-new steel barge. At an estimated $1.2 million, at the time approximately the current cost of a dented, used vessel, we could have a shiny new steel barge, with a smooth exterior and a basin ready to contain the pool. On April 9, 2001, I assigned the naval experts Charles Cushing and Kent Merrill to prepare a design and send it out for bids from several shipyards.

IN POLITICS A PRESS announcement may be seen as a commitment by a city official. But for the commitment to remain active, it requires that the official remain in office. And in Hoboken that was not to be. On May 1, 2001, Mayor Russo stood for reelection to a third term and was defeated by Hoboken city councilman David Roberts. The floating pool had been Russo's project. In addition, my ally, Michael Krieger, had completed his city assignment and was no longer involved with the floating pool. The person who had brought me across the river to Hoboken was gone. I was angry and crestfallen, and for a time I blamed the Russo administration for moving too slowly.

However, on learning that Cassandra Wilday had been appointed by Roberts to be Hoboken's director of environmental services, I decided to try to stay in the game. I had known Cassie since 1988 when, as director of waterfront planning at the New York City Parks Department, I had hired her as part of a team to produce a waterfront management plan for all of the Parks Department's waterfront parks and open spaces. Three months after Russo's defeat, in August 2001, I met with Cassie and a few new and some holdover Hoboken city officials. In my follow-up letter to Cassie, I reiterated the need for a formal agreement, this time by December 1, all the while thinking that there was no way I could buy a ship unless they signed on.

I continued to be pulled in different directions. I attended another meeting with officials in January 2002, again without reaching an accord. Then, at a subsequent meeting in June 2002 with the Department of Buildings to discuss codes and egress issues, it seemed as if the officials were trying to accommodate the pool. I wondered, though, as Jonathan wrote to me, "were they posturing?" That was our last meeting. No doubt to sustain my belief in the project, for months I kept believing that Hoboken officials were still thinking about the floating pool when they really weren't. The facility had been put on hold by the Roberts administration. They feared maintenance costs would be over budget, environmental permits would be a problem, and the pool might be too large for a redesigned Pier C, whose construction had not even begun.

In my own professional life, I had learned that election cycles result in new leadership with new or different agendas. During Mayor David Dinkins's administration, I was in office at the EDC as vice president for waterfront planning. In 1994, shortly after Mayor Rudolph Giuliani took office, I was fired by the incoming administration. A similar political wave hit me in Hoboken.

At a press conference on December 10, 2000, Mayor Michael

Russo, the pool's advocate, held aloft an architect's rendering of a floating pool to open on his city's Pier C. Six months later, Russo lost his reelection bid to city councilman David Roberts who, at that time, had no interest in the project. Although this delay was disappointing, I turned it to good account, using the time to start a foundation, put together a team, fundraise, and purchase a barge. The results of the Hoboken election were instrumental in terminating that version of the project; in fact, it was a win in disguise for me. Pier C did not open until November 2010. Meanwhile, a new mayor in New York City and a new governor in Albany came along and allowed the *Lady* to open three years earlier in New York than she would have in New Jersey.

In retrospect, I was the naive one in this process. I had let my enthusiasm get in the way of good sense. I had expended a great deal of time and effort on a public project expecting that logic and righteousness would prevail—even when there was always the risk that the project would meet political and regulatory resistance. But all was not lost. With designs in my backpack and hat in hand, I figuratively traveled back home across the Hudson to begin phase two: the seven-year process of donating a floating swimming pool to the City of New York.

ON A COLD, RAINY day in November 2002, six months after I had departed Hoboken, I was in Jonathan Kirschenfeld's below-grade office on Tribeca's North Moore Street and was missing the chocolate croissant and café latte that I used to pick up from Balthazar on my way to Jonathan's former office in SoHo. A large, glass window faced the painted brick wall of the adjacent building. Lit by skylights, the dripping wall appeared to be in a cold sweat. Jonathan and I were joined at a long, black, rectangular table by Kent Merrill. Also with us was Johann Mordhorst, the first employee in Jonathan's newly formed single practice that specialized in projects for public benefit. Together, the two men were working on an American Institute of Architects award-winning residence for formerly homeless and mentally ill people, and on the floating pool. The residence would take two years—the pool, five.

The purpose of our meeting was to discuss the construction budget for the brand-new steel barge that over a year earlier I had assigned the Cushing team to design. To fundraise in a rational manner, I had to verify our earlier assumption that new was better and not significantly more expensive than refitting an old barge. If we had had a commitment from Hoboken to place the pool there, the time to accomplish this would have been a problem. Without a Hoboken contract, there was no rush. Nonetheless, to make this unique public project real, it would take time to find a container that floated, the money to pay for the still unknown costs, and a New York City location.

At the meeting in Jonathan's office, the men had laid out on the black table a detailed engineering plan for the new marine structure to contain the pool and the final architectural design for the structures to be housed on the upper level. A space for Jonathan's snack bar was shown, along with dressing, bath, and shower rooms, plus an office for the staff. We had an in-house estimate of the cost of a new steel barge, but we needed prospective builders to verify or refute our number. Kent had done his homework and located eight marine construction firms from Rhode Island to Wisconsin, Florida to New Orleans. He told us that the plans were in the mail. I awaited the responses full of uncertainty. Would companies be interested in working with us at all? Would there be any welcome (or unwelcome) surprises?

If the price for the marine construction work was within reason, I had to make sure that there would be money in the bank to pay for it. This required me to be successful in fundraising, a skill that was not topmost in my repertoire. Then I recalled the tradition of annual galas of the nonprofit Council for Parks and Playgrounds that, as a newly minted community activist, I had founded with then city councilman Henry Stern and state senator Jerome Wilson in the 1960s, nearly a half century earlier. We started with a small goal: to convince post–Robert Moses parks commissioner Newbold Morris to make the playgrounds more inviting by changing the depressing color of play equipment from battleship gray to a variety of bright colors. We also gathered a cohort of mothers in all the boroughs to speak up for improvements to their local parks. Eventually, we needed to raise private money to pay for a small staff, publications, an office, and related expenses. In addition to seeking grants from the city and state, we added yearly fundraising events to appeal for donations from private individuals. These events still occur annually, and the proceeds go to New Yorkers 4 Parks. Despite hating to ask for money, I, with the help of a few others over the decades, was one of the primary fundraisers for this cause.

There must be as many ways to raise money as there have been campaigns to raise money. In my case, I essentially reeled from one benefactor to another, plodding on without a prepared road map until I reached the goal, nearly $2 million to build a floating pool. A "naming" was one possibility, so I made a list. A company could sponsor the pool with a donation large enough to encompass the barge's construction. In return, the corporate logo would be shown in a prominent place. Imagine airplanes flying into one of the city's airports, and below them passengers see SPEEDO© painted in huge letters on the bottom of the pool! And with one act of charity my work would be done. I put my ideas together and practiced my pitch.

Here, as with many of my needs, friendship was important. In spring 2001 I called Edward Meyer, CEO of Grey Advertising, and the husband of one of my best friends. He put me in touch with Jared Moses, CEO of Grey Alliance. Jared and his staff connected companies that sought Grey's marketing help with philanthropic organizations. He immediately understood that companies seeking to expand their brand via the floating pool might appreciate this unique way of getting their message out. Concurrently, he knew whose product might be a good fit with a floating pool. Since there might be a concession stand, some of the companies he suggested produce food and beverages, such as McDonalds and Coca-Cola. Others, such as Reebok, Speedo, and Coppertone, were more pool-specific with their swimsuits and sunscreen. Jared's efforts to fund the pool as a marketing vehicle, while clever, had sadly netted us nothing by February 2002. The Trump organization, with residential towers that heralded the Trump name rising near the Hudson below West Seventh-Ninth Street, did not respond. Neither did

Speedo after being contacted twice. At Reebok, the ask was "in the process of being passed around to a few more people."

Once the corporate sponsorship idea was determined to be a non-starter, and with Kickstarter and other crowdfunding sources not yet existing, I reached out to my network of friends and family with one-on-one personal requests. It was easy for me to put together a list of family members, friends, and acquaintances who might be interested, but the harder part would be to ask, again and again. I chose two likely supporters for my first asks. On November 8, 2001, I addressed a request to an executor of the Estate of Edith K. Ehrman. Didi, as Edith was known, was a longtime friend who shared my love of pools. In 1980 she opened a pool that she donated to the town of Armonk, New York, in memory of her daughter, Anita Louise. The facility was a gathering place for the community, where families who did not belong to country clubs could bring their children to swimming lessons and the elderly could exercise. I had spoken to Didi about the floating pool concept on various occasions in the last years before her death in 2000, and she had been very receptive.

I followed up Didi's interest with what for me was a bold request to her executor: a contribution of $1 million to support the creation of a floating swimming pool. To show that there was "bang for the buck," I was careful to include the information that the pool, still in late 2001 optimistically planned for Hoboken, could hold 230 swimmers who had no nearby access to public swimming facilities. The ask concluded with one more pitch: I offered a naming opportunity.

I sent only one more personal letter during this period and it was to David Rockefeller, Sr., on January 25, 2002. I had described my dream to Mr. Rockefeller in the 1980s after he had read my op-ed article about floating pools. Twenty years later, I sat on the board of the National Parks Foundation, a position to which I had been appointed earlier by President Bill Clinton. David Rockefeller, Jr., was the board chair and a friend. I told David that I would like to speak to his father about my pool project, and he suggested that I write to him directly. Because I was still awaiting confirmation from Hoboken, I mentioned to Mr. Rockefeller the possibility of having two pools, one there and another in New York City. I enclosed a financial plan and descriptive graphics for him to review and asked if he would be interested in helping fund this endeavor.

Still waiting for a contract with Hoboken, on January 17, 2002, I received a check for $1,914,450.20 from Didi's estate. My kickstarter did not request a naming. Then, in May, David Rockefeller Sr.'s check for $5,000 arrived. With the addition of eight word-of-mouth gifts—four from my immediate family, three from friends, and another from a more distant relative with a passion for revitalizing historic passenger ships—by the time of our meeting in Jonathan Kirschenfeld's office in November 2002, the Neptune bank account held over $2 million. This was all due to the unique nature of my relationships and the ability to fundraise among people who have a long-held interest in a similar vision. Inexperienced in project overruns, I expected this would be more than enough to cover the total bottom line in the pro forma budget.

WITH THE FUNDS to pay for what I thought would be a brand-new barge, the question as to where I would put the vessel once it was transformed into a floating pool became more urgent. During the time I was working with Hoboken officials, I had also begun a series of public relations forays to determine the interest of various New York City officials in having a floating pool on their waterfronts, and moreover, in supplying funds to maintain such a facility. My Parks Department friend, Joshua Laird, gave me a list of eleven potential sites to visit. When the Hoboken option collapsed, these sites were suddenly vying to be my new plan A.

Fortunately for my project, the urge to add recreation to New York City's waterfronts had finally entered the psyches of municipal officers. Elected officials and agency heads, urged by community activists and not-for-profit parks-oriented organizations, were turning their sights from private high-rise apartment houses to public recreation on the waterfront. As in Hoboken, the Port Authority piers in Brooklyn were no longer being used for shipping. Many in Brooklyn Heights and beyond clamored for recreational open-space replacement, without housing, on the waterfront. In 1996 the US

Coast Guard moved out of Governors Island, leaving ninety acres of waterfront land in the lower harbor open for city and state recreational planning. Here, by law, housing would be excluded. The demise of Westway resulted in state legislation in 1998 for a planned Hudson River Park on Manhattan's West Side, which would extend along the east side of the Hudson from Battery Place to West Fifty-Ninth Street. Certain commercial uses—retail, sports clubs, restaurants—would provide a tax base while functioning in a more synergetic way with parks. Here too, housing was excluded. My floating pool appeared to have found its political and policy moment.

There were several places on Joshua's list of interest to me and, without responses on the price for constructing a new vessel or offers of a site in New York City to place a pool, I spent the next eight months checking off that list. The EDC was ready to develop a set of blocks inaccessible to the public around 125th Street. With a push from Columbia University and some residents in the local community, Jeannette Rausch, my former intern at EDC, was involved in sending out requests for proposals (RFPs) not only for developers who would build new housing on the upland but also for partners who would add waterborne recreational and transportation activities to the existing piers. EDC had received three responses to its RFP for housing and water-related developments A floating pool could add a river-based recreational facility to all of them.

On the Lower West Side, in 1998, the state was already constructing the first section of Hudson River Park. Perhaps a pool could be established at one of the rehabilitated piers to serve Battery Park City residents and students from Stuyvesant High School and the Borough of Manhattan Community College. The city's 2012 Olympic bid package was also in the works and included housing for athletes on Hunters Point in Queens. A floating pool could provide a practice site nearby. In Brooklyn, the Brooklyn Bridge Park Conservancy (BB Park Conservancy) awaited the Port Authority's move out of Piers 1 through 5; and the Parks Department and EDC along with an actively interested community hoped to transform Transmitter Park on Kent Avenue. A floating pool was an enticing addition to all of these projects, but the leaders with whom I met had big questions about its implementation and problems they feared might arise once in operation.

My first visit with a possible site partner was to Emily Lloyd in February 2002, at the time the executive vice president for administration at Columbia University. Emily saw the pool as a potential addition to the university's athletic facilities and a much-needed venue for children from West Harlem to recreate. But when I asked if Columbia would underwrite the pool, she demurred. The university might make a donation to the pool, but total funding was out of the question. Although many people like Emily offered fundraising ideas, also like Emily, no one was willing to commit to providing either capital or maintenance money for the pool itself. (Unknown to both of us, Emily, in another role, would one day provide major government financing for engineering work that would allow the pool to open.) My fundraising success to date was not applicable to long-term questions about operation of the pool.

In March 2002 I sought siting advice about a pool at West 125th Street from people with knowledge of the West Side waterfront: Terry Lane, president and chief financial officer of the Upper Manhattan Empowerment Zone Development Corporation, and Jeannette Rausch at EDC. Lane had more questions than answers: Who would operate the pool? Improve the bulkhead? Carry the insurance? What state environmental laws applied? For Jeannette, who knew the physical territory from her work on the RFP, docking at West 125th Street might compete with a ferry landing that had been promised to the community, and the water in the remaining area might be too shallow to float the pool safely.

In October I met with Connie Fishman, executive vice president of Hudson River Park, for advice on the Lower West Side waterfront. Pool patronage was not on her list. Connie had an array of physical difficulties in mind. Wakes from ferries and boats in the Hudson River might knock on the pool barge docked at Hudson River Park too severely and cause patrons and workers to fall or become seasick. Wakes might also damage the barge's structure. More important: access to the required utility connections was problematic.

National historic resources laws forbade any piercing of the nineteenth-century bulkhead—the retaining wall at the park separating the river from the shore—making modifications difficult, if not impossible. With each conversation, I was learning more about the myriad factors that needed to be reckoned with in order to site my pool or undertake any water-based amenity.

A pool for athletes at Hunters Point in Queens was quickly shown to be a chimerical idea. As a member of a volunteer committee chaired by Daniel Doctoroff (before he became deputy mayor) to advise on New York's bid for the 2012 Olympics, I knew that a floating pool installed there for swim practice would not be needed for another dozen years. This was long past the time by which I intended the pool to open. Furthermore, there was no assurance that New York would be the selected venue.

The questions and comments from my several meetings awoke me to the reality of what I was getting myself into and the complicated work that was ahead. As I struggled to come to terms with the responses and tried to understand the real possibilities for a floating pool, I also learned that an outsider's idea, no matter how novel or potentially enriching for the community, would inevitably face resistance from local officials, for whom implementation of their own plans was primary.

WHILE THE WAIT for a vessel continued, in September 2003, with no word on the costs or curiosity from barge construction companies, Joshua Laird let me know that interest in securing the pool for Transmitter Park on the East River in Greenpoint had heated up. He handed me proof of the intent: a complete breakdown of costs for the city to prepare the site. I immediately began the journey to meetings regarding a floating pool at Transmitter Park, still without a vessel.

Little had changed on the Greenpoint waterfront since the spring of 2002, when the Department of City Planning approved the 197-a plan. A photograph by the McLaren Engineering Group (as late as 2006) titled "Community Barriers to the Waterfront" is starkly reminiscent of Tom Fox's photograph of a white-shirted man trying to reach the Hudson River in 1992. In the McLaren photograph, an elderly man stands on a hole-filled asphalt lot, leaning on an umbrella and gazing at the East River through a ten-foot-high chain-link fence.

But there was hope. With newly elected mayor Michael Bloomberg in office and a short recession over, the political will existed to create parks and esplanades along the rivers and harbor. New York began to reclaim its waterfront. The Planning Department was surveying all 578 miles of the city's waterfront in preparation of a report on its future. Educational institutions, environmentalists, groups banding together for recreational opportunities, and community organizations were getting on board. The Harbor School opened deep in Brooklyn's Bushwick in 2003. Its principal and eight teachers began a marine science and technology program that introduced 125 low-achieving students to the harbor and all of the waterways. In a few years, after moving into a former infirmary building on Governors Island, the students would begin planting oyster shells to clean up the rivers. In Manhattan's Hudson River Park, the River Project, begun in 1986 by founder Cathy Drew, was studying and teaching about the estuary and the biodiversity of fish and invertebrates that the project had found in the Hudson. Brooklyn's Community Board 1 (CB1) added the Waterfront Committee to which I would offer a floating pool, and Mayor Bloomberg charged the EDC, with its access to state funds, to begin the paperwork for Transmitter Park.

Then, on February 19, 2004, the same day when I would finally receive the shipyard bids confirming the cost of a new barge, I picked up a call from Marianna Koval, executive director of the Brooklyn Bridge Park Coalition. At the time, she was dedicated to reclaiming the land and the outdated Port Authority piers and warehouses below Brooklyn Heights for the creation of a public park. We had met two years earlier to talk about the pool, but all I had then was a design, and the Port Authority still owned the piers. On hearing through the Brooklyn parks' grapevine that my pool might end up at Transmitter Park, Marianna put in her pitch.

"Could we have the floating pool ready to open at Brooklyn Bridge Park in the summer of 2004?" she asked, to which I answered, "Would that the pool was built!" Intriguing as her proposal was, there was no way I could meet Marianna's deadline, a mere four months from her request. Then, in a rash move, I said, "Aiming for summer '05," to which she boldly responded, "Summer 2005 may be perfect." Then she added an idea that was outside my train of thought, saying, "There are changes afoot in the new Brooklyn Bridge Park Development Corporation and a commitment to creative interim uses." Marianna, head of a recently formed nonprofit organization, was the first semipublic individual to meet my idea with a plan rather than a long set of questions.

On the day of Marianna's call, fifteen months after our initial meeting in Jonathan Kirschenfeld's office on the subject of bids for a new steel barge, our intrepid naval architect and relentless investigator Kent Merrill finally had answers. Was I ever surprised! My original assumption in 2001 when I asked Charles Cushing to design a new steel barge without rust or dents was that it would cost in the low $1 million range. Three years later, we received six bids for a steel barge shell with deck plating and all of the necessary internal structures, including bulkheads for strength and buoyancy and mechanical space for water and sewage tanks. (The pool-related equipment would be priced and attached separately.) The lowest three bids were roughly equal at approximately $3 million each, triple my original assumption. The highest bid was $5 million, a five-fold increase. The difference between our budget and reality was breathtaking. The reason? A skyscraper construction craze in Asia and the Near East had caused the price of steel to skyrocket. What a letdown!

Providentially, while the cost of steel had risen over time and would continue to rise, the price of used barges had declined. Single-hull deck barges were, by law, being replaced with safer double-hull barges. The result was a glut on the market of this type of vessel. Perhaps we could find one of these barges in sufficiently good condition for sale at a price within the floating pool budget.

Believing, as my father often told me when I was ready to give up, that "there is value in trying," I asked Kent to take a look at all available deck barges costing under half a million dollars.

Then, to add to the complexity, on March 8, 2004, nearly three years after I had discontinued discussions with Hoboken about the floating pool, I received a copy of an article in the *Jersey Journal* from John Carbone, who had helped direct my project to the city's former mayor, Anthony Russo. According to the article, Hoboken was back in the news and apparently back in the game. On a call to me the day before, Mayor Russo's successor, David Roberts, wanted to know if the floating pool was available for Hoboken (I guess to save his hide ex post facto). I admitted to Roberts that as of that time, the floating pool did not have an official home. More forcefully I added that because talks with the City of Hoboken had not progressed, I was now discussing the location of a pool with officials in New York City, and these discussions were "progressing satisfactorily." Roberts twisted this conversation to his political advantage and told the press that the pool was in Hoboken's plans. I was once again fed up with the political confusion in New Jersey. Without an agreement in hand or a sure home at Pier C, then not scheduled to open until 2006, I made the decision on February 12, 2001, to put all of my efforts into pursuing a berth for the pool in Brooklyn's Transmitter Park. I discontinued further negotiations with Mayor Roberts and put Marianna's invitation to Brooklyn Bridge Park on the back burner.

After feeling elated that Brooklyn officials wanted the pool and might even wait for it, I also now knew that it would be impossible to build it. I was disappointed and fed up. I also began to doubt myself and thought that it was time for me to reassess my ability to continue the project. Loath to move beyond my preset financial goal, I put building a new pool on hold for six months. This would give Jonathan and the Cushing team time to try to reduce the costs to within my budget and to go back and explore used barges. It would also give me time to work on a book that I was contracted to write on the history of Governors Island. A break seemed so much more imaginable.

So Kent went shopping for a used metal barge within our price points. But the possibility of another type of structure to contain the pool appeared on his desk. On June 1, 2004, three years after I had asked for a proposal for a made-to-order concrete deck barge, we heard from Wayne Fillingame, the general manager of Stolt Offshore Inc. It was an appealing idea. We would have a brand-new, complete facility—a cement barge, with a pool and service area—deliverable in just six months. But we also had concerns, two of which were not fiscal but physical and environmental. The barge's freeboard, or the height measured from the water line to the top of the pool deck, was too low. Waves and swells in New York City's waterways could spray the deck and make it slippery, as well as spew dirty river water into the pool from the still-existing combined sewer outflow pipes and from the oil that continued to seep along the south side of the bulkhead in Newtown Creek. In the opposite direction, the barge's draft, or the distance in feet from the water line to the bottom of the barge, was too great, requiring deep water for the vessel and thus ruling out berthing the barge at a shallow water site such as Transmitter Park. The third and major concern was financial: I did not have, nor had I planned to raise, the extra $845,000 that Stolt required to design and build a concrete floating pool. I wondered if this was a sign that the purchase and retrofitting of a used barge would also cost more than originally budgeted.

This time, though, the water gods were on our side. On June 21, 2004, three weeks after the receipt of the Stolt proposal, intrepid Kent emerged from the Louisiana bayous, where he had spent many days inspecting the steamy undersides of retired deck barges that were for sale and looking to give them new purpose. Kent, already an engaged team member, described the adventure and process by saying, "I inspected each barge carefully to find the one barge that, while no longer quite up to the extreme rigors of carrying thousands of tons of equipment in the open ocean, still had many years of life left for recreational use in New York Harbor." Kent was searching diligently "for the perfect barge for the project." He found two worth considering, and from there the complexity escalated.

One, the *Santo Domingo*, might have been free if the owner

decided to make the barge a (tax-deductible) donation. The other, bearing the forgettable name C500, could be negotiated down to $450,000, the amount listed in the budget of our original pro forma. That same day, our attorney, Steve Crainer, called Stolt's general manager to thank him for the time he had spent on his intriguing concrete barge proposal but also to inform him that we were returning to our original idea, a new pool built into a used steel barge with the only concrete component being the deck pavers—and as those were a composite, Stolt was taken off the project.

Kent spent the next week in Larose, Louisiana, examining the *Santo Domingo*, which he found in such poor shape that the expense for repairing it would be an additional two or three times our target total budget of $450,000 for the vessel. A reduction in the price of the barge (perhaps to zero) might have helped, but the owner, probably noting our interest, had changed his mind about the idea of donating it. Kent then went to Morgan City, Louisiana, to survey the fallback option, the C500. The ship came alive to me in his description: "a retired, ocean-going deck barge that in her working days transported a wide variety of heavy industrial equipment hundreds of times between numerous ports on the US Gulf and East Coasts." According to Kent, the C500 looked "pretty good." Then the bargaining began, with Kent acting as an intermediary between our attorney, Steve Crainer, and Enrique Esparragoza, the Colombian owner's representative.

Kent, writing on Neptune's behalf on July 14—three weeks after finding the C500—offered $450,000. The following day the Colombian owner lowered his original asking price to $475,000. Then, thanks to Kent's Internet vigilance, he found a website that showed the C500 offered for $460,000. He told the broker to go back and ask about the discrepancy in price. Assuming we would get our way, Kent asked me if I was ready to wire down a 10 percent deposit so that the barge would be secure while he and Steve Crainer worked out the specific contract terms. I sent the sum of $45,000. Four days later, on July 19, 2004, Enrique Esparragoza messaged me in Spanish accepting my purchase bid of $450,000. I had to catch my breath. I was going to buy a gigantic barge! This move would be the first physical evidence—tons of it—of my dream becoming reality. I called Jonathan, who had been copied on all of Kent's digital correspondence, to celebrate. I also wanted to ask if his construction drawings were in order.

PREPARING A CONTRACT for barge ownership brought new issues, the first of which was registration. The C500 was originally registered in the United States and now was comfortably docked in Berwick, Louisiana. However, as were approximately 18.5 percent of all vessels in the world at the time, she was registered in Panama and carried the Panamanian flag. Still, I had no intention of allowing the floating pool to enter the Lower Bay of the City of New York without an American flag waving from her stern. Could we fly another flag from her? Changing the flag of the vessel did not mean simply changing the colors from blue, red, and white to red, white, and blue. The barge would have to meet the various standards and requirements of a key US agency: the Coast Guard. Further questions arose: Was the C500 really a "vessel" and hence under the control of a maritime agency? Or was it a "substantially land-based structure" and therefore only obligated to meet New York City local authorities' building, electrical, fire, health, and safety codes?

I had spent my teenage summers sailing a Moth sailboat in the Chesapeake Bay, where the only supervisory requirements were those issued by my father: a properly caulked boat to prevent sinking and a curfew for my return to shore. Years later, and on the verge of possessing a vastly larger vessel, I was perplexed. My love of boats and the open water was founded on a blissfully naive experience. What were the rules? Where could I turn for answers? And once I had answers, could we be assured that the C500 would satisfy the requirements of the Coast Guard and other agencies?

Charles Cushing, with his vast array of ship and boat design commissions, came to the rescue. I was no longer just a client. He was another team member who shared my passion to build a floating pool. Within days of the decision to start working on a purchase and sale agreement, Charles ushered me into the elegant offices of his friend and one of his firm's attorneys, Brian Starer of Holland &

Knight. Charles must have provided some background information on this lady and her idée fixe, for although I felt welcomed, Brian pressed me to give the elevator pitch for the floating pool, the community it would serve, and the larger goal of opening up the city's waterfront. When I had finished, Brian said, "Got it!" and ended the short meeting. As he shook my hand, he agreed to do some (which became a lot of) pro bono work for the Neptune Foundation.

Cushing and his specialists in the New York and Washington offices of Holland & Knight thoughtfully and efficiently cleared up a portion of my jurisdictional concerns. They explained that when moored, the barge would be substantially a "land structure" and thus a matter for New York City regulatory authorities, not federal agencies. However, because the C500 would remain afloat at all times, at some point the Coast Guard would be in charge, particularly in the process of changing the flag. The extent and impact of that agency's authority remained to be seen. Kent began to secure and fill out the appropriate Coast Guard reregistration forms, but that work stopped when he was diverted to concentrate on the purchase of the C500.

Along with the registry change, the draft agreement from the seller contained wording about the name of the vessel, indicating that we must remove or cover markings that included the name. As the name change was negotiable, Kent, who would have to arrange a repainting, asked me for choices. Was I to retain the barge's alphabetical and numerical nomenclature, C500? In 1982 Bergeron Industries of Braithwaite, Louisiana, had built the vessel under the equally inspiring name of CBC 2264 for the Canal Barge Company. Subsequently, under the possession of others, the barge had carried a variety of other names: *Tide Mar 264*, *Tide Mar 265*, and *Gulf Fleet 265*. These handles obviously meant something to the owners, but they only made me laugh. I needed to rename her immediately, but I didn't feel ready. The barge felt like an alien, a frightening possession that I needed to chase away. I vacillated as to what to do. I could paint over the "C500" and leave a blank space on the barge's hull, as the seller originally required, but that would obliterate her existence. The final option would be to keep "C500" on her hull for the time being, giving me a chance to accept and welcome her as mine. Perhaps, when the floating pool was ready to move to New York, I could assign the task of painting a new moniker on her to the shipyard hired for the retrofitting. I opted for the latter choice.

Insurance was next on the to-do list. Several weeks before the acceptance of my purchase bid, Kent informed me of "additional issues" that would come with barge ownership. "Various types of insurance," he wrote, "may be needed throughout the different phases of the project." I was forewarned but not forearmed. Finding someone who could procure the various types of coverage we needed would be a challenge. Although the variety of insurance contracts we needed to acquire would be good business for the insurance companies, the professionals feared the unknowns with respect to a floating pool for which they lacked algorithms for adequate risk assessment. The floating pool was a hybrid that required short- and long-distance towing; that could be damaged while under construction; that could be destroyed by an "act of God"; that would hold a pool, hence posing risk of death by drowning or bodily injury by slipping on the deck; and, most intimidatingly, that kids could jump off of for fun and be carried out to sea. All of these risks, some pertaining to regular barges, others pertaining to swimming pools, and others never before (to believe the insurance regulators) considered, had to be accounted for in blanket coverage at a price affordable to the Neptune Foundation. By the end of August, I appointed Kent, our courageous barge shopper, as the designated and interim insurance finder too.

Carter Craft reentered, and the contact wake was lengthened. Carter knew a stellar marine insurance agent, John Keenan, through family and waterfront work. (Keenan's wife, Catherine, was a South Carolina relative of Carter's.) In the 1990s Keenan had volunteered his help to Carter and Kent Barwick to set up the Metropolitan Waterfront Alliance. Tall, handsome, and imperturbable, Keenan was an inveterate sailboat owner and racer, a Coast Guard–licensed captain, and, more importantly for Neptune, the founder and owner of Keenan Marine Insurance Agency in Ardsley, New York. In that role he had insured a decommissioned police boat in private hands, and according to Carter, he could "handle weird projects." Keenan joined the Neptune team for a fee two days before Christmas in 2004, which was three months after the purchase of the barge.

SINCE JULY 19, Steve Crainer and Kent Merrill had been busy behind the scenes with the owner's representative, Enrique Esparragoza, fashioning a final agreement for the purchase of the barge. Steve began with a boilerplate from the seller and worked with Kent as well as Charles, who was experienced in maritime purchases. Insertions and outtakes by both sides continued for several weeks. I signed the agreement on August 31, and there was an immediate glitch—a possible breach of contract. The seller did not return the signed papers until it was too late for me to wire the $45,000 down payment, which the agreement required that I send no later than three business days after the signing. Unfamiliar with Labor Day and the holiday for US banks, the owners had to accept a delay of several days in receiving the payment.

Added to all the other unknowns in taking possession of a gigantic barge, there was one more blank to fill in: the closing date of the sale. "Closing" meant the delivery of the barge from the seller (Transatlantic Cement Carriers, Inc.) to the purchaser (the Neptune Foundation). The first draft of the agreement indicated that the closing would take place on an unknown date in August. The final agreement listed September 20, but the date changed twice after the final draft was accepted. At first, to accommodate one of the principals who could not attend, the closing date was moved up four days to the 16th, which was good. The second change was a postponement to September 23 due to an "act of nature," namely, Hurricane Ivan. This was the first of such acts that would hinder our progress in the coming year. The storm began in the Atlantic in early September and grew to a category 3 hurricane on its way to a dreadful landing on the Alabama/Florida coast on September 16, the day slated for the closing. On the 13th, I nervously watched the storm's path. I also asked Steve for directions to send the seller the remaining $405,000 of the final purchase payment, adding a punch line to my email: "I realized this morning that it's the Jewish New Year. I'm either going to be damned in hell or very blessed to be spending money on such a high holy day!" The seller also must have been concerned, but for reasons other than meteorological ones. An hour later, I read that the barge was being moved from its berth in Berwick to a "secure location." Closing that day was out of the question. Finally, on September 23, as the hurricane changed course and landed as a tropical depression in a southwest corner of Louisiana, the closing took place.

The purchase did not mean we had the pool ready to float. Neptune paid the rent for the C500 to remain at Conrad Shipyard in Amelia, south of New Orleans, until we found a plant to undertake her retrofitting into a floating pool. But having bought a vessel and persevered through the complexities of choice, price, naming, and a storm, we assumed that we had a place for the vessel ultimately to land.

CHAPTER 6

Contracts and Crawfish

THE PURCHASE OF THE *C500* was complete and all we had to do now was find a place for her to become a floating pool and bring her to New York City. Never had I envisioned the good: meeting the barge and the human beings who were turning my dream into a reality. Nor, even though I had worked in city government, had I fully understood the many challenges that I, with the help of a knowledgeable team, would have to meet and overcome for the dream to survive.

It was time for another meeting with the Parks Department, for an update on EDC's progress on Transmitter Park. I entered the meeting on September 9, 2004, with the assumption that the Walcavage design for the park had reached the stage of working drawings, and that my pool was both in her plan and on the Greenpoint community's to-get list. But, having learned my lesson from Hoboken about the need for all major players to be committed to the floating pool, I needed a "yes" from the city agency that would manage the facility.

In the room sat Liam Kavanagh, first deputy commissioner. On either side of him were both male and female members of the agency's Brooklyn Capital Projects and its central planning offices. Unlike the 1950s, when I dared not enter the inner sanctum of Robert Moses's successor, Commissioner Newbold Morris, Kavanagh welcomed me and began the proceedings with the following news: the Parks Department was committed to the floating pool project, had the capital dollars to prepare the site, and would also provide the means to run the day-to-day operations of the floating pool. I was momentarily overjoyed. Then came the kicker: the powers that be would like to have the pool ready to station at Brooklyn's Transmitter Park in Greenpoint for the following summer, June 1, 2005. I took a deep breath and agreed with the group that the barge had to be under construction for the retrofit within three months (December 1, 2004) and that the DEC permit had to be under way for approval by then. Commissioner Adrian Benepe then emerged from his adjoining office through a side door at the end of the meeting to give the gathering official sanction. Although I had no formal notification of this, Adrian must have convinced Mayor Bloomberg that his goal, after he assumed office in 2002, to expand public access to the waterfront, could be met by placing a floating pool at Transmitter Park.

The pressure was on. In nine months, the time it takes to gestate a baby, the Neptune team would have to deal with the boring but necessary details of a construction job. Kent, holed up in the Cushing office on Lower Manhattan's Vesey Street, had to finish the working drawings for the marine work—including inserting a large enough hole into the barge to accommodate a pool. Jonathan Kirschenfeld, in his office farther north in Tribeca, had to clarify the details of his land-based architectural designs for workers used to building ships. Kent must find a shipyard and, with Steven Crainer, negotiate a favorable price, and write and sign the work contracts. And our newly minted John Keenan had to obtain various kinds of insurance. Eventually, and preferably on time, it would be up to Kent to get the barge north to Transmitter Park by summer 2005.

Thankfully Kent had already asked for bids from five shipyards to convert the C500 into a floating pool on an aggressive schedule. But the delays had already started. A month past the construction start date of December 1, which had been agreed on with the Parks Department, negotiations began with two companies, Conrad and Bollinger, both in Morgan City, Louisiana, who had priced the job in the low $300,000s to fit within our total budgeted $2 million.

Purposely omitted from this retrofit was the installation of approximately $800,000 worth of items such as pavers, pool gutters, plumbing lines, privacy screens, cladding and roofs for the changing pavilions, railings, and an upper water play area with jets. These mainly structural and partially decorative items had to be installed in New York City after the initial phase of construction as they might crack, blow away, or suffer unknown mechanical damage when the floating pool was under tow. Assuming that work in either bidding Louisiana shipyard would be fast enough to counter any more delays, I needed to secure a slip somewhere in Brooklyn for May and June 2005, where local contractors could work on the barge and complete the job. The Erie Basin and Atlantic Basin, once active shipping terminals in Red Hook, and the Port Authority Piers 1 through 5 were on the list of possible locations.

What I perceived initially as a few easily accomplished tasks became an ever-elongating list. Along with locating a shipyard in Louisiana and a riverside workplace in New York, we also needed to find companies with workers who would outfit the floating pool on its arrival in northern waters. For this, our team hired architect Steven Sivak, an associate of Jonathan's, as construction manager. Sivak left his Building Arts office in Ann Arbor, Michigan, and found temporary lodgings in New York. He swiftly bored into the project and helped guide us through the arduous task of bringing the pool to completion. To do so he made time charts showing what needed to be accomplished when. He constantly updated the costs, which often changed weekly. He also began a relentless search for independent contractors who would commit to signing contracts in 2005 to work on the barge immediately when it arrived. There would be eleven contractors in all: installers to clad the pavilions with prefabricated, opaque, cement boards; painters to paint these panels; steel fabricators to weld metal strips to form roofs; electricians to install wiring; plumbers to connect water and waste pipes to sinks and toilets; installers of pool equipment such as filters, chlorine tanks, and depth markers; installers of flooring, tiles, cement pavers, and gutters; and a bench maker. Steve made sure the whole Neptune team and associated contractors were working efficiently with no lags or delays. We had not a moment to spare to meet the June 2 deadline. Indeed, we were, by the estimate of the Parks Department, beginning behind schedule.

COMPREHENSIVE AND FORMIDABLE as Steve's job was, there was other work to be done. One of these tasks was to engage the community. Despite the successful meeting with the Waterfront Committee of CB1 in July, many residents were not fully committed to having a pool attached to their new park. Landscape architect Donna Walcavage, who had been hired by the EDC to lead the park design team months earlier, in line with contemporary park planning that required public participation in workshops called charrettes, brought the larger Greenpoint community into the planning process. The CB1 Waterfront, Parks, and Transportation Committees met for a workshop in the auditorium of the Greenpoint Savings Bank on January 5, 2005. If the community remained lukewarm or passive, what would the consequences for the pool project be? The administrators were in agreement, but the community needed to be convinced.

By now I had memorized my sales pitch and was entirely comfortable when Donna introduced me to the group as the representative of the Neptune Foundation. Some of the faces of the twenty-some-odd attendees were familiar, including Julie Lawrence, chair of the CB1 Waterfront Committee, and influential Greenpoint resident Adam Perlmutter. This time, rather than talking about the idea of a floating pool or justifying its planned existence, I was there to bring the group up to date on Neptune's progress. The pool was scheduled for completion in June. It could remain in Greenpoint as long as it was wanted, or until another neighborhood needed it. The pool and its location would be a subject of the workshop. The feeling in the room was not hostile, but it would have been hard to describe it as enthusiastic.

When the floor was opened for questions things began to look bleak. Of the twenty-six questions and comments, nine could be construed as negative. Three people looked directly at me and said the pool was a bad idea. Another announced that it should be put in the Hudson. Some citizens were afraid that the barge would block views. Homeowners were concerned about the influx of outsiders and long lines on hot days. Others worried that the pool would compromise elements wanted for the park, such as a place to sit, sunbathe, and simply enjoy the sounds of the surf. Fishing (probably for sport, definitely not for eating), unlike the pool, was a way to connect to the river in an uncontrolled environment. When they thought of the pool, people imagined the ugly and odiferous scene of children swimming (in partially chlorinated water) near the local storm drain outfalls discharging raw sewage around the barge. Fishermen and environmentalists stated that the shadow caused by the vessel would kill the fish finally returning to the East River.

One other person in the group repeated a statement from the CB1 meeting in July. "It's eye candy and distracts attention from the restoration of the McCarren Park pool." This was obviously and correctly a hot-button issue in the Greenpoint community. A floating pool should never compete with a new McCarren. Along with his ten other WPA-sponsored pools, Robert Moses had opened the McCarren Park pool, his largest, with a capacity of 6,800 persons, in 1936. The facility was integrated, and the well-kept and well-staffed pool comfortably served Puerto Ricans and African Americans who came by bus and the walk-in, nearly all-white Greenpoint-Williamsburg residents for decades. The citywide fiscal problems in the 1970s brought unpleasant changes to the community and to the McCarren pool. Factories closed, residents lost their jobs, and, similar to conditions all over the city, the white population fled and racial conflict, vandalism, and criminal activity were rampant. Cuts in city services hit the McCarren pool as the Parks Department had no funds for its maintenance. But by 1979 the Parks Department had the money to repair a pool that had deteriorated to an unusable state. At the end of summer in 1983 the pool was closed for restoration, but protestors fought the beginning of that work. Allegedly in an effort to control the user population, the community board voted for demolition of the McCarren pool and for a smaller one to be built in its place. Without local support, and with a need for the funds to be used elsewhere, Henry Stern (who had been appointed parks commissioner by Mayor Ed Koch in 1984) closed McCarren pool, and thus it remained for twenty-three years. Given the history, I thought perhaps the floating pool could be the smaller replacement for the Moses pool. But by July 2004 members of CB1 were fighting for the reopening of a facility with a capacity over two thousand that was yet to be designed and funded.

After the January 5 charrette, Donna distributed questionnaires to all of the attendees so that, as she told me, "people who don't like to talk, or don't like to oppose their neighbors, had a chance to give their input." Donna thought I would be pleased with the twenty-one responses. Only three people were opposed to the pool, thirteen thought it was a good idea, four were undecided, and one questionnaire was returned with no response. So what did this mean for twenty-first-century community support, and what difference did community support mean for our project?

With a history in the not-for-profit world I knew the importance of having all of the parties in line, but I had only some. The search for a yard to begin the barge conversion was under way. I had made my pitch to the community but with limited success. Not heard from were the people at multiple agencies who had to approve the floating pool and complete their tasks for its installation in five months.

Topmost on the list was the need to secure DEC's approval to bring a floating pool to Transmitter Park. Just after the CB1 January 2005 workshop, as a follow-up to the September meeting at the Arsenal, I met with Jonathan, Paul Ersboll (the Parks Department's deputy chief of design), and DEC regional staff. A major issue for DEC was still the size of the barge, the shade it cast on the water, and the fear of a consequential loss of fish habitat. Neither we nor DEC had proof that our barge would have a negative impact on local fish, but perhaps we could lessen the agencies' fear of that occurring with some ecologically positive strategies, unscientific though they may be. We suggested that the waterway's mollusk population might increase as new habitat was secured on the barge's undersurface. We offered to set up monitoring stations on the barge to keep tabs on the daily cleanliness (or detritus) in the East River. Or we could create educational programs for the park rangers with exhibitions depicting the history of swimming as recreation, or the types of marine life that had once been found in local waters. These ideas were left on the table.

We needed to prove that the pool in the East River at Transmitter Park could pass DEC's "reasonable and practicable" and "water-dependent" tests. Theoretically, it was "reasonable" to insert an in-ground swimming facility upland where, since the days of Robert Moses, public pools had always been located. Also remembering the price difference between the Progressives' floating baths and the in-ground bathhouses, I argued that for our project this was not "practicable." On-land locations were scarce and would be more expensive than utilizing the hundreds of miles of available state waterways. DEC's counterargument was immediate: if, perchance, the agency did allow this floating structure to be in state waters for a time, and it proved to be a success, it would be difficult to require future pools to be built on land. So we read between the lines that DEC staff was worried that the pool might be a success.

I still had to grapple with the DEC staff's assertion that the floating pool was not a water-dependent use. Correct, it was not a marina, or a floating ferry landing pier. As was shown with Westway, where a highway on landfill was not considered a water-dependent use, this point was (and remains) crucial in the agency's approval process. After wracking my brain and talking with others, I still had no way to define a pool on a barge that floats as water-dependent. And then I realized that the responses from the agency had a subtext and were motivated by administrative anxiety. To allow a floating pool might open the floodgates to other projects, such as floating generators, gas stations, or even apartment houses, which could eventually fill up and despoil the natural waterways.

At this January meeting there was no way to create a surefire argument that would be acceptable to DEC, because, while all these possibilities regarding auxiliary uses were nice, the primary purpose was still a swimming pool, which would traditionally be sited upland and built in the ground. Ultimately, and thankfully, rather than close the case, all present agreed that Ersboll as a representative of the Parks Department, which had been committed to the case from the beginning, would prepare a draft application for a DEC permit to place the floating pool adjacent to Transmitter Park.

Despite the willingness of the leaders of the city's Parks Department to take on the future costs of the floating pool and prepare the DEC permit document, we were confronted with delay after delay as we slugged through the morass of various other levels of government bureaucracy. When the pool arrived, even though it was built to move to other sites, the waterfront engineers would have to create a sturdy landing for it in Greenpoint. This meant securing the barge to pilings anchored deep into the mud under the East River. Enter the Army Corps of Engineers (ACOE), a federal agency that, since codification of the Rivers and Harbors Act of 1899, has had authority over the navigable waters of the United States. To ensure that the sinking of these new pilings would not harm the waterway, the Parks Department needed a timely submission of drawings and calculations so that it could secure a permit from the ACOE. How quickly would the city agency act, and the federal agency review the plans and grant the permit? Additionally, before we could moor the barge, it had to be deemed seaworthy by another federal institution, the US Coast Guard. The priority tasks of developing working drawings and conducting legal negotiations had long ago pushed aside Neptune's application for a Coast Guard certificate. To fill in the blanks on the Coast Guard form, Kent, dressed in khakis and a T-shirt, was in his Vesey Street office in Manhattan searching through a fairly neat, but high, pile of papers to find proof of the barge's tonnage and its original size (which would change in a few months when the reconstruction would add overhangs to the sides of the barge) to once again assert that the facility was "recreational." Even so, once the application would be ready to go, because of its unusual combination of parts, Kent had no certainty that an anchored, floating swimming pool even fell under Coast Guard jurisdiction.

ON JANUARY 25, 2005, we were now two months past the agreed-on cutoff date for the start of construction, and without complaints or, in fact, any word from the Parks Department, we continued on our way to convert the C500 into a floating pool. Steve Crainer, in his small office in the Radio City Music Hall at Rockefeller Center, accepted Bollinger's final bid—now raised to $1.6 million, four times that of the original bid, and $0.3 million above Kent's original estimate. Over the next five weeks, Steve was negotiating the vessel modification agreement. On March 9 I signed the contract, which estimated a five- to six-month work period. I wired a check for the initial payment, all the while blithely assuming that the Neptune Foundation was putting big money down on the building of a pool that would be ready by June. Fortunately, or not, included in the contract was a $45,000 penalty for late delivery.

I sent a payment to insurer John Keenan to cover the premium on a $3.5 million builder's risk policy, and another for the premium on $1 million in coverage to tow the barge the eight miles from Basin Marine in Berwick, Louisiana, where we had berthed her since purchase, to the Bollinger Repair Yard, where the work would begin. The underwriter now worried that the delay in forging the contract and making the coverage effective meant that construction would now run into September: the height of hurricane season. To mitigate that increased risk, the guarantor added a $100,000 deductible for windstorm losses. When Keenan explained that "windstorm" wasn't just any storm, it meant "a severe storm to which the national weather service gives a name, e.g., a hurricane," I lost it.

The insurance costs were only some of the expenses not listed on the original pro forma. A barge conversion cost estimate from December 1, 2004, had shown a new category: dockage, towing, and a disconcerting throwaway "etc." Insurance premiums (during the shipyard period and during the tow to New York) were listed at $110,000. The towing to and positioning in New York added another $110,000. The grand total presented to me in this document for the entire project was $3,684,528. That was some costly overrun! It was time for me to raise additional funds.

Again, I opted to go personal. I compiled a list of relatives, plus friends and acquaintances, who might be able, or care, to lend their support. With the editorial help of my best speech and letter writer, my husband Larry, I wrote the pitch. It told how I felt reluctant to ask for help. I described the project as a philanthropic endeavor that was meaningful to me personally. I wrote that the purposes of the pool were to serve recreationally deprived New Yorkers and to offer them access to the city's waterfront. I admitted that we (the Neptune board) had already bought the barge and begun the retrofit without waiting to amass all of the funds needed. Finally, I listed the $4 million projected total cost of the project and the approximately $3 million already raised. The ask: I needed to find $1 million more to finance this dream and was compelled to turn to my personal circle of friends and family for help.

Private fundraising for a public cause has an inherent problem. Many might ask, "Why should I pay extra for a good, such as parks, for which I pay taxes?" But the fiscal crisis in the 1970s, with the decline in the city's tax base to virtually nil, and the resultant lack of money to maintain public parks, changed that point of view. In 1980 the Central Park Conservancy was founded to raise private funds for the restoration of a historic park that, like the McCarren pool in Brooklyn, was in total disrepair. Many of the donors to my floating pool had also been longtime contributors to the conservancy. But I thought my ask would be more difficult. The floating pool, because it was to be located along a waterfront where residents lacked recreational facilities, was not going to be placed in an upper-class community.

I first took the chance that close relations (my husband's two brothers and three cousins) might have an affinity to my project regardless of where it landed. Theirs were the largest gifts. My brother-in-law, Peter, clarified the reason for his gift in a handwritten letter. "You can count on me to provide precisely the support you have requested because of my honoring family bonds," he wrote. And he continued, "If you have a dream, then surely, I should be a part of helping you realize it."

Next, I approached friends. For some, the specific cause might not matter. I had made donations to further their interests out of friendship, and now, as was the norm among our group, they could reciprocate without restriction. Just as I had proselytized in the various agencies where I had worked, I also told dinner partners or new acquaintances (if they asked me what I was doing) that I sought to improve recreational opportunities for underserved New Yorkers. Days later a small gift might appear in the mail. On reflection, the pitches worked and I got all the financial help I needed: the Neptune Foundation had received $1 million in gifts and pledges, and if all else went well, I would be able to offer the floating pool to the City of New York for the summer of 2005.

And there was an additional upside. One of the donors had sent a check through the not-for-profit Jewish Communal Fund. To meet the fund's requirements for donations, Neptune had to expand its board. I remained chair, our attorney Steve Crainer became secretary, and Kent Barwick remained a faithful member. As it was inappropriate to have two family members as directors, my husband Larry resigned. Replacing him was Robert Douglass, a much-respected friend since my time at the Downtown Alliance where he was board chairman. Bob had relied on me for advice on "offbeat ideas" that related to the waterfront. An adviser to Governor Nelson Rockefeller and Chase Bank, he played a key role in the revitalization of Lower Manhattan after the terror attacks of September 11, 2001. Carl Weisbrod joined the board as a favor to me. My mentor since my first government job at the Department of City Planning, Carl was in constant motion running the Downtown Alliance, providing planning advice to cities throughout the country. When I invited him to join the Neptune board, he was head of the real estate division of Trinity Church. David West was our most recent addition. A recent graduate from business school and a protégé of our insurance guru, John Keenan, David came on board to help me keep dozens of vendors' insurance forms up to date. With the board rearranged, the Bollinger yard needed to rearrange the C500.

While waiting, on March 14, 2005, in response to a call from me, another Joyce, Joyce Purnick, wrote an update for the New York Times on the "old woman and the pool." Her Metro Matters article on the front page of the Metro section dealt with the then positives and negatives. Purnick explained that Hoboken was out of the picture and that the new mayor, Michael Bloomberg, liked the idea of a floating pool (which I had assumed ever since the Arsenal meeting six months before). The words of parks commissioner Adrian Benepe, quoted in Purnick's interview, were, "Your pool project was visionary but not quixotic." The article then pointed out that Greenpoint had been selected as the New York City site, but—and didn't I know it—problems may lay ahead. The river depth in Greenpoint may be too shallow, and the shadow cast by the barge could harm the "marine environment." The article ended with a quote from me that I should have put on a sign and hung around my neck for the next two years: "Don't congratulate me till it's done."

The press coverage was gratifying, even though the *Times* quote suggested that I was putting a brave face on a logistical mess and a schedule about to be blown. On March 17, seventeen days after the contract signing with Bollinger, his yard finally came into focus. After a postponement while we sought a replacement tug company, since Basin had lost their vessel captain (a foreshadowing of later tug problems), the barge finally arrived in Amelia. Work began immediately. Three weeks later there was another delay as workers tried unsuccessfully to use two cranes to remove a portion of the heavy steel deck that would be put aside on land until the pool's innards were ready for its replacement as the pool's bottom. The next day we all cheered when Kent Merrill's digital description told us of burly construction men finding a way to lift the section in two pieces using a single massive crane. We not only had a bottom; we had an opening large enough to create a half-Olympic-length swimming pool.

I was thrilled. The barge retrofit was under way. Still, I should have seen the warning signs that all would not go well with Transmitter Park. Only now, in March, after asking many times, was I finally told by Parks Department staff that ACOE was finally reviewing the Transmitter Park permit application for driving piles into the bottom of the East River. This construction should have begun in January. Then, out of the blue, came the final blow. On June

20, 2005, just weeks before the park, the landing, and the pool should have been finished, I attended another meeting at the Arsenal with Liam Kavanagh, Paul Ersboll, Joshua Laird, and others. They informed me that EDC, the lead agency for building Transmitter Park and its waterfront amenities, had erased the floating pool from the plans. But there might be another site for the pool in Brooklyn.

In retrospect, I believe that politically my one vote did not match up to all of Greenpoint's. Mayor Bloomberg, and hence EDC, had to listen first to the community, who, more than a pool, wanted a new ferry landing pier. The Walcavage designs for extending the park out into the East River now showed airy walkways of a type that was structurally unfit to handle a multiton barge. I was baffled, worried, and angered, but also relieved. I was building the boat. I had used personal capital to make up the budget shortfall. Now the floating pool was homeless again, but delays and delivery problems had disappeared.

I CONTROLLED MY STRONG emotions and stayed focused on the mention of a Brooklyn site, the Port Authority Piers. I knew that the bistate agency had been in control of twenty-five finger piers between the Brooklyn Bridge and Atlantic Avenue for nearly half a century. In the late 1950s the agency had widened slim piano key landings and covered them with huge gray-blue sheds to serve very large freighters. Six of these piers and sheds stretched below the Brooklyn Heights residential area and the Brooklyn Queens Expressway, from Fulton Landing to Atlantic Avenue. Similar to their property in Hoboken, containerization was the death knell to these piers, which had been derelict since the 1980s. Ships had disappeared and a few of the sheds were on month-to-month leases for construction or storage of coffee beans and other items.

This set of six piers was a year away from being transferred to the Brooklyn Bridge Park Development Corporation (BB Park Corporation). This public entity had been created by the state in 2002 to construct a waterfront park to be known as Brooklyn Bridge Park. Here, in a process not unlike the park design stage of the Hoboken Piers, suddenly was my next (and hopefully my last) choice to land the floating pool, now six weeks under reconstruction, with more than $1 million spent. My efforts to place the floating pool here, under state leadership, were joined by members of the Parks Department, as well as the very patient Marianna Koval and her not-for-profit conservancy, who had been sending me digital messages asking about the floating pool since 2002.

Joshua Laird, the parks commissioner's point person on the pool, dragged his heels until October 2005—four months after the Transmitter Park disappointment—to agree to talk with Wendy Leventer, the state official in charge of the park's Development Corporation. Josh was often notoriously slow in moving my pool ahead. This time was he just too busy with other city parks matters? Because this was now a New York State project, had he been waiting in line for a meeting? Or, anticipating Wendy's reaction, was this an effort to let me down lightly? Wendy had completion of the park on the top of her to-do list. A floating pool was not in the landscape architects' original design, and introducing a pool now might adversely affect an awaited and necessary DEC permit, causing new and undesirable obstacles for her. Perhaps Wendy and her landscape architects were also concerned that once berthed at Pier 2, the floating pool would be in such demand that it would become a permanent fixture at this site. A favor for a summer season or two could develop into an annual budgeting and programming commitment for the Development Corporation, and it would delay, not further, the construction of Brooklyn Bridge Park. The move down the Brooklyn waterfront, or to any riverine location, would be a challenge. Those who did not like the project would attack it, no matter the site. Those who supported the pool feared it would be too successful or impede other plans and projects.

This reminded me of my stint at the Parks Department in the late 1980s when I was director of waterfront planning. I had lobbied singlehandedly for the addition of a floating pool to Battery Park in Manhattan. But there were no funds in the agency's capital budget for my venture. I was still many years away from creating the Neptune Foundation, and Parks had no interest in putting a floating pool into the city's budget. At that time, with Commissioner Henry Stern's blessing (perhaps the first step toward his later commitment to run but not pay for the pool's management), Joanne Imohoisen, the assistant commissioner for revenue, allowed me to send out an RFP to private developers to construct a floating pool at Battery Park in Manhattan. No sooner was my RFP on the radar than I received a call from Justin J. Murphy, the chair of the Downtown–Lower Manhattan Association, a group David Rockefeller Sr. founded in 1958 as part of his efforts to reinvigorate Lower Manhattan via the development of pockets of new residential and commercial projects built into the East and Hudson Rivers. Over the phone came Justin's admonition: "Ann, a floating pool at the Battery will interfere with our plans for developments on landfill in that area. Once [the pool is] open, the community will never let it leave." In other words, I understood Justin to say that the pool's popularity might stand in the way of the future commercial and residential development that would contribute to the tax base in ways a recreational facility never would.

While I waited, after the October 2005 meeting, to be introduced to the powers that be at the BB Park Corporation, my primary concern was finishing the work on the barge. Compared to city and state administrative politics, it was a process that I had a better chance of controlling. Once again, I was disappointed. Instead of progress there were delays. Over a year earlier, in July 2004, when we were trying to figure out which regulatory agencies would apply to the floating pool, Kent Merrill had recommended that we classify the barge with the American Bureau of Shipping (ABS). Similar to the US Coast Guard, ABS certification means that a ship is seaworthy and its systems meet a high standard of safety and reliability. His suggestion introduced me to another type of bureaucracy, that within the private sector.

Kent's idea was theoretically a good one. While not a replacement for the Coast Guard, the agency that would have to give permission for the vessel to travel to New York, classification with ABS might help lower Neptune's insurance costs even as we proceeded with the plan for the retrofit. What's more, it might help unravel some of the regulatory threads. If a recognized maritime agency certified the barge, perhaps the New York City Department of Buildings might back off from trying to apply its regulations to what is obviously not a land-based building. But theory in this case did not concur with reality.

Instead, the retrofit met with challenges. In May 2005, three months after Bollinger had begun the conversion, and a month before EDC had scuttled the Transmitter Park plan for a pool, ABS demanded replacement of large portions of the barge's steel foundation, which would have been appropriate if the barge were headed back out to do offshore work in the open ocean—but it wasn't. This demand meant that Neptune would owe Bollinger extra payments of hundreds of thousands of dollars to do the additional work. And, surprise! Bollinger needed approval from C. R. Cushing & Co. to add that work. Kent or Charles would have to sign "change orders."

While I sat at the desk as Neptune's one and only secretary, writing thank-you letters with accompanying tax-deductible notifications, and paying bills with the foundation money in the bank, the private bureaucratic delay continued. In an effort to keep extra costs down, Cushing, appropriately, needed to analyze the additional scope of work to ensure it was cost effective and that the extra steel replacement made sense. This took time, and the Bollinger workers assigned to the pool were, for the time being, relegated to other jobs in the yard. On May 27 Bollinger stopped the project. The Cushing team had to regroup and had thankfully decided that it would not be cost effective to classify the floating pool with ABS. Eventually, work resumed in the Bollinger yard as per the original charge. The work stoppage persisted for four months, across a summer when the floating pool should have been open for swimmers in Transmitter Park. During that period, planning for Brooklyn Bridge Park continued but without a floating pool or an appropriation of funds to implement the plan for a park.

AS MY MOOD WORSENED and my anxiety mounted, meteorology—an actual storm, not a projection on an actuarial table of an insurance firm—intervened. Hurricane Katrina hit the Gulf Coast with a vengeance in late August. I waited at home in New York, in sympathy and shock, for a very long week watching the humanitarian disaster on television like everyone else. According to Kent, the physical facility, a floating pool, was fine. The old barge had proved herself worthy in the teeth of one of the most destructive storms in US history.

Countless news reports, books, and movies have documented the tremendous physical, social, and emotional upheaval caused by Katrina. In contrast, her effect on the floating pool was minuscule. All we lost was time. Now-homeless shipyard workers had been lured by the Federal Emergency Management Agency (FEMA) from Amelia to New Orleans with promises of housing and earning higher-than-average wages at temporary jobs repairing the damage done to the city. Despite a large banner on Bollinger's website that read, "Bollinger has employment opportunities at every location," the manpower situation remained bad. In January 2006, three months after Katrina, only ten people were working on the floating pool, but a total of forty would be needed to finish the work by May or June of that year. FEMA would probably still not start laying off the temporary workers for at least a month. And if a sufficient number of workers ever returned to the ravaged town of Amelia, where would they live?

We were in a holding pattern, and New Orleans and its environs were under water. Given the scale of the tragedy, rebuilding levees and floodwalls, making caskets for the dead, and building new homes had to come before retrofitting a barge to house a floating pool that when finished would leave Louisiana to serve New Yorkers. On January 17, 2006, sixteen months after my meeting with Commissioner Liam Kavanagh, I sent a message to the Neptune board members: "In view of the circumstances post-Katrina, please understand that we have no delivery date."

The next day I called Donald T. Bollinger, owner of the Bollinger Shipyards, for his assessment of the situation. It was to be our first personal contact, and I was apprehensive about whether I'd be able to hold my own with this much-talked-about friend of President

George W. Bush, nicknamed "Boysie," pictured in the press as heavy-set with thick eyebrows and a ruddy face. I was direct and asked, "When will your workers get back to the pool?" He was less direct, because human needs came first. He was securing temporary housing for the workers who had lost their homes. He expected to start hiring in several days. From a business aspect, finishing our job was the top priority, but its accomplishment was uncertain. Bollinger had no idea how many workers would come back.

Hoping to speed up the process, I tried another approach: flattery. Bollinger had recently been appointed by New Orleans mayor Ray Nagin to help in the planning and rebuilding of New Orleans. Fortunately, Nagin was in the room when I called. I thanked Bollinger for taking on the task of building the country's first modern floating pool in his yard. I added that, on completion of the novel project, the press would surely be at his doorstep. Given the recovery and reconstruction efforts that the "Bring New Orleans Back Commission" was discussing, I made a suggestion: Why not bring the floating pool back to New Orleans the following winter? "The barge," I said, "having been retrofitted by the Bollinger shipyard, could be one of the post-Katrina projects to be delivered to New York City. It will serve as a great piece of public relations for New Orleans, as well as a connection between these two resilient and vital cities." The mayor, listening in on our conversation, was interested. But his interest did not bring workers hurrying back to Amelia.

Only fourteen people were working on the barge by February 2; a day later there were fifteen, and five days later there were only eighteen. On February 15 Bollinger notified me that his shipyard was slowly making progress on hiring more employees, but progress was gradual. He hoped to begin work on the superstructure—housing for changing rooms, lifeguard/manager's office, and bathrooms—soon. But now the holdup was not New Orleans. Even though we were a year behind schedule, Jonathan Kirschenfeld, sleeves-with-holes rolled up, had not completed his drawings for the pavilions and upper-level work, and without these drawings Bollinger could not order the construction materials. "At this rate,"

Boysie wrote, "we will be finished in May. . . . We WILL overcome the challenges." Naively, I understood Bollinger's words "will be finished" to mean "the pool will be on its way to New York."

IN MARCH 2006 Kent Merrill, Jonathan Kirschenfeld, and I left the skyscrapers of New York City and boarded a jet plane bound for New Orleans. It was the day I was to meet my 2,540-ton dream and see an amazing group of hard-working men. Although I had spent time in both Annapolis, Maryland, with its shipyard that served the Naval Academy, and in Mamaroneck, New York, with a facility that repaired private yachts, Bollinger's Amelia repair yard was way beyond the scope of my experience. Scan Amelia, one of many Bollinger shipyards: it is on a narrow peninsula surrounded by offshoots of the Intracoastal Waterway and bayous. Seen on Google Maps from above, it looks like an African bib necklace, each spoke an earthen jetty surrounded on three sides by water and hanging from a half circle of rough roadway. The sides of the jetty are chockablock with ships afloat, each vessel looming larger than the last. Suddenly, one is face to face with the C500.

I stood up to my full five feet, three inches on the ground and looked up at her, lost in the vast shadow cast by the huge semi-rusted blue leviathan. The C500 seemed to be a sad giant gazing down on me, the tiny person who had given it a second chance. It had been a long road for me and this floating hunk of metal to meet here in this boatyard. We faced each other. "It's real," I thought.

But the breakthrough moment came when, with the help of several burly men in hard hats, I was pushed and pulled up a very tall ladder to come aboard. I finally saw, beyond the day-to-day process and bureaucracy, the human labor required to reconstruct the C500 into a floating pool. On deck, men of all shapes and sizes knelt, squatted, pulled, and lifted. One man wearing a yellow hard hat, his face covered with a gray, metal visor and his neck with a light green gaiter, worked lying on his side. He wore heavy leather gloves with fingers many sizes larger than his own. In his right hand he held what appeared to be a power tool with an orange plyer-shaped handle that he used to poke a hole through the side of the barge. Sparks flew.

I toured the vessel with Corey Phelps, a handsome, muscular, earnest young man who was totally in charge of his team and the work. As a leader of the group, he wore a white hard hat with the Bollinger logo center front. We walked around the rectangular hole left after removing a portion of the deck a year before. Two large sheets of steel waited on land nearby, tucked among cranes, metal siding, and machinery the uses of which I could not fathom. Barring another "windstorm," these cranes would soon lower the 50-by-115-foot section of the former topside into the barge to become the pool bottom, elegantly reusing the metal and leaving footprints of the barge's history. I asked Phelps what he thought when he heard that he would be working on a floating pool. Like me, he couldn't fathom how a city surrounded by water like New York should have no place for a person to swim. "Here, anywhere there's water," he responded, "you can pretty much swim."

Work on the barge ceased for lunch. At a restaurant on Route US 90, the highway that runs through Amelia on its way from Seattle to Boston, I hoped to have a bit more interaction with Phelps and some of the floating pool workers. But this was time for a treat, not talk. A waiter placed a giant Styrofoam container on the table. It held multiple pounds of boiled, red, shrimplike creatures with antennae, long tails, and small claws. These were the first of the crawfish, a local delicacy, to come into season since Katrina. In the midst of this feast, my face splattered with Cajun red pepper mix, my hands smelling of seafood, I finally had the opportunity to meet the man who, over a year ago, had given me a chance to pursue my dream. In walked Boysie Bollinger. I feared his reaction. Would he ignore me? Had my odd job been only trouble? No, this human encounter evinced a combination of pleasure and satisfaction. Not only did Bollinger envelop my grimy hand, he called his friends over from the bar to introduce them to the "lady whose floating pool I am building."

Our trip to the Bollinger yard had confirmed that the barge was on her way to completion. Yet once released from Amelia, we had

PLATE 1. Boss Tweed opened the first floating baths in 1880. Residents and workers from the tenement houses ventured to the baths for a half hour, theoretically cleansing dip in an open-air pool. The usually single-story rectangular wood structures had a well of river water in the center, floated on pontoons, and were attached to land by a gangway. Slats on the sides of the pool and on the bottom kept swimmers contained and allowed a constant flow of river water to pass through. Throughout their sixty-seven years on the waterfront, the baths were extremely popular. Crowd control was essential, and in keeping with the social norms of the age, the floating baths were sex-segregated. An insert in this engraving by Harry Ogden depicts the exclusion of men at a pool on opening day. **CREDIT:** "Opening of the Free Baths in New York," drawn by Henry Ogden, *Harper's Weekly*, June 6, 1883.

PLATE 2. In 1998 the not-for-profit Neptune Foundation hired architect Jonathan Kirschenfeld to design a twenty-first-century floating pool on a retired, flat-top barge. Jonathan proposed a design not like the nineteenth-century floating baths but in the style of the 1950s beach clubs of Long Beach, Long Island. These were a collection of cabanas that surrounded a communal space. The roofs under construction as seen from above in the Bollinger shipyard in Louisiana in 2006 are whimsically painted and have open-air skylights. **CREDIT:** Bradley A. Kelly.

PLATES 3 AND 4. The design of the twenty-first-century floating pool was only the first step. A multiyear search for a berth for it began in Hoboken, New Jersey, in 2000. A decade earlier, the Coalition for a Better Waterfront, a 150-member group of local residents, had proposed ideas for a development plan that differed significantly from past plans for the waterfront: instead of high-rise residential and commercial structures that closed off the shoreline to public use, the coalition's map shows passive and active recreational facilities right on the piers, and low-rise housing and commercial structures on the upland. A continuous public walkway and a floating pool attached to a pier invites the public to enjoy the estuarian environment. By 1999 a waterfront park with two recreational piers was finally in the works. Pier A had become a park, but a plan for Pier C was at a standstill. In March 2000, in the spirit of the earlier coalition's plan, I offered Hoboken's Mayor Russo the donation of a floating pool. In August, at a meeting with Hoboken city officials, architect Dean Marchetto unveiled a preliminary Pier C development plan. There was a pavilion for summer activities with a pool floating on its south side. Next to the pool, but absent from this image, was a handwritten comment: "future." **CREDIT:** Fund for a Better Waterfront and Dean Marchetto, FAIA.

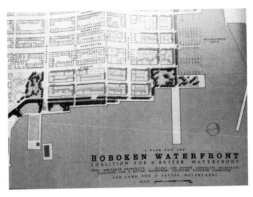

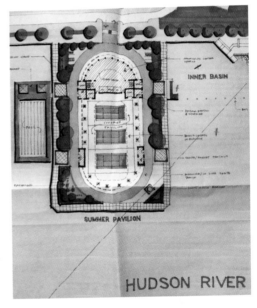

PLATES 5 AND 6. With the promise of Hoboken apparently nailed down as a location, it was necessary to find a barge. The first choice was a used steel cargo barge with a flat deck, a portion of which could be removed to allow the pool to be constructed within the opening. However, no barges were available at the budgeted price. A three-year hiatus ensued. Hoboken's Mayor Russo lost his reelection bid, and the political will to bring a floating pool to Hoboken disappeared. In July 2004 Kent Merrill, Team Neptune's naval engineer, emerged from Morgan City, Louisiana, with the *C500*. In 2006 shipyard workers added her new name, the *Floating Pool Lady*, in white.
CREDIT: Kent Merrill and Ann L. Buttenwieser.

PLATES 7 AND 8. With the purchase of the *C500*, it was time to transform the former cargo barge into a floating pool. On April 18, 2005, cranes at the Bollinger repair yard in Amelia, Louisiana, lifted two enormous sheets that had been cut out from the top of the barge, leaving a hole for the construction of a half-Olympic-size, seven-lane pool. A small portion of the human labor required for the barge's reconstruction may be seen walking on the deck and resting next to a dumpster. The 50-by-115-foot section of the former topside would be reused as the pool's bottom, leaving footprints of the barge's history. Instead of tons of cargo, the floor would be weighted with water to a four-foot depth, and up to 174 swimmers at a time. A year later, members of the Neptune team visited the barge. The rectangular hole remained, but the empty deck had become a two-story structure, with Jonathan Kirschenfeld's as-yet-unpainted pavilions for offices, shower and bathrooms, and changing rooms in place. The floating pool still had no berth to open in New York City. **CREDIT:** Kent Merrill and Ann L. Buttenwieser.

PLATES 9 AND 10. On October 30, 2006, the *Floating Pool Lady* arrived at the Brooklyn Bridge. A barge had transported her on a 1,592-mile trip from Amelia, Louisiana, around the Florida Panhandle, and up the East Coast—with a stop to weather a storm in Cape Hatteras—and into New York Harbor. Here two tugboats circled her around the Brooklyn Bridge waiting for permission to land in Brooklyn. But that permission was not granted. She was held up in Staten Island by bureaucratic requirements Neptune had not met, and then by a nearly monthlong wait for more available towboats. Finally, on November 27, the tugs *Susan Miller* and *Tracy Miller* inched the *Lady* into her berth between Piers 3 and 4, near the entrance to six former Port Authority piers that had been waiting since 2002 to be transformed into Brooklyn Bridge Park. Here began the final phase of the barge's construction and the search for a temporary berth in the future park for a July opening. **CREDIT:** Kent Merrill and Ann L. Buttenwieser.

PLATES 11 AND 12. The finishing touches on the floating pool were under way. The scale of the canopy hovering over the collection of cabanas was perfect, turning the area into a communal space. On the deck, pavers still needed to be laid; flooring needed to be installed in bathrooms, showers, and changing rooms; and the lanes on the steel bottom of the pool would be painted a marine blue to match the doors of the nearby former maritime warehouses. **CREDIT:** Ann L. Buttenwieser.

PLATE 13. Six years after Neptune's disappointing exodus from New Jersey, New York State officials were in charge of getting the floating pool open by July 4, 2007. The berth between Piers 4 and 5 became its temporary location. The *Floating Pool Lady's* stern would be attached to a man-made beach by two gangways (shown here lying on the upland). Two Miller's vessels adjusted the *Lady*, with water sloshing around in the pool, while off in the distance, workers on an MTA barge added post-9/11 security protections to underground subway lines. **CREDIT:** Jonathan Kirschenfeld.

PLATES 14 AND 15. Opening day for the press was on board the *Lady* on July 3, 2007. In response to a reporter's question about the project, I replied: "Normally it takes nine months to gestate and give birth. This baby took twenty-seven years, and here she is!" Standing behind a podium, I addressed an audience of dignitaries and a small crowd of children waiting to be the first to jump into the pool. On my left stood Rep. Nydia Velásquez and (obscured) Brooklyn borough president Marty Markowitz. From left to right in the back row, I was joined by Brooklyn Bridge Park Conservancy executive director Marianna Koval, who believed that the interim use of a floating pool would draw a constituency to support the long-awaited Brooklyn Bridge Park; former state senator Martin Connor; former New York State Assembly member Karim Camara; and former State Assembly member Joan Millman. **CREDIT:** John Muggenborg.

THE FLOATING POOL LADY A QUEST TO BRING A PUBLIC POOL TO NEW YORK CITY'S WATERFRONT

PLATE 16. With the speeches out of the way, Brooklyn borough president Marty Markowitz and parks commissioner Adrian Benepe, whistle in hand, stood with several dozen children ready to leap into the pool. The commissioner called out, "Are you ready, kids?" Then he laughed, blew a whistle, and everyone jumped. **CREDIT:** John Muggenborg.

PLATE 17. July 4, 2007, dawned cloudy, but Marianna Koval stood at the entry to the gangway to welcome everyone who stood in line to be among the first swimmers to try out the unique pool. That day four thousand individuals came to the barge and over a thousand of them swam. At 9:00 p.m. visitors sat on the beach, with Lower Manhattan office buildings and the Brooklyn Bridge in the background, and watched fireworks, celebrating both Independence Day and the opening of the *Floating Pool Lady*. **CREDIT:** Philippe Baumann.

PLATES 18 AND 19. During the six weeks that the facility was open, Marianna Koval took time off to enjoy floating in water on water. I also visited the pool to see how the public was enjoying the facility. One day I introduced myself to a group of eight-year-old girls and one of them looked me straight in the eye and asked, "Why did you make the pool free for us?" **CREDIT:** Julianne Schaer and Ann L. Buttenwieser.

PLATE 20. The pool closed in Brooklyn on Labor Day 2007, having served a diverse population of nearly sixty thousand people. "Bring her back!" were the three words heard over and over from the public. A week later the barge left to winter in New Jersey and to await the transfer of ownership from the Neptune Foundation to the New York City Department of Parks and Recreation. New York City mayor Michael Bloomberg opened the *Floating Pool Lady* at her permanent berth in Barretto Point Park in the Bronx nine months later. At the podium for that event are (left to right): parks commissioner Adrian Benepe, Mayor Michael Bloomberg, an unknown boy, and two students from the Point, a local nonprofit. I am holding a photograph of a nineteenth-century bath that once floated in a nearby Bronx location.
CREDIT: NYC Parks/Malcolm Pinckney.

PLATE 21. The Barretto jump! With the Rikers Island jail in the background, Mayor Bloomberg and Commissioner Benepe joined local children who had walked through an industrial area in flip-flops to reach the only pool in their community. Every year thereafter the pool welcomed from thirty to nearly fifty thousand patrons, more than any pool of the same size in the Bronx. **CREDIT:** NYC Parks/Malcolm Pinckney.

PLATES 22 AND 23. At the opening of its eleventh year of operation at Barretto Point, two girls, their backs covered with free sunscreen, watched the activities in the pool below. Having reached the pool via the boys' or girls' dressing rooms, their walls decorated with images of fish that once swam in the East River, children enjoyed their first day of summer vacation. **CREDIT:** NYC Parks Department/Malcom Pinckney and Charles Truax.

NEW YORK'S HARBOR AND RIVER SYSTEMS TEEMED WITH SHAD, TUNA, WHALES, SQUID, SALMON, TROUT AND THE MOST FAMOUS

THE FLOATING POOL LADY A QUEST TO BRING A PUBLIC POOL TO NEW YORK CITY'S WATERFRONT

PLATE 24. Having relished the scene of kids having fun in the pool, I was invited to sit among a group of swimmers for a photograph. The *Floating Pool Lady* is more than a floating pool and more than the realization of a personal dream. She reflects New York's storied immigrant past and continues to inspire future waterfront projects in New York City and beyond. **CREDIT:** Ann L. Buttenwieser.

proof of neither New York City's financial nor New York State's political investment, and, most important of all, we still did not know where the *Lady* was going to land, even temporarily.

Although the New York City parks commissioner had verbally committed to running my floating pool in 2004, Brooklyn Bridge Park, the second site where we now sought to land, was under the auspices of a subsidiary of a state-run entity, the Empire State Development Corporation (ESDC). Now we needed a friend in Albany. Eliot Spitzer, an acquaintance of my husband since the late 1990s when Spitzer had run for state attorney general (and who knew me through the Buttenwieser name), was going to take office as governor of New York in January 2007. Following up on Marianna Koval's 2004 invitation, and with Joshua Laird finally in action, in mid-March 2006 we had our first meeting with staff of BB Park Corporation, the ESDC subsidiary. I hoped that personal connections, limited as they were, would facilitate progress, but instead the reality was foot-dragging with obstacles (or objections) coming from state agency bureaucrats whom I would never meet.

I arrived at the BB Park Corporation meeting on March 13 with my team, now expanded to include another paid member, Malcolm McLaren, whom I then considered (and still do) to be the best waterfront engineer in the United States. Sturdily built, gray-haired, and mustachioed, Mal could explain technical terms regarding barge placement and anchoring to all of us in the room in plain English. Furthermore, having worked on innumerable state and city waterfront projects, he commanded respect and confidence in important quarters, and he could later effectively argue with officials regarding our needs at city hall, as well as in Albany, if required.

We approached the meeting hoping to discuss an agreement for the floating pool to dock temporarily at one of the former Port Authority piers in order to finish the work on the pool and both decks. At the least, I hoped to achieve a move-in date, the lease terms, and information about the types and amount of insurance the state would require. Jamie Springer, a young go-getter and project manager at the BB Park Corporation, was open and cooperative. He considered the pool to be an excellent temporary use for the park. But his hands were tied by Wendy Leventer, who, because the state gubernatorial election had not yet occurred, was still head of the corporation.

Because Wendy was still in control, Springer's agenda for the March 2006 meeting was a step backward. He proposed to discuss how to proceed if, not when, my request was deemed feasible. On the top of his list was an update on the phasing and schedule for building the park and the amount of land we would be allowed to use on the upland between two empty piers Jamie and the Brooklyn Bridge Park's landscape architects had chosen, Piers 2 and 3. For them, the first priority was for work to begin on the park ASAP. They planned to start with environmental remediation of all of the property once used by the maritime industry. For this, their schedule showed large amounts of dirt-based fill arriving on the upland in eight months. On hearing this my imagination ran wild. At minimum Neptune needed room for ten to fifteen parking spaces, room for the base of the stairway onto the barge, and sufficient width to place a crane now and again. Although this bulkhead, a former asphalt parking lot for shipping containers, certainly had sufficient width for both needs, I saw trucks arriving, and wind blowing black dirt into the workers' eyes, and a just-painted-blue pool. But that was the least of my worries.

The meeting had to address an agreement. Confusion ensued. Since the pool docking was to be the first use of the former Port Authority property, should this be a lease, a permit, or a license? If the barge would be ready to depart Amelia in July, as promised by Bollinger, Springer would need to have a contract in place, whatever its legal title, by May 30, because the floating pool would soon arrive in New York Harbor, ready or not.

Before the meeting ended, Jamie asked a strategic question: Where were we regarding securing a permit from the DEC? Nowhere, I said. The Parks Department deputy chief of design, Paul Ersboll, who was supposed to have handled this matter, had moved to another job. He was no longer at the agency, his position was unfilled, and no one in the office was conversant with the DEC permit. We left the meeting stuck at a seemingly permanent square one.

THE NEXT SIX MONTHS were a time of surprising progress in the Bollinger yards. A report from Kent Merrill on May 24, 2006, described status of the conversion work after Hurricane Katrina. Jonathan Kirschenfeld's upper-level pavilions housing the changing facilities and offices on the barge were built. Sinks and toilets were on order. The barge had been dry-docked to get its hull sandblasted to bare metal and to receive many coats of deep blue ship's paint. The pool had been filled with water for testing, and indeed, the C500 held water. But the best news in Kent's report was that Bollinger had stated in writing that their delivery date would be July 31, 2006.

There was also persistent dysfunction. In July I received word from Steve Crainer and Kent that the long-standing Coast Guard application—which had been put aside amid delays and revisions in contract and design work—required a name. When the barge was in dry-dock, without instruction from Kent, workers had simply started painting the letters that years ago had been welded to the side of the hull in bright white. And it wasn't even C500! It was her previous name, CBC2264.

After days of debate and discussion, Jonathan came up with the perfect handle: "Ann, when you went to the Brooklyn CB1 Waterfront Committee meeting, they greeted you with 'Here comes the Floating Pool Lady.'" Thus, with my approval and with white paint instead of champagne, several men rechristened the barge: the *Floating Pool Lady*. Back in New York City, with the help of the Panamanian consulate, Steve Crainer finally completed the documents to return the vessel to US registry. We no longer had a foreign homeport listing of Panama City on what we hoped would become a New York City treasure. The barge had a name and was an American citizen.

It might appear that by now, with all of the delays, the BB Park Corporation would have given up on our project, but in June attorneys on both sides finally got to work on a document giving us permission to land at Brooklyn Bridge Park. This was great news. Since this kind of work was well outside Steve Crainer's area of legal expertise, that month we added another pro bono attorney from my husband Larry's firm, Jaimee Schwartz, to our team. On June 10 Jaimee sent me the first draft of a license agreement. Mark-ups of this, and subsequent drafts would shuttle back and forth between the state and Neptune for the next four months, while matters at the state came to a standstill and the city disappeared. Once the *Floating Pool Lady* departed Amelia, Wendy Laventer would have to sign the papers to let us land. Before she could sign Wendy faced a bureaucratic nightmare affecting many levels of state government. She would need approval from the internal insurance group of the ESDC, the BB Park Corporation's lead agency. In turn, the two men in that group required approval from others in an office in Albany for the insurance that Neptune and the companies, or subcontractors whom we had hired to complete the work at Piers 2–3, would need to carry. Here was the issue.

In my most nonsensical moments, I imagined two men who, from nine to five daily, sat side by side at computers, like something in the movie *Brazil*. In consultation with their superiors in Albany, I supposed that they did nothing but decide how many millions of dollars in exotic types of insurance coverage they would require. A word salad of insurance terms such as builders risk (which we had but needed to renew), commercial general liability (CGL), commer-cial property, and pollution liability regularly flew by this neo-phyte's computer screen. The dollar amounts were over the top. For a small nonprofit entity, the bureaucrats demanded liability cover-age in the amount of not less than $5 million. I was stunned by the amount and confounded by the legal nomenclature.

Depending on three familiar and potentially chaos-inducing fac-tors—hurricanes, the availability of a tug, and work on the barge still to be done—the *Lady*'s arrival was now due around October 16. On September 20, Jaimee Schwartz circulated a draft of a license agreement approved by both Neptune and the BB Park Corporation. She left section 17 (*Insurance*) open pending further discussion in-house and negotiations with insurance officers in Albany. For now, we expected that the nine-to-fivers in charge of our insurance fate would move very little from their proposed terms.

On October 2, 2006, I sat in Collect Pond Park in downtown Manhattan on a lunch break from jury duty reading the latest draft of the license agreement to dock the floating pool at one of the Brooklyn Bridge Park piers. Items such as the barge's location, utilities, and nightly security were fairly standard. The language in section 10, *Option to Use the Pool*, made me believe that the *Lady* had finally found a home for her first summer (now 2007) in the city. This part of the agreement granted Neptune an option "to use and occupy the Pool . . . for recreational purposes, including swimming, from and after July 1, 2007" with the end date to be determined. But my optimism was short-lived. There was a catch. The recreational occupancy required the Parks Department to agree to "operate and finance the operation of the pool" during the months of the option. Worse still, in less than a day I received the following notice from parks commissioner Adrian Benepe: "It is unfortunate that you will not be able to stay in Brooklyn Bridge Park during the summer of 2007. It's hard to find another site at this time especially given the number of permitting and capital infrastructure issues still to be resolved. The Department has no capital funds for utility or infrastructure." And the Parks Department's expense budget had no funds for operating the pool. The city was out. On reading this note from the man who had supported and encouraged my efforts from day one, I was appalled and felt terribly let down. Yet Adrian's missive also mentioned that he was working on securing a site for the *Floating Pool Lady* in the Bronx for the summer of 2008. I had learned from the history of the floating baths that new programs require patience, but how far ahead can one look to be assured of success?

In early October 2006 I had to act decisively in the face of a very uncertain future. Since my inspiring moment in the Battery Maritime Building in the 1970s, I had dreamed of bringing floating pools back to New York City. My aspiration was reinforced by the Neptune Foundation's charter, which gave us permission to construct three prototype floating pools for the New York/New Jersey region. Without further deliberation I reminded myself of my decision, after the pool was removed from the plans for the Transmitter site in Greenpoint, that the Brooklyn piers were the only proper place for the floating pool to open and operate. That being so, I would not accept a no from Commissioner Benepe or anyone else. In retrospect, this decision was not naive; it was strategic.

On October 10 the team began to arrange for the voyage to Brooklyn, assuming a departure from Amelia eight days later. By October 16, and in record time, Kent found an available tow company at a price that we could afford, Steve Crainer fashioned an acceptable contract, and Keenan procured the necessary insurance. Both sides had accepted the wording of the agreement with the BB Park Corporation (without the option for a summer venue). However, Jaimee Schwartz continued to correspond daily with the nine-to-fivers in New York City regarding the insurance policy numbers and amounts. She also pushed back against a totally new requirement: proof of the Neptune Foundation's automobile insurance. Neptune did not even have a car!

Meanwhile, to the chagrin of the state publicity office that was trying to curtail any announcement about the *Floating Pool Lady* until her arrival, the *Daily News* and the *New York Post* had reached someone in the Parks Department for a scoop on her imminent departure. She weighed anchor in Amelia at 8:30 a.m. on October 20, 2006. In the care of *Tiger Pride*, the lead tug, and *Miss Claire*, the tail tug, she made an uneventful downriver passage to the Eugene Island, Texas, sea buoy. There she rendezvoused with an ocean tug with the wonderful and (I hoped should a tropical storm arise) equally appropriate name of *Ataboy*.

The trip from there to the Sandy Hook, New Jersey, buoy was a total of 1,592 miles. Eric Dreijer, *Ataboy*'s pilot, estimated that the approximate trip time would be ten days with a projected arrival on Halloween eve. Under light winds and with a two-foot chop in the water, this second tow commenced the sea voyage to New York at 4:30 p.m. on October 20. My barge was moving and so was I, running between computer screens to watch the Google map track the *Lady*'s passage in the Gulf of Mexico. I imagined Dreijer to be Edwin T. Hyde escorting his fleet of floating baths from the Bronx to Manhattan for the start of the swimming season over a century ago.

This much smaller fleet of two vessels—tug and barge—made a three-day beeline from Texas to west of Key West, hugging Florida's tip to reach Alligator Reef south of Miami on October 24. I gently patted the photographs on the screen sent to me by Kent. They showed her, shining in the sunlight, and a dark silhouette in moonlight, being towed pool-end (bow) first by the two-story white-and-black *Ataboy*. Just as the *Lady* and her escort *Ataboy* passed Miami and entered the Atlantic, we finally received good news from Keenan. He was able to find the $5 million commercial general liability coverage at a price Neptune was willing to pay. At the last moment we now had almost all we needed to berth the *Lady* for the winter in New York Harbor.

The voyage continued uneventfully up the concave US coast from Florida past Georgia and South Carolina. As the pair neared Cape Hatteras, on October 27, they encountered heavy weather. Winds of thirty miles per hour and fourteen-foot seas forced *Ataboy* to heave to or bring the tug and barge to a complete stop. I held my breath. They waited out the storm just offshore. The delay might have been helpful because we were still experiencing bureaucratic delays: Jaimee Schwartz was still working with the state operative for approval that our insurance was in order, but she was getting little response. "He still needs to speak to some folks in Albany, but he promised to call me this afternoon," she wrote.

On Sunday, October 29, at 4:45 p.m., with winds lowered to twenty miles per hour and waves reduced to six feet, *Ataboy* and the *Floating Pool Lady* were back under way. Their ETA: 9:00 to 10:00 a.m. on October 30, at Sandy Hook, New Jersey. From there, the trip would take two additional hours to reach the Verrazzano Bridge. Another tow company, Miller's Launch, with license to work in New York Harbor, awaited the handoff of the barge from the ocean-going *Ataboy*. Miller's would do their best to get to Pier 2 around 3:30 p.m. to begin docking the *Floating Pool Lady*.

But that was not to be. At 10:48 a.m. Jaimee forwarded a message to me. I sat down and swore in the four languages in which I was conversant while reading: "*Please note that NO WORK MAY BEGIN ON THE SITE OR THE POOL MAY BE BROUGHT TO THE SITE UNTIL THE*

AGREEMENT IS FINALIZED AND CGL INSURANCE FOR THE NEPTUNE FOUNDATION IS SIGNED OFF."

Under clear skies but with an uncertain future, on Halloween Eve 2006, the *Floating Pool Lady* arrived in New York City. She had gone through a hurricane undamaged, and many time-consuming changes, for the better. I had learned what it was like to work through politics and the multiple levels and types of agencies to get the job done. But the *Lady*'s paperwork to allow her to land in Brooklyn, New York, was incomplete.

CHAPTER 7

Kafka on the Pier

IT WAS 3:30 P.M. on Monday, October 30, 2006, Halloween Eve. I hugged the fence at the very edge of an upper terrace under construction at 55 Water Street. On my left was my daughter, Jill, slender with her long dark hair blowing in the breeze. Above us and to our left loomed the Brooklyn Bridge. In front of us, gliding up the East River, was an apparition in blue. Jumping up and down, I screamed: "There it is! There she is! She's here!"

"How do you know that's her?" Jill asked.

"I can't miss her. I know her structures. Look, you can see the pool!"

Unknown to me, two other members of the Neptune architectural team were nearby. When naval architect Kent Merrill, who for ten days had supervised her voyage from Louisiana, got word that the *Floating Pool Lady* was on her way up the East River, he charged out of his office on Vesey Street, camera in hand. He too found an overlook on a third-level balcony at the South Street Seaport's Pier 17. Before long Kent spotted the *Lady* coming around Governors Island and watched as she passed where Jill and I stood, slowly making her way up to his vantage point.

During the last leg of the barge's journey, architect Jonathan Kirschenfeld had been running back and forth along the Brooklyn Promenade, above the East River, trying to alert the media as to the precise time she would arrive. The various media outlets, including the *New York Times*, were getting impatient. When he got word that the *Floating Pool Lady* was in the vicinity, he left the Promenade and ran onto the Brooklyn Bridge. In 2018 Jonathan wrote to me, "Just as I arrived, . . . a white tugboat from Miller's launch, the Staten Island marine transportation company that had taken over from *Ataboy* a few hours earlier, was maneuvering the barge into a U-turn under the Manhattan Bridge." From Jonathan's vantage point, the tug's name was obscured, or not seen by him as his eyes were focused between the posts on the edge of the barge. He saw greenish water from the storm in Cape Hatteras, sloshing in what should have been a dry pool. "It was a completely unexpected and glorious vision," Jonathan wrote, "as though ordained by the Gods as reward for our faith. And standing next to me was the *Times* reporter with his cameraman."

Thus arrived the *Floating Pool Lady* for me, an ugly duckling turned into a swan. Her body was sleek and resplendent in her deep blue paint and her gay pavilion roofs red, yellow, gray, and orange. Blue mooring lines punctuated the four-foot-high white railings required by code to keep children from falling into the river.

The tugboat pulled the *Floating Pool Lady* up the East River as if she were on a leash. Under the Brooklyn Bridge, she made a bow to the press. With the tug nestled adjacent to her gleaming blue port side, she was supposed to dock temporarily between Piers 2 and 3 in Brooklyn, in order for work to be completed for a summer opening elsewhere. But the state had not accepted a letter stating that Neptune had no cars and therefore required no automobile insurance. Until Neptune submitted a hired and non-owned automobile insurance policy, the vessel was prohibited from landing. It was now 5:38 p.m. and the *Lady* was near home but could not berth on the east bank of the river.

After multiple radio transmissions between Kent, the tugboat captain, and the tug's home base, Miller's Launch, it was decided to abort this landing. Slowly the tug pulled the lines attached to the *Lady*'s stern to the right, passed the outer ends of Piers 2 and 3, and proceeded south, not from whence she had come, but to Staten Island, New York, where a tab for renting space to berth would begin to accrue.

At 9:22 p.m. I sent a message to the Neptune board members that expressed anger: "The *Floating Pool Lady* is currently at a rental dock at Miller's Launch as the State continues to create hurdles for us to jump," as well as hope: "Once we receive State approval, we should be good to go." But a new environmental issue intervened. Held up by the stuck-in-the-mud USS *Intrepid* Sea, Air, and Space Museum, a 920-foot, 27,000-ton former aircraft carrier, it would be twenty-eight more days of dealing with public and private bureaucracies, tides, insurance, and additional unforeseen costs before the *Lady* reached home base in Brooklyn.

INITIALLY I EXPERIENCED a few good days. Several months before, at my own expense, but at a reduced price, I had hired a public relations firm, Sharp Communications, Inc., to help generate media attention for the pool's arrival. The firm had contacted reporter James Barron to cover the story of the pool's arrival. When I awoke the morning after, the *New York Times* had a flattering article titled "Two More Ladies in the Harbor, a Floating Pool and the Woman Who Had the Idea for it." The story captured my joy at the pool's arrival but also my pessimism about its future. Barron quoted me saying that my dream was "two-thirds realized." Still, there might be "unforeseen delays."

Then late on Wednesday, November 1, two days after the *Floating Pool Lady*'s unwelcome arrival in New York City, Neptune's attorneys heard from ESDC's nine-to-five insurance managers—still working under the aegis of upper-level officials in Albany—that we were good to go. Neptune's lack of auto insurance was fine. The agreement was "acceptable." The woman who still had her hands full securing permits and completing an environmental impact statement for the pending park, president of the BB Park Corporation Wendy Leventer, had signed the license agreement. We had the approval "to bring the pool to the site and start the work on completing the pool and its accompanying structures." In speaking with Wendy shortly thereafter, her intelligence and humanity were evident. "Sometimes," she said, sympathizing with Neptune's bureaucratic situation, "it feels as if you've woken up in a Kafka novel."

Additionally, I realized that the state bureaucrats whom I had nicknamed "the nine-to-fivers," Nazim Nasroodin and Naresh Kapadia, were human beings with their own concerns, trying their best to do their job. They had not selected me for some especially torturous part of the project. Perhaps it would have been better for me to have gone to their office and express myself face to face, introduce myself so they could see the child in the water, share my dream and passion, and want to be part of the team. This scenario would have required more emotional maturity than I had during the most stressful moments, so instead of reaching out, I got angry and shut up. My experience points out a need for changes in the way the bureaucracy works or fails to work. Change the culture. Give bureaucrats more of a say. Let them own the project and be rewarded for finding solutions instead of putting up obstacles. Give them a process but also the ability to question requirements that are out of line with reality.

Kapadia had posted a tagline: "Good luck with your project." But luck was not with us, and the "otherworldly" tale continued. As in Kafka's parable "An Imperial Message," in which the messenger struggles to leave the palace to deliver the emperor's dying message, various members of the Neptune team and I would continue to push through the sediment to bring the *Floating Pool Lady* to her assigned landing. Also, like Kafka's messenger, we often felt as if we would never wend our way through the muck to complete our mission.

The barge waited in Staten Island for the Miller's boats to tow her back to Brooklyn, and more unbudgeted costs accrued: $1,365 per day for 260 feet of berthing space at their launch plus the $750 rental of two large cylindrical rubberized tubes, known as Yokohama fenders, to protect the barge and the Miller's berthing site from damage. We needed to bring the *Lady* back to Brooklyn ASAP or our marginal budget would balloon. But the Millers did not intend to initiate the tow until eleven days later, at high tide on Friday, November 10. There was a very compelling reason for their refusal. The *Intrepid* needed an overhaul, so all available tugs were at her beck and call to move her from her Hudson River base at Pier 84 in Manhattan across the river to a dry dock in Bayonne, New Jersey.

Nevertheless, Kent Merrill made the rounds of the usual tug suspects, but there were no takers to finish the job Miller's had started. Captain Pat of McAllister, a towing company that operates thirteen tugs of various sizes, all but one of which they named after a member of the McAllister family, was enthusiastic, but he had sixteen other ships to move; he couldn't spare a boat for us. In addition, at 9:20 a.m. on Monday, November 6, a full moon high tide would reach its crest, and the McAllister Towing and Transportation Company would join others in the *Intrepid* move.

Led by the *Christine McAllister*, dozens of tugboats (probably including some from Miller's Launch) were now on alert in the river waiting to assist as needed—and they were needed! The *Intrepid*, docked at Pier 84 for twenty-three years, was stuck in a mass of mud that had collected under her hull. Elected dignitaries at the pier for the occasion watched six large tugs strain at the ropes attached to them and their load for an hour. The ship had moved a mere fifteen feet. The propellers of the *Intrepid* were wedged in mud until the next lunar high tide in early December, so she was for that day unmovable. The *Floating Pool Lady*'s wait to move would continue.

With the *Intrepid* delayed for another lunar month, shouldn't tugs now be available? Kent continued his search. The vessel from Miller's Launch that had picked up the *Floating Pool Lady* in New York Harbor eleven days earlier was missing parts. The timing of her repair was unknown. On Thursday, November 9, Kent found Vinik, a tug company in Keyport, New Jersey. They enthusiastically proposed to use one of their vessels, with the help of eight line handlers from Miller's, to move the *Lady* from Staten Island and tie her up to her mooring in Brooklyn. My new goal was to execute the move of the barge on the following Monday, the 13th, with Vinik in the lead.

But every day that the *Lady* was in her rented hotel cost Neptune serious money. A story floating around the harbor might explain why Glen Miller, president and owner of the eponymous launch, and Sven van Batavia, the vice president, were charging a do-good not-for-profit daily rent. The culprit: a vessel called the *Lila* under the auspices of the Floating Hospital. Begun in 1876, following the tenets of nineteenth-century Progressives, who thought that ill-nesses might spread from the tenements to the elite and that wash-ing cleaned both body and soul, the hospital provided relief to New York City's impoverished sick children. While there were doctors and nurses aboard, at the time there were no medicinal cures, and a day in the harbor with sunshine and fresh air was thought to be therapeutic. Around the time that New York City's floating baths were opened, the Floating Hospital added tubs with salt water from the outer harbor where children could become clean and, because it was a medical facility, get rid of dirt and illness-causing germs.

Jacob Riis's social thought may be found in the Floating Hospi-tal's first trip. A Riis-like managing editor of the *New York Times* had seen policemen ordering newsboys off the grass in City Hall Park onto the hot concrete pavement. He appealed to the newspaper's readers for money and succeeded. Under the auspices of the St. John's Guild, a boat was chartered to take the boys for a day's outing on greener shores. Two years later sick children were added to the outing.

The Floating Hospital in its later years had trouble finding a home. She berthed near Forty-Fourth Street in the Hudson River, then shuffled between South Street Seaport's Pier 17 and Pier 11 at the foot of Wall Street. She was not damaged by the September 11 at-tacks, but as with the floating baths, commerce pushed her out. Having sick children near tourist venues at the Seaport might turn away business. In view of their need after the attacks, the city en-larged Pier 11 to accommodate more ferries. The Floating Hospital arrived at Miller's Launch during her wayward period, never paid a cent, and never left. The rule after that: everyone pays! Neptune was paying the price for the bad behavior of another not-for-profit.

Carter Craft, my insurer finder and my hero of the harbor, came to the rescue. In a letter to Glen and Sven that captured what I was trying to accomplish but also made me blush, he wrote: "It was very NICE of Miller's launch to let her berth there . . . but I don't think she should be put in the same company of the floating hospital. . . . Ann's work and the Floating Pool is really a pioneering effort to help a whole new generation of people connect to the waterfront and experience the Harbor. I hope as you settle up with her you can give her every consideration because she and the project deserve it." That afternoon I wired Miller's a check to cover the initial tow and two days' berthing charges. Then Glen Miller let me know he had stopped the clock on all rental fees billed to the Neptune Foundation until November 15 at sundown. "How felicitous," I thought. "That's my birthday!" The rental problem was solved, but we did not meet either my or Glen's departure deadlines. A meteorological factor once again caused a delay. The tugs were available to bring the barge to the bulkhead between Piers 2 and 3 at high tide, but high tide on November 15 began at 5:00 p.m. Darkness would preclude a landing.

It was a confused and pressure-filled twelve days. Two teams from the state, both new to us—an engineering consultant firm and the property manager—suddenly required a complicated assemblage of heretofore unknown other items that had to be accomplished before the barge's arrival, whenever that would finally be. Kent rushed back and forth from the Cushing office to the state's, preparing and delivering a site plan that showed, for example, the ramp with stairs attached from the upland to the barge. From Miller, Kent submitted the procedures the tug company was going to use to wedge the barge into the narrow space between two piers, without damage. Neptune's construction manager and taskmaster, Steve Sivak, sent out one of his "all-hands-on-deck" alerts that summarized the stressful time. "Team," he wrote, "It's time to pull out the stops. . . . The gangway needs to be bought. The electrical/water lines need to be installed. C. R. Cushing needs to handle all activities that relate to accommodating the barge in NYC . . . AND A WHOLE HOST OF ACTIVITIES NEED TO BE DONE IN TIME AND ON TIME."

Finally, on Wednesday, November 22, just over three weeks since her long-awaited arrival in the East River, I wrote to Neptune's attorney, Steven Crainer, that "barring weather, the floating albatross is due in Brooklyn around 2 p.m. on Monday . . . FINGERS CROSSED!" I was reaching a state of exasperation, and my indefatigable hopefulness seemed, even to me, a mere habit.

ON MONDAY THE 27TH the Neptune contingent descended on Brooklyn. The earliest to arrive, Jonathan set up his camera on the Brooklyn Promenade around noon. By 1:00 p.m. Kent, cell phone in hand, stood waiting on the quay between Piers 2 and 3, close enough to touch the *Lady* (if and) when she arrived. While they were getting set up, I was in transit to a higher perch so as to get good pictures as she came up the East River. I boarded the number 6 train at Eighty-Sixth Street and changed to the number 3 at Fulton Street. I exited at Clark Street in Brooklyn and sought an unimpeded location to see my barge in the distance. With my camera flopping on my chest, I rushed south on Henry Street past low-rise apartment houses and turned west on Love Lane only to reach a viewless dead end. I ran farther south, onto Hicks Street, then west, passing townhouses on Montague. Breathless and scanning the river, north and south, in anticipation, I entered the Brooklyn Heights Promenade. A cool breeze fanned my damp forehead.

Looking up, the sky was clear, and the absence of the Twin Towers of the World Trade Center made me stop for a moment to remember that September day in 2001, when the towers were hit by two hijacked jet planes. In those attacks 2,753 men and women had died, and nearly five hundred thousand dust-covered people had been left stranded south of the towers in Lower Manhattan. Looking down at the East River, I also remembered that on that day the waterways were plied with every type of boat imaginable transporting people off the southern tip of Manhattan to safety or closer to home. The Coast Guard came onto the scene immediately, and over nine hours the flotilla totaled 134 vessels: fifty tugs from Miller's Launch and other companies; thirty-three public and private ferries; seven Circle Line sightseeing vessels; three fireboats and various police boats; and more. Today, in contrast, the river was calm and only the orange blaze of the Staten Island Ferry was in motion far off to the southwest.

Then around 2:00 p.m. a multi-appended vision slowly came into view in the Upper Bay. Two tugs from Miller's Launch (the larger *Susan Miller* and the smaller *Tracy Miller*) and an unnamed launch were towing a large blue rectangle with what appeared to be multi-colored umbrellas arrayed on its top deck. After a month's wait, Miller namesakes were back in business for our quirky one-time job. Now I ran north on the Promenade, not thinking for a moment that I might trip and fall over the railing on my right onto the expressway below. My intention was solely to keep my eyes focused on what had begun as a speck in the distance. I watched it increase in size and its components become more recognizable as it passed Governors Island and entered the East River.

An hour later, the *Floating Pool Lady* and her entourage met at the entrance between Piers 2 and 3. I watched in amazement at the pilots' precision as they guided her into her berth without damage. The barge was 260 feet long, and the distance between the piers only about 275 feet. In just fifteen minutes they brought her stern first, parallel to the piers. Then, when she was about a hundred feet out from the seawall between the piers, they started to pivot her ninety degrees. Next, inching her sideways between the piers, the tugs maneuvered her to within about thirty feet of the quay, with only feet to spare between the ends of the barge and the two piers.

The smaller *Tracy Miller* and the launch then shimmied her sideways to her final destination, parallel and close to the cement bulkhead. Then immediately another cast of characters went into action to make sure that the *Lady* didn't wander. Line handlers on the barge fit the loops, or eye ends, of the blue mooring lines that had been thrown to them from land to the cleats on the barge. Then, leaving the ropes slack enough to accommodate both low and high tides, handlers on the shore pulled the lines and wrapped them around the bollards and cleats on the piers at her bow and stern, and along the recently placed protective fenders at the bulkhead.

The Miller vessels and their handlers departed with a toot. I took my last photos and exited the Promenade running down Old Fulton Street to the river, hoping to at least touch my newly moved prize. But a state security employee had locked a high barbed-wire-topped gate at the northern entrance to all of the piers. My entry to the site was stymied. It was nearly dark. Like Kafka's messenger, I still had not reached my destination, and the obstacles would continue.

The difficulties of arranging the *Lady*'s arrival at her working berth were contemporaneously offset by the ease of hiring a field superintendent to oversee the final phase of the construction. Corey Phelps had had this role at Bollinger. Steve Sivak, who could have worked with Jonathan to oversee the completion of the latter's designs, had decided to resume his architectural practice in Michigan. As associate vice president of the Downtown Alliance in 2002, I had led a task force to develop a concept plan for the Downtown East River Waterfront. Frank Sciame, the founder and CEO of Sciame Construction, whose offices were happily (for me) located downtown near the East River, was a participant in meetings with the community. During a coffee break at one of those sessions in 2002, I told Frank about my floating pool project. His eyes lit up and, in what was doubtless a weak moment, he offered to provide any construction assistance that I might need—for free.

Now, four years later, I had taken Frank up on his generous offer and asked for a small favor. Neptune's license for the *Floating Pool Lady* to land in Brooklyn Bridge Park required the installation of protective fenders alongside the bulkhead between Piers 2 and 3. Could Sciame, with its construction experience along the East Side waterfront, help Kent with the installation of the fenders? But that was not all; my main ask was for a field superintendent. Jonathan Kirschenfeld raised his hand to work on this with Frank and his group. He invited Joseph Mizzi, the company's president, over to his office to show him the half-finished video we had made on the Amelia refitting, hoping he would fall in love with the project and its public aspirations. According to Jonathan, he did.

Joe Mizzi was another gift from the sea gods. Standing in for

Frank Sciame, Joe agreed to help us with the fenders and offered to finish the construction at a highly discounted rate. He would provide us with a full-time field superintendent for five months, beginning in January 2007. The superintendent would have odd jobs that included finding an office trailer and a portable toilet. But most important, he would make sure the site and the workers were safe and secure, and he would oversee and coordinate the work of all of the trade contractors (subs), many of whom our construction manager, Steve Sivak, had hired as early as 2005 but were waiting to begin their jobs. These subs would board the barge to connect the plumbing pipes and electricity wires, add cladding to the pavilions, paint where needed, install hundreds of cement pavers and the pool's scuppers, and, lastly, cart away remaining debris and fill the pool with fresh water.

The cost to Neptune of Sciame's oversight was not to exceed $60,000 (a minimal rate of $75 per hour) plus compensation for the required insurance. And there was a kicker: if Sciame's services cost more than the budgeted amount, they would provide them pro bono. On September 22, 2006, five weeks before the *Lady* would arrive from Louisiana, Steve Crainer began to deal with Mizzi, who requested a contract. A month later the first draft of that agreement was circulated. After so many frustrating and costly surprises we had a deal that assured us that five months would be smooth sailing as far as superintendent and supervising were concerned.

BUT BEFORE THE FIELD supervisor could begin work on readying the barge for a summer opening, the civil servants in the ESDC insurance office had found that now that the barge had arrived, Neptune required a new certificate. The reason was that individuals associated with the *Floating Pool Lady* would be working on or near "navigable waters of the U.S. and engaged in maritime employment such as loading, unloading, repairing . . . certain vessels (USL&H). These ever-observant individuals now required the addition of United States Longshore and Harborworkers' Compensation" to its portfolio.

The minor aggravations that occur in any project continued, and the lines toward solutions were never straight. On December 5 I met "a bump in the night." Apparently, the *Lady* got bumped by a standing object when towed from Amelia en route to the meeting point with *Ataboy*. We had photographs of the damage, but we needed to determine its extent. For that, we needed access to the barge deck, which depended on all hands—the subs, Sciame Construction, and Neptune—having the proper insurance, and, access to the barge.

And then, two days later, the BB Park Corporation's property manager for the piers, John Vigario, suddenly lost the upper hand to the water. When he and the marine surveyor were on board checking out the floating pool, a small wave came. As it approached, the two men dashed down the gangplank to the bulkhead. In seconds the wave knocked the gangplank off the barge and into the water, leaving no way to access the *Lady*. Standing on the bulkhead, Vigario sighed in relief as a second wave approached and pushed the gangway back onto the barge. But it was a no-go. The ramp, now cracked and useless, would have to be replaced.

The list of additional faults in our planning was lengthy. There was a problem with the mooring lines, which we had agreed to inspect daily. They were already abrading from rubbing against the edges of the barge and the quay. Once the lines were eaten away, the barge would be untethered and at sea. The expensive Yokohama fenders protecting the barge from hitting the quay and piers were useless. The lines keeping the barge from bumping against shoreside structures were too loose. Missing were costlier service items: periodic line checks by experienced handlers and a towboat to tighten the lines further, daily if needed, but at minimum before and after "wind or weather events."

Security was also inadequate: the tall chain-link fence at Pier 1 that on the afternoon of the barge's arrival had precluded my entry to see the *Lady* up close was supposed to prohibit entry to all of the piers. But there was no guard for the fence or the barge. And the barge itself was vulnerable. If someone was bold enough to hop the fence or come to the pier in a small craft, the passage to below decks, where the electric lines were attached and the tanks for

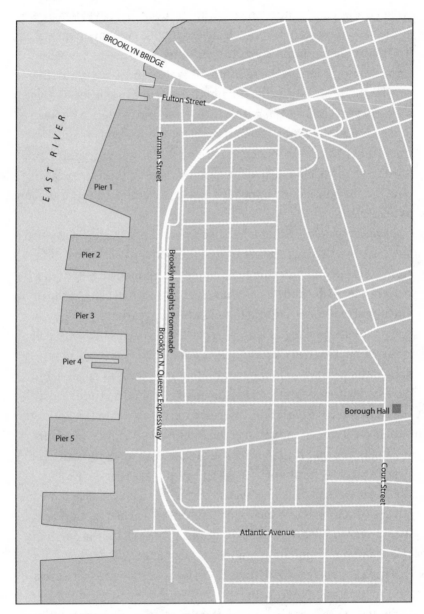

MAP 3. Brooklyn piers, without subway lines

waste and water were stored, was open. The railings, although built to code height, were unsafe because the space was too great between the bottom rung of the rail and the deck. Missing were a gate at the base of the gangway, enclosures for open compartments, a line under the railing—known as a lifeline—to prevent someone from slipping beneath the rail into the water, and more: a life ring similar to the one my father did not throw to me in the South River so many years before, but with a throw line and ladder, to retrieve persons from the water. One last problem was the pool itself. The water that had caught Jonathan's eye on the barge's entry into the harbor was possibly a destructive annoyance. It might freeze and damage the pool sides. We needed a pump to empty the pool as soon as possible.

It was very evident that it had been years since this property had been in use as a maritime venue and the *Floating Pool Lady* was far from fully outfitted for this or any subsequent mooring. Kent Merrill had a lot to do, and we landlubbers had a lot to learn. As the instigator of this mess, I told someone who days earlier had congratulated me on the *Lady*'s arrival "that I had a baby with colic."

As we approached Christmas, the good news was that a new gangway sat attached to the barge, allowing access as needed. But occupied with preparations for the holidays, I had no time to visit the *Lady*. Kent, with a smile, informed me that work in the Bollinger yard had increased the value of the *Floating Pool Lady* nearly fourteenfold, from her initial purchase of $450,000 to $3,400,000. Yet despite the rise in value, there was no guarantee that the post-Bollinger work to finish her would begin in January. The Sciame insurance document was incomplete. Then we learned that a crane would eventually arrive to lift large pieces of steel for the pavilions. Needed was additional insurance: riggers liability!

Three days before Christmas Keith Behnke, Sciame's vice president for operations, wrote me that "we were good to go." On December 29, just three days before the start of what would hopefully be a New Year with calmer waters, I signed the Sciame contract. The next day, in a message with the subject line, "Happy New Year!" I wrote to Steve Crainer and Kent Merrill, "Sciame is starting work on

Tuesday morning. The subs' papers are in order." Exhausted but much relieved, I left the city for Westchester County to spend New Year's Eve with Jill and other members of my family. It had been a very long two months since our Halloween Eve visit to the East River and the *Floating Pool Lady*'s first and abortive attempt to dock between Piers 2 and 3.

CHAPTER 8

Perspective Matters

A PROJECT SUCH AS the *Floating Pool Lady* engenders as many perspectives as there are people involved. When I started the project, I wanted to build a floating pool to be placed in a recreationally underserved community. I'd worked with a team whose members loved the project but each from his own perspective. Jonathan Kirschenfeld saw the opportunity to "make a piece of architecture that floated." Kent Merrill, whose associates in the marine world thought he was crazy when he told them about the project, when faced with the prospect of a cement barge that he would finish, lobbied for a steel barge, which he worked on for three years. Boysie Bollinger, whose yard had built thousands of ships, added to that perspective to take on a barge with a pool, and found it to be "one of the most unique projects he had ever tackled." Commissioner Adrian Benepe, who had spent his career knowing only recreation in land-based, in-ground pools, became an advocate of the *Floating Pool Lady* because it would open up the city's waterfront to recreation. As we worked to find a summer site and finish the pool, new perspectives clouded the *Lady's* future.

On February 1, 2007, the day after my return from a month's

vacation in South America, I finally reached the *Floating Pool Lady*, to touch her railings, to walk on her deck, and to see up close her painted pavilions and her pool. I accompanied a young filmmaker, Doug Cabot, who was producing a video titled *Just Add Water*, to watch and listen to him conduct interviews with our subs, finally at work, and I was greeted with additional perspectives.

We were met on the quay by Chris Sedita, the field superintendent assigned to us by Sciame Construction. Sedita, a man of few words, stood there in his pristine white polo shirt with "Sciame" embossed on its left pocket. His close-buzzed black hair came to a point in the center of his forehead. Black-rimmed wraparound sunglasses gave him the look of a cool dude. We shook hands and he pointed to the bottom of the new access ramp. As I started to climb, I recalled the very tall ladder waiting for me, stationary on the ground, in a Louisiana bayou to meet the *C500*. This time, with the renamed *Floating Pool Lady* in the East River, the climb was rockier than on land, but much shorter. When I stepped onto the pool deck, I was surrounded by yards of electric cables, dozens of brown boxes encasing I did not know what. On my left was a waterless, rectangular pool wearing a dirty, light-green base coat.

On top of the walkway leading from the pool to the upper deck, I found Shawn, Mike, Sheldon, and Courtney, four electricians wearing black T-shirts adorned with the yellow logos of Broadway Electric. They were splicing electric lines and attaching them to metal boxes with electric screwdrivers. On our arrival they immediately silenced their tools and began to chat with us. They explained that they found it strange to be working "on a pool on water," a catchphrase that I committed to memory. I sympathized as the well-built young men commented on the queasy feeling they got in the morning when the East River had traffic and the *Lady* rolled from side to side a bit, in the waves streaming landward from other boats' wakes. They assumed that the pool would be steadied at some point. I was particularly interested in the young men's perception of the purpose of the pool. They knew the facility would be moved around to serve "kids who don't have pools." Sounding like the nineteenth-century Progressives, they seemed to like the concept since it would keep children and teens off the streets and out of trouble.

The pleasure on many of the workers' faces was evident as they put the finishing touches on the *Lady*. Lenny Grand, supervising plumber (L&G Plumbing and Heating, Queens), with his shock of gray hair, plastic-rimmed glasses, and blue polo shirt, smiled while he talked about the job and the artfulness of the pool. For him the floating pool was unique. He had installed pipes in buildings over water, he had even worked underwater, but he had never worked on a ship. Lenny was encountering some problems on this job, yet he was not deterred. For him the aesthetics were important, and he praised the project in words similar to those of the electricians: "An absolutely beautiful swimming pool on the water."

A month later, on March 6, 2007, I was once again in the Parks Department conference room at the Arsenal. Seated there, with sun streaming through the enormous windows, I felt as if the history of the *Floating Pool Lady* was a part of this landmarked building. In 2004 we had sat in the same room to discuss opening the pool on Brooklyn's Greenpoint waterfront. Now talk was again of "the where," a landing in what would become Brooklyn Bridge Park.

IN THE EARLY 1980S, when shipping had moved to large container ports, in addition to its vacant property in Hoboken, New Jersey, the Port Authority of New York and New Jersey owned six unused former break bulk piers in Brooklyn, which with the upland and the land underwater covered forty-eight acres, or one-eighth the size of Brooklyn's Prospect Park. In various widths, the piers jutted out into the East River from Old Fulton Street, just south of the Brooklyn Bridge, to Atlantic Avenue (see map 3).

With redevelopment of urban waterfronts in its portfolio, the Port Authority sought to sell the six piers and the upland to developers for higher and more profitable uses. Here was waterfront property with excellent access via public transportation and with an incredible sweep of views from the Statue of Liberty to the

Brooklyn and Manhattan Bridges, and across to the towers of Lower Manhattan. The benefits of the site's location caused planners to focus on uses similar to Battery Park City.

A look at some of the reactions from public agencies involved with waterfront planning during this period gives a sense of the multiple desires for Piers 1–6 over time. During Mayor Edward Koch's administration, development ruled. In 1985, as the Port Authority struggled to find a new use for its Brooklyn property, the Public Development Corporation (PDC), with the power to recommend development plans, was put in charge of the waterfront. PDC had already been working with the Port Authority and the Department of City Planning in an agreement to study the potential development of the piers. The results were a study released in 1986 that recommended the construction of luxury housing, an international trading center, conference and research facilities, and a world-class yacht and charter marina. A throwaway public access and open space were listed but not a park that would entail capital costs but no income for maintenance. The intent of the Port Authority and PDC was to issue an RFP in a year and construction to begin in 1989.

As soon as the Port Authority's report became public, residents of Brooklyn Heights, who lived above the piers with unobstructed views, and had for decades watched the shipping activities and more recently enjoyed the quiet, rose up in opposition. Along with neighboring communities they formed the Brooklyn Heights Association and latched on to a very different park, one with zero profitability use. The battle that ensued (well documented elsewhere)—involving a public authority with only one interest, to sell the piers at a profit; elected officials, whose interests and support for a park waxed and waned with election cycles; and community activists, whose single-minded advocacy for a park resembled Jane Jacobs's battle to save Washington Square Park in the 1950s—continued for two decades.

New York governor Mario Cuomo brought a state entity into the fracas that was going nowhere in 1991. Cuomo had been on the side of the Brooklyn Heights Association since 1989, when he intervened in the Port Authority's intended sale of the piers to developers. Having favored the community, which was now a coalition of multiple groups, and taken away a Port Authority opportunity, Cuomo charged the Port Authority, the New York State Urban Development Corporation (UDC), and the PDC to prepare a plan for the disposition of the Port Authority property. Although development with financial return was the role of the agencies involved, this would be the beginning of joint planning for a park. The group hired the Boston-based firm of Carr, Lynch, Hack and Sandell to work with the agencies as well as the coalition. Alternative 1 was a modification of an all-park venture that the coalition had put forth three years before. Here on forty-five acres were to be thirty-five acres of open space and some commercial, income-producing uses, but no housing, the highest-valued use.

In the early 1990s, with Mayor Dinkins in office, I was in charge of a waterfront planning office at PDC's replacement, the EDC, and the city's sentiment regarding development in the waterfront softened somewhat. The DCP's 1992 *Comprehensive Waterfront Plan* contained a section titled "The Public Waterfront." The upfront goal of this chapter was to reconnect the public to the waterfront via a variety of methods, including parks. Nonetheless, perhaps because the economy was slowing, "substantial open space" but not specifically a park was in the plan for Piers 1–5. (Pier 6 was rented out for coffee bean storage.) Without mentioning acreage, recreation, open space, and a marina were listed along with the usual income-producing elements, and housing was back on the list.

While the UDC awaited consensus on a plan, the Port Authority was once again on its way to put the piers up for sale, because the piers were in need of repair, one of them was about to collapse on a subway tunnel, and soon the property would have no value. More coalition and wider community outrage, along with help from the governor's office, stopped the Port Authority once again. Then the coalition and borough president Howard Golden, with broad community participation, composed a document known as *The 13 Guiding Principles to Govern the Redevelopment of the Downtown Brooklyn Waterfront*, and in July 1992 the coalition, Golden, and local elected officials sent it to the UDC. Five years later the state had done nothing to advance the *Principles*. Frustrated by the inaction, in December 1997 local elected officials, including borough president Golden, stepped in and created the Brooklyn Waterfront Local Development Corporation (LDC) to take charge of the design and development of Piers 1–5. The order given to its president, attorney Joanne Witty, was twofold: convince the Port Authority that its development plans should be a public park and create a plan for that park based on the *Principles*. Two years later the Port Authority turned the pier property over to the LDC for use as Brooklyn Bridge Park, and in 2000 the LDC published a plan for the park. Seven years later I was at the Parks Department discussing a summer home in the park for the *Floating Pool Lady*.

THE VIBE IN THE room was good. Together, we were in the who-will-pay-for-what and the how-to-secure-a-permit stage of the sausage-making process that I hoped would result in the opening of the *Floating Pool Lady* in July. Many of the attendees were familiar to me. Commissioner Benepe sat at the head of the conference table. I was to his right with architect Jonathan Kirschenfeld. To Adrian's left sat my friend Joshua Laird—now elevated to assistant commissioner for planning and parklands—and his sidekick from DCP, Jennifer Kao. There were also newcomers at the table, but having worked in the department, I needed no introduction. Steve Des-Noyer, from the Capital office, was the point person for reallocating capital funds if the agency opted to have a financial role in setting up the floating pool. As Adrian had written to me the previous September, the department had no money in its budget to run the pool, but it might pay for hooking up the barge to the land-based connections such as electrical, water, and sewage services. Neptune's maritime engineer, Malcolm McLaren, sat next to Jonathan. As it had been when Transmitter Park was to be the site, Malcolm's job was to design the anchorage for the barge. But first he needed to know who had the essential information: What type of soil will surround the pool? Will it be sandy or muddy? How deep is the water?

Councilman David Yassky, who had secured city council discretionary funds for Greenpoint's Transmitter Park in 2004 and had been following the floating pool ever since, was at the meeting because these monies were as yet unspent. Yassky had intended for the funds to be used to repair the sinkholes that made parts of the Transmitter site unsafe. A year later, the city allocated new funds for open-space repairs in the Bushwick/Greenpoint community. By 2007 Yassky's donation was no longer needed for its original purpose and was therefore easier to move elsewhere within his district. His choice: Brooklyn Bridge Park.

I hugged Marianna Koval, the executive director of the BB Park Conservancy (formerly Coalition). We whispered to each other, "Let's do it!" as she positioned herself next to several conservancy board members, who were there because the floating pool fit perfectly into the not-for-profit's perspective for funding and constructing Brooklyn Bridge Park. They needed interim uses to build a broad-based constituency in favor of the park. Three years earlier, "The Brooklyn Bridge Park Interim Use and Programming Survey" had listed a floating pool.

The pro bono attorney from Cleary Gottlieb, Penelope Christophorou, had come to the meeting to find out more about a crucial issue: the DEC permit. Was it a possible deal breaker that could prohibit the pool from being opened? The two women were ready to go to work on the politics, the permits, the fundraising, and the agreements, and with boots on the ground, to assure the opening of the pool in Brooklyn Bridge Park in the summer of 2007.

In my glass-half-empty mood, I silently considered another deal breaker. As willing as Adrian and Parks Department staff were to take on some of the costs of the floating pool's installation for the coming summer, I knew, from my tenure as director of the agency's Waterfront Planning office, that it would be impossible for the pool to open in summer 2007. For that to happen, Steve DesNoyer's Capital office would have to send out notices describing the setup work for the pool to several contractors on a prequalified list; receive their descriptive and financial bids for the job; negotiate the contract; and finally hire the team (probably the least expensive one) to do the work. Even if begun immediately, the procurement process would take several months, and we were already in March. Letting out a deep sigh, I turned to the half-full glass to consider alternative solutions to getting the work done. Perhaps Neptune could hire the contractor and get reimbursed? Maybe money allocated to the conservancy by the state could be used? Or perhaps I could donate the floating pool to the Parks Department now, with the intention that it would be on their watch to get the facility open on time.

Ostensibly, we were all around the table at this meeting on March 6 to help Parks Department administrators and staff complete the task that Adrian had accepted three years ago: to take on, and run, the *Floating Pool Lady*. But it was Penelope's concern that had to be placed at the top of the list of things we needed to address. Unstated, but known by some in the room, were the words "The DEC prohibitors hated the pool categorically."

Joshua Laird provided background. A few weeks before the Arsenal roundup, he and others from the Parks Department had met with Steve Zahn, John Cryan, and other staff members of DEC's regional office. The question was a familiar one: What needed to be done to gain approval for a floating pool in New York waterways? For me, the meeting was as Yogi Berra once quipped: "like déjà vu all over again." Keeping to the bureaucratic stance the staffers had taken at my first visit with Joshua in 1999, as well as in a subsequent visit in January 2005, they stated once again, unequivocally and unalterably, that the pool barge was *not* a water-dependent use, and that the vessel, if it sat in one place in New York waters for a prolonged period of time, would cast shadows that kill aquatic life and thereby violate the Clean Water Act. Then came the positive-negative throwaway. Even if it ultimately received approval, the pool would have to be temporary and move to different sites for short stays. But they hoped that it would be gone from the harbor in five years. We knew that as in the past, John Cryan was the least hostile member of the DEC team.

My initial meeting at the DEC Region 2 office in 1997 had been to test the waters about bringing a floating pool to New York. Indeed, that day I had listened to many environmental concerns. I had exited the meeting feeling that the door to securing the agency's water quality permit had been left open. Now, ten years later, I had purchased a barge, converted it into a floating swimming pool, and brought it to a former Port Authority pier in Brooklyn to ready it for a summer 2007 opening. Before the first adult or child could enter the barge to swim, however, Neptune would have to secure that permit. But there was more, my worst nightmare. At least one member of the DEC regional office, who was not at the meeting that Joshua attended, was angry that I had brought the *Floating Pool Lady* to New York, period!

Since the go-no-go deadline for opening the pool for the summer of 2007 was fast approaching, it was essential that we take time at this meeting at the Arsenal to figure out how to lessen DEC's enmity toward our project. We discussed mitigation. Perhaps we could minimize the effects of the shadow cast by the pool by showing DEC that the Parks Department had recently eliminated shade elsewhere and would keep that area shadeless in perpetuity. This mitigation was at work in Riverside Park. Commissioner Benepe and Mayor Bloomberg would soon put a shovel in the ground to begin the construction of an overwater path in Riverside Park between West Eighty-Third and West Ninety-First Streets. The objective was to repair the erosion that had caused the roadway to collapse into the Hudson and force bikers, joggers, and others seeking recreation to detour, effectively closing off the waterfront. In negotiations with DEC to offset the environmental harm caused by covering the Hudson (which the road collapse had left open), the department might be allowed to compensate with an offsite project, where the river had been opened when making improvements.

To make up for the shade that the pool caused, the agency might remove disused piers or pull back the land. If we spread the mitigations to various locations, it might even give the perception that the floating pool was a temporary facility and would be moving around from place to place. I thought this was a bit of a stretch. After all, the regulators were intelligent; they might not have vision, but they had sight. Nonetheless, Joshua started a bank of environmental offsets.

On the list was Brooklyn Bridge Park, which at the time had a net loss of land due to erosion. Ironically, some of the river's edge to be removed in constructing Transmitter Park might also be applicable.

Then we came to the idea I liked best. Perhaps we didn't even need a DEC permit. If the barge stayed only eight to ten weeks, was anchored by temporary spuds (removable pilings anchored deep in the mud alongside the barge to hold it in place), and nothing was left behind when she was towed to her postseason storage facility, perhaps the floating pool could be classified as a vessel and therefore exempt from DEC's major concerns. Initially I thought this was a clever way to get out of the whale's belly. Then I remembered that such a move would lead us into additional expenses and the jaws of a different, potentially problematic agency: the US Coast Guard. Their regulations required the barge to be crewed, twenty-four seven.

Finally, we discussed politics. The Brooklyn piers had lost one of their advocates, Governor Pataki, who had declined to run for a fourth term. While in office, Pataki had been a strong proponent for building a park on the piers. In 2002 he had joined Mayor Michael Bloomberg in a memorandum of understanding wherein a newly created state entity, the Brooklyn Bridge Park Development Corporation, would build the park, and the city and state would jointly dedicate funds to its construction.

Eliot Spitzer, New York State attorney general for seven years, was now in the governor's office in Albany. As attorney general, understanding the reality of climate change, he had litigated against President George W. Bush on loosening the federal government's air pollution regulations. In 2002 Spitzer, along with Mayor Bloomberg, was involved in saving 198 community gardens that (much like the Port Authority on Piers 1–5 in the 1990s) the city planned to eliminate in favor of development.

All of Spitzer's environmental lawsuits had been backed by active coalitions, but until the floating pool had been open for a season, such groups would not exist for us. Since he had not yet appointed his environmental staff, we could only hope that Spitzer's Department of Environmental Protection (DEP) commissioner would be friendly to the pool. In the interim, Joshua suggested we request a one-year reprieve from the governor while the Parks Department applied to new officials at DEC for a permit. With this delay, the pool could achieve two goals. It would be open this summer, and it would provide the interim activity needed to raise a constituency for Brooklyn Bridge Park, which had a fabulous design but not one inch of it built. Marianna, who had attended Princeton with the new governor, might be the go-between who could make this happen. The meeting at the Arsenal ended with not her okay but total frustration. She had hoped to get Parks Department confirmation that Brooklyn Bridge Park was a go. "I can't believe you guys are not going to get it together to open this," she said. *"We have the place."*

It was now time for me to lobby, something that for years I had carefully avoided because of my lifelong timidity. When I was a child and my father was an economic adviser to Franklin Roosevelt, members of the administration were invited to our apartment for working dinners. They included figures such as Secretary of Labor Francis Perkins, my father's prior boss; Roosevelt's closest adviser, Harry Hopkins; and Benjamin V. Cohen, a member of Roosevelt's brain trust and drafter of significant New Deal legislation. Shy and fearful of having to speak, I would hide alone behind the bookcase in the front hall until my father pulled me out to say hello to his guests.

As a married adult I was still shy, especially to ask for favors. Yet my husband's civic consciousness was certainly an advantage. Larry was finance chair for Robert Abrams's successful run for the office of New York State attorney general, and for several unsuccessful attempts at the mayoralty by such candidates as Richard Ravitch, Orin Lehman, and Mark Green.

Many of the relationships that made the *Floating Pool Lady* a reality were unique to me because they stemmed from my career working in city agencies. I knew people in government who would answer my call or letter, and most surprising to me was that their assistants recognized my name. Henry Stern was a friend from the time when we were young parkies inventing the Council for Parks and Playgrounds. When he became parks commissioner, and

Adrian Benepe and I were both working for the department, Henry was our boss. He was the first agency head to say a conditional "yes" to my offer to donate a floating pool to the city, and Adrian was the commissioner who accepted the *Lady* without constraints.

My lobbying followed two paths, the state and the city. The 2007 honoree of the annual awards dinner of the Citizens Budget Commission (on whose board my husband Larry sat) was the (for me) long-awaited governor Eliot Spitzer. Here, I thought, was the opportunity to put the floating pool on the governor's agenda. Instead, it was the perfect example of a governmental runaround. When Spitzer finished speaking, I took a deep breath and, knees shaking, stood in line with others wanting a word with him. Finally reaching him, I introduced myself (the name Buttenwieser rang a bell), complimented him on his speech and his award, and said: "Floating Pool Lady." The governor replied that yes, he had heard of it, and then he introduced me to an associate, saying: "Tell him what needs to be done." The young man gave me his card and told me to send him the details. I responded with a fact sheet about the *Floating Pool Lady* with a photograph, and a note saying that opening the pool in Brooklyn Bridge Park should be top on the ESDC agenda and that we needed help with DEC. I knew the matter was now in the hands of the highest level of New York State government. A loud silence rang from Albany. I believed that Spitzer had dropped the matter.

Undeterred, in mid-March I tried the city route. I avoided calling on the phone, which made me nervous (what if the answer was "no"?), and instead I drafted a letter to Dan Doctoroff, deputy mayor for economic development and rebuilding. I had known Dan for several years. He was familiar with my pool idea and had thought it could be a practice venue on the Queens waterfront if New York City were chosen for the 2012 Olympics. As a member of Mayor Bloomberg's cabinet, Dan had served on the initial board of directors of the BB Park Corporation. My letter asked the deputy mayor for two assists with getting the *Floating Pool Lady* to Brooklyn Bridge Park for the summer. Would he give the project a push by expressing his approval of the pool to the appropriate person at ESDC? Would he also speak to the now soon-to-be-appointed DEC commissioner, Pete Grannis, to communicate his excitement about and support of the pool, which would soon be coming before a very recalcitrant DEC? Again there was silence. Not until midsummer, when Dan visited the pool in operation, and when Larry and I bumped into Mayor Bloomberg in a restaurant, did I find out that he, Dan, and others in the mayor's office were working on it. But they too were meeting resistance from DEC on other environmental matters.

Also in mid-March, Marianna let me know that there was new leadership at the ESDC. Governor Spitzer had appointed a former law associate, Patrick Foye, to be the downstate chairman. To my surprise and pleasure, Spitzer had actually listened and had charged Foye with getting the pool open in Brooklyn Bridge Park. Foye passed the task on to Jennifer Rimmer, for whom the semidysfunctional state bureaucracy was a far cry from her former work running a Long Island environmental/smart growth nonprofit, Residents for a More Beautiful Port Washington. Intelligent, exceptionally well organized, and with an impressive take-charge presence and attitude, from her office on Third Avenue in midtown Manhattan, she oversaw the work of several ESDC subsidiaries. Two of these entities were going to build twenty-first-century parks. The BB Park Corporation was Rimmer's favorite.

The leadership changes at ESDC were the perfect opportunity for Marianna to introduce interim uses such as movies, games, and educational programs to Brooklyn Bridge Park and thus open the way to the larger task: getting the community involved and pushing for the park to be built. On March 16, at a meeting with ESDC's Rimmer and state intergovernmental relations representative Darren Bloch, Marianna brought up the floating pool. Apparently, the group, which included the LDC's board members, never stopped talking about a range of ideas. "Your floating pool," she told me, "was just the most exciting and captured people's attention." Always thinking ahead, she reasoned, "Now we should bring ESDC into the steps needed to open the pool."

Although Rimmer took the lead, the project still had to be approved by the LDC board, and knowing how many years they had been at work, one could not blame certain members who felt that the pool was a distraction and the state should concentrate on getting a shovel in the ground for the park. But park construction still awaited DEC approval, timetable unknown. This left an opening for an interim use that was ready to go in three months. A few days later I received a call from Jennifer Klein, project manager for the park. This was good news. She asked for the same utility hookup information and measurements that Jamie Springer had requested in October 2005. I took the opportunity to ask for the missing soundings and subsurface information that Mal McLaren needed for designing the pool's anchorage.

On March 23, two and a half short but seemingly endless weeks after the Arsenal meeting, the BB Park Corporation board approved locating and opening the floating pool in an area between piers with a safe entry area and no immediate plans for construction. The exact site remained undetermined for a few more weeks as the two southernmost piers with the best pedestrian entryways were still in use. On Pier 5 a developer was storing construction materials for the conversion of a former manufacturing building into a residential development called One Brooklyn Bridge Park. Pier 6, with access to Atlantic Avenue, was still under lease for coffee bean storage. Then things began to move even more rapidly. On March 28 we received the subsurface information that allowed Mal McLaren to start work on the spuds that would be driven into the ground to hold the *Lady* in place. Five days later Marianna gave a tour of the park-to-be to key people from ESDC. They boarded the barge and came away convinced that this indeed was the interim use needed to energize Brooklyn Bridge Park and spur its development.

AS ACCEPTANCE OF THE pool by the BB Park Corporation approached reality, on-time completion of the pool became essential, but it was days of hurry up and wait. All of the Neptune worker bees were diligently employed. Jonathan Kirschenfeld climbed aboard the barge to check on the canopy over the pavilions. Weeks before, when workers started outfitting the *Lady*, he had found major problems with dimensional accuracy. In some cases, the hired structural steel fabricators had to reposition and reweld steel elements. Jonathan was very satisfied with this visit. The scale of the canopy hovering over the collection of cabanas was just what he had hoped for. The area was becoming a communal space. Besides enjoying his canopies, Jonathan walked through the project with the paver and Kalwall (wall enclosures for the pavilions) installers who, according to Jonathan, were "exceedingly competent professionals, very excited about working on the *Floating Pool Lady*."

On the other hand, Chris Sedita, whom Sciame Construction had hired as field superintendent to finish the pool's structures, had a big problem: garbage. Although the subs' contracts required them to clean up their own mess and deposit it in Neptune-supplied dumpsters, the deck was cluttered with papers, wood shavings, and empty wooden pallets. Unusable bags of wet sand that had arrived in the pool from Louisiana were still there, making the pool an attractive nuisance. Electrical wires, ropes, plastic strips, and corrugated boxes—some whole, some flattened—lay here and there on the pool's bottom. In one corner on the pool were more pallets. Some held pool gutter parts and circular tubing, while others, piled higher than the four-foot depth of the pool, held unopened packs of concrete pavers. The scene was both an aesthetic headache—what if I brought donors to see the project now that the weather was improving?—and, as construction manager Steve Sivak wrote, "on the verge of being dangerous" were someone to trip. I sent Eagle Rubbish Removal a check for $1,500 for a day's work. Another unforeseen cost!

The two Steves, Sivak and Crainer, had contracts on their desks. From his office in Ann Arbor, Michigan, Sivak sent me the signature page that confirmed Neptune's agreement to pay the tile setters. These men started the installation of flooring in bathrooms, showers, changing rooms, and other parts of the pavilions now sheltered by Jonathan Kirschenfeld's canopies. During this catch-up time, Steve Crainer and I corresponded back and forth with Naresh Kapadia in the ESDC permits office about lengthening our stay between Piers 2 and 3 from the original contractual end date of April 30 to June 30. By then, although it was not for sure, we hoped to be at another pier for the summer. To keep the tenor mild, nonconfrontational, and nonbureaucratic, I originally suggested putting this request to Kapadia in a letter. The process, however, stayed on the usual bureaucratic path. But unlike the previous months of hassle over insurance, it took less than three weeks for agreement and to have a contractual amendment to Neptune's license agreement with the state ready to be signed.

On April 15 a nor'easter was about to pound the region. Marianna Koval wrote me, "Can I go lash myself to the deck?" (to protect the ship). Beginning in the Carolinas, the storm reached New York at dawn. Winds with 48 mph gusts hit Kennedy Airport. Tides swamped local beaches, rain flooded roads and subways, and over seven inches of water fell in Central Park—an amount second only to (by then) the wettest day ever, in 1882. The *Floating Pool Lady*, without Marianna's help, rode out her third major storm with grace between Brooklyn Piers 2 and 3 and was unharmed.

It was time for everyone on the expanded team to act. A month earlier, in mid-March after her visit to the pool, my other me, Marianna as a one-person band, began to lead. Dedicated, driven, vibrant, bubbly, and upbeat, this nonstop, high-energy-force woman, prone to using earthy language and who refused to take "no" for an answer, was the perfect complement to my quiet, reserved demeanor. We also had several commonalities: we were two stubborn personalities with big dreams. We were both good at raising money, and both willing to pursue our dream, no matter how many noes we encountered, and regardless of how long it took.

Marianna's was a very complicated program. She began by examining maps to choose the interpier site that had the best public access, had room for a beach on land alongside the pool, and would not be required in case—in the best of all possible worlds—work on the park began while the pool was still there. A beach? Patricia O'Brien, Marianna's mother, describes her daughter's motivation: "We had to have a beach, otherwise the experience was incomplete."

Her first choice for pool and beach were the water and land that occupied the area between Piers 4 and 5. That effort was immediately frustrated. Paul Seck, the landscape architect for Michael Van Valkenburgh Associates, the firm that in 2003 had been hired by the BB Park Corporation to design the park, would only consider a location that would not interfere with putting a shovel in the ground. That location was Pier 6. In mid-April the firm arranged for Marianna and the state agency's staff to visit that site.

This time the Port Authority—not the water gods—came to the rescue. The Authority, still in ownership of that coffee bean storage pier, refused to provide access. Grudgingly, according to Marianna, Seck and company acknowledged that Pier 6 would not work. She jumped into the opening and begged the landscape architects to design a plan for the pool and beach that worked with their construction needs at Piers 4–5, Seck's second-choice location. According to Marianna, that group had "seemed to relent," but final word had to come from Rimmer. And I, in an aside, reacted joyously that others were getting bogged down in bureaucracy, writing to her: "I LOVE IT! The powers that be who want Pier 6 can't even gain access!"

An attorney by profession, Marianna Koval began discussions with the conservancy, ESDC, and Neptune lawyers regarding licensing agreements, of which there would be four. She even contacted the Department of State's Coastal Zone Management office, where she asked for help in dealing with the environmental restrictions. Their answer indicated that even other state agencies lacked the power to intervene: "Prior history suggests we won't be able to smooth this with DEC—best to make nice and proceed." Would ESDC also be powerless?

Next, Marianna prepared a preliminary budget for the conservancy's side of the deal. She needed money to cart 3,200 tons of sand dredged from Jones Beach to turn a former Port Authority parking lot into a beach and to purchase brightly colored umbrellas and lounge chairs. Because the funds for civic projects coming to the park from state legislators' member items were finite, Marianna also checked out the income she might derive from renting the pool out for special events like corporate parties or photo shoots.

To assure that the pool would be ready for the beach, watchdog Marianna checked in with Jonathan Kirschenfeld almost daily for updates on the schedule, prodding him to finish the pool. While Jonathan respected Marianna's sense of responsibility, her apparent lack of trust in the team's collective ability to deliver on time was a constant strain on him and Neptune's construction manager, Steve Sivak.

WHEN JENNIFER RIMMER, president of the BB Park Corporation, arrived at the ESDC office at 633 Third Avenue in mid-March, she was greeted by her boss, Pat Foye, a man with a serious white mustache and beard speckled with gray, with the following charge: "Get this done. I want this to happen." This young woman looked up with her amazing deep-set blue-gray eyes and realized that she had only ten weeks until opening day. As Rimmer described it, to accomplish Foye's command was "not a small feat." Opening the pool required constant watch over Neptune, the conservancy, and the not-yet-hired pool operators to ensure that the all-too-familiar state and local permits, insurance, and legal contracts were moving forward. She had to secure the cooperation of elected officials, some of whom had funds to contribute, and residents who feared noisy outsiders who might leave garbage on their streets and disrupt their neighborhood. There were also other sensibilities to consider. Observant Jewish, Mormon, or Muslim men walking on the Brooklyn Heights promenade "might find the view of the pool sinful." A problem with any one of these elements could prevent the opening.

On April 5 Rimmer put the pool project on a fast track by instituting weekly meetings in the ESDC thirty-sixth-floor conference room. These meetings were held weekly (eight in all) through May 22. Jonathan described the scene:

> It was the first time in the years-long history of the pool that we had powerful people gathered around a table all focused on getting the project to the finish line. Finally, there were heads of agencies (ESDC, the Park Corporation, the Conservancy, the Parks Department, DEP, and construction managers, architects, engineers, and more) coordinating their roles and time-frames for the July 4 opening. I was finally

convinced that with so much expertise and good will in the room that we were over the big hump of disbelief. The weekly gatherings kept me going full throttle and I was completely energized after having struggled for so long to push the project forward by Neptune's team alone.

Although his reaction to the meetings was positive, Jonathan took a large risk when he assured the group (as he had assured me when we first met) "that construction would be complete and all permits signed off by Independence Day."

Pressing all of us for updates was only a small part of Rimmer's task. Neptune and the conservancy had emotional skin in the game. The pool and the park were our passion. Less committed were the internal bureaucrats: lifelong ESDC employees, outside insurance agents, internal and external attorneys, and staff who pushed the permitting papers, all of whom stated categorically that there was no way to open the pool in the time allotted. Rimmer needed to convince them that it could be done, and that instead of losing the project in a morass of slow-moving, bureaucratic details, they could rush to the finish line and be winners.

Like me, Rimmer had a degree in urban planning, and like Marianna Koval and me, she refused to take no for an answer. Unlike my timid persona, Rimmer's was bold and she seemed able to take on all comers. During our time together, she had my total respect. But at one of the early meetings, she informed me: "You know, Ann, there is the elephant in the room . . . DEC might prohibit you from opening." Was it water quality and dead fish, or had DEC changed its perspective and was now questioning the validity of our current working stay at Pier 2? With my having full knowledge of the obstacles, Rimmer added something along the lines of, "Leave it to us, we are handling it." Despite the fact that at the time I was wearing a bright red dress to give me courage, I felt pushed aside by Rimmer and Richard Dorado, the ESDC attorney handling negotiations with DEC. Too shy to persist, I backed off and, in doing so, miscalculated that others were working as much in my interest as I would. It had never occurred to me to bring the Neptune lawyer to the table to ask questions.

Up to now Marianna and I had been focused on the physical elements of our project: finishing the beach and the pool. It was not until Asphalt Green appeared on the radar that we turned to maintenance. In March, even before ESDC and the BB Park Corporation were fully on board, Marianna, with eyes always out for improving the park experience, had learned that Asphalt Green located in Manhattan needed to close their indoor Olympic pool on June 24 for repairs. They were looking for practice space for their swim team. As my commitment to the project was to finance the floating pool and give it over to others to run, Marianna and I together took on the task of enticing Asphalt Green, the prime competitive and community swim facility in the city, to manage and operate the floating pool.

On March 5 we met with Asphalt Green senior program director Paul Weiss. Ten days later I was asked to lunch with executive director Carol Tweedy, perhaps to ascertain whether my commitment to them was real and (as usual) what powers I had to get state approvals and permits in time to open. In a week Asphalt Green submitted their business plan. In mid-April Steve Kass, founder and president of the American Leisure Corporation, put in a bid. Twenty years earlier Kass had been coauthor of the Parks Council's feasibility study for a floating recreation center. According to the study, the pool would be operated by an independent management company, similar to Kass's business. Hearing that a floating pool venture was under way, Kass called me to offer his services to run the pool. We had a brief conversation. I told him that Asphalt Green was on the case and pushed "save" on my computer. But somehow I felt that our ducks were not in a row.

With discussions ongoing about entry fee, practice schedules for the team learn-to-swim programs for neighborhood kids, and lap swims for the general public, on an impulse, and to cover all bases in case a deal with Asphalt Green fell apart, I tried another approach: donate the *Floating Pool Lady* to the Parks Department *now*. If Parks owned the facility, they could operate it, and as a city pool it would be self-insured. Neptune would be out and Asphalt Green would have to find another location. In April I called Commissioner Benepe and asked if I could donate the pool to the Parks Department immediately. He liked the idea and thought the paperwork and approvals for the donation could be accomplished in time for the summer opening. Pleased with Adrian's response, I wrote to Neptune's attorney, Steven Crainer, with a subject line that indicated my feelings about the prospects: "I'll believe it when I see it."

I was right to be concerned. Two weeks later an attorney for the Parks Department let me know that they would not be able to have an agreement ready in time for a summer opening. Why, I asked myself, was it so difficult to give something to the City of New York for free? I would find out later, when the *Floating Pool Lady* was finally gifted to the city, that even with Adrian on my side, it would actually take eight months, innumerable meetings on the DEC permit application, changes to the wording on the transfer document, trips to Bayonne, New Jersey, to examine the gift, and more for a donation agreement to be fashioned and signed.

In mid-May staff from Asphalt Green, including swim coaches, instructors, and lifeguards, climbed up onto the barge to assess the situation. Jonathan Kirschenfeld, who accompanied the group, was excited. Being on the *Lady* with other people gave him a sense of the dimensions. He was already planning a party with a band playing. However, the visitors from Asphalt Green were less enthusiastic. What they saw was a general state of disarray with an empty pool, unfinished pavers, missing "Do Not Dive" markers, and workers scurrying around upstairs and down. To serve their competitive swimmers without interruption in their practice schedule, Asphalt Green needed a pool that would be open by July 4. Their assessment was that we (Neptune and the conservancy) just couldn't do it. Could we?

With less than seven weeks until opening, the pressures on me were no longer to buy a barge, to fundraise to pay for its retrofit, or to lobby for its home; it was to find an operator for it, immediately. At the end of May I picked up my rotary phone and called Steve

Kass. Two weeks later the conservancy's pro bono attorneys began work on American Leisure's contract.

THE SESSIONS IN THE ESDC meeting room concerning getting the floating pool up and running had been moving along smoothly, now on a weekly basis, until finally the long-feared elephant lumbered into the room. On May 21, six weeks before the pool was scheduled to open, Richard Dorado, the ESDC attorney, gave me a draft copy of an order of consent from the DEC. Contained within it was, in writing, my worst nightmare. The order charged the BB Park Corporation, the BB Park Conservancy, and the Neptune Foundation with violating article 15 of the State Environmental Conservation Law. Referring to our rent-free stay at Pier 2, we had placed and had been allowed to place "a wharf, platform, or other structure in and on or above waters without prior approval." (Really? a DEC permit?) The order imposed on all of us "jointly and severally" a whopping financial penalty: $61,000! If we paid up immediately, the fine would be reduced by $11,000 to $50,000. But that was not all. Once the fine was paid, the structure and all of its ancillary equipment would have to be removed from the site by September 15, 2007.

Mouth agape, face red, heart palpitating, I, like Alice in *Through the Looking Glass*, had entered a world that I did not understand. Like the Bandersnatch in "Jabberwocky," the poem Alice encounters in a mirror-written book, I was the frumious Ann. I wanted to shout out, "But it's not a structure." I had to get myself together and regroup.

It was time for me to drop all outward signs of timidity and start a countercharge. And I did. The *Lady* was in trouble. I put Steve Crainer in touch with Dorado. After all, this was only a draft; there must be room for compromise. First on the agenda: remove the word "structure." We are a "vessel" and under that description did not need a permit to work at Pier 2. I asked Mal McLaren to confirm that in his experience as a waterfront engineer, we did not need a permit to work on a barge at former working piers.

It had been a busy four months. Perspectives such as Adrian's, who still advocated for the pool but was unaware of the length of time it would take to secure it, had stayed the same. The DEC had changed its perspective from the need to follow certain environmental rules to punishing Neptune for bringing the barge to New York and coming to work at the Brooklyn piers. Asphalt Green saw a pool unable to meet the timetable for its pre-Olympic swimmers; Steve Kass saw an opportunity to help those less fortunate. The stress and anxiety took its toll. Privately, I lost sleep and ten pounds of my 105-pound body. I cried a lot. But publicly, my perspective was to go full steam ahead and damn the torpedoes.

CHAPTER 9

The Orwellian Bureaucracy

THE MONTH OF JUNE was to be devoted to completing the barge's construction. Outside, pavers needed to be laid, and inside, tiles needed to be attached to the bathroom walls. Finishing touches (including painting the pavilions' exteriors and the pool's interiors) had to be applied. When I arrived at the Brooklyn piers on June 1, I expected to see a commotion surrounding the pool. What I did not expect was a site minus its workers and, by mid-month, more bureaucratic problems that to the eleventh hour would imperil the pool's opening.

It was 6:16 p.m. on a Friday, and no one had notified the BB Park Corporation that we needed to work overtime, and on the weekend, if we were to have a shot at starting on schedule. The work site between Piers 2 and 3 was in stasis. The river was still too, except for a white wake trailing a ferry in the distance. Two empty trucks that appeared whiter than the wake being kicked up by the ferry sat on either side of the gangway to the barge.

On board the pool was dry, and neither workers nor supervisors were on deck. I was pleased to see that the pavilions' roofs were in place. They were wearing white protective coverings that matched the off-white concrete pavers that workers had laid at both ends of the pool. Simple, modern, white steel railings framed the outside of the barge. Only two colors, both reminiscent of a maritime past, punctuated the scene. A marine blue, matching the doors on the adjacent former Port Authority sheds, reflected on the unpainted Kalwall pavilion enclosures, as well as shone in the shadows cast by sunroofs at the bow of the vessel and on the ropes attached from the barge to Pier 3. Orange netting, the color of the pool's life rings, covered the white railings' bottom rungs.

All of this was lovely until I stopped to do the math. At our first group meeting in April, Jennifer Rimmer had targeted June 15 for completion, with a week's safety audit to follow. That brought the time to finish at fifteen days. Subtract from this the move to our finally chosen summer venue, between Piers 4 and 5, where the *Lady* would be accessed from Marianna Koval's beach by two gangways. Once we arrived at this new location, workers would have to connect the multicolored lines on the barge to electricity, water, and sewage outlets on land. This process would take several additional days. "But what if we have issues? There's no slack at all!!" I sent out the familiar all-hands blast: "Any chance of our people working the next few weekends?" Yes, for a fee.

Our original construction manager, Steve Sivak, returned from Ann Arbor to crack the whip during the last critical weeks of work. Fortunately, but without knowing why, my math had been inaccurate. The Neptune team would have until the last minute, on July 3, 2007, to ready the *Lady* for her opening. Sivak would obtain last-minute materials, answer questions from subcontractors as rapidly as possible and then, with Jonathan, assist in performing work focusing on what needed to be done to get the final approvals.

Besides me obsessing about finishing the hat, there were others on the team who needed to act. Jonathan could start meeting with the Department of Small Business Services. That city agency considered the hybrid barge a structure (not a boat). Hence, we required a building permit. Maritime engineer Mal McLaren could finally design the mooring system. He determined that anchors could be deployed more quickly than spuds—"a win-win situation." The water depth was suitable, making it easy to depart and return to the site by tying the barge to anchors already in place. This movability might help us with the DEC regulators. Jonathan was pleased with the artistry of this solution; big ugly pilings would now not protrude above the lovely pool, obscuring its lines. To my delight (and the benefit of Neptune's budget), the anchors would also be less expensive.

But was it really a win-win? An agency not previously on the team's get-their-approval list was literally in the way: the MTA, the hydra-headed corporation responsible for all public transportation, from buses and subways, bridges and tunnels, to railroads in the New York Metropolitan region. The agency is in charge of four two-way (a total of eight) subway tunnels that run under the Brooklyn piers. Opening in the early twentieth century, the tunnels served as a new mode of transportation that brought workers and residents back and forth between Manhattan and Brooklyn as the population grew. Barges working on three of these tunnels were the cause for our concern.

The IRT 4 and 5 express lines' two tunnels run underneath Pier 4. These opened first in Manhattan in 1904 to connect merchants—who complained that poor transportation was going to affect business—from the Battery to uptown residential areas. The 4 and 5 were extended to downtown Brooklyn in 1908, from Lower Manhattan to, and under, Joralemon Street. Although they didn't have the voice of the business community, this subway line could have brought workers living above Manhattan's Ninety-Sixth Street to a manufacturing district located around today's Brooklyn Borough Hall. In 1915, with a citywide population growth of over one million, overcrowding of the 4 and 5 lines caused the officials in charge to open another set of tunnels that today are overlain by Pier 2. At that point there was IRT 2 and 3 local service from Manhattan to a growing residential area in Brooklyn around Clark Street. That overcrowding continued. By 2007, at the time we met the working barges of the many-headed agency, a report about to be issued to the MTA showed that subways running in the IRT tunnels under Piers 2 and 5 had morning and evening rush-hour passengers squeezed so

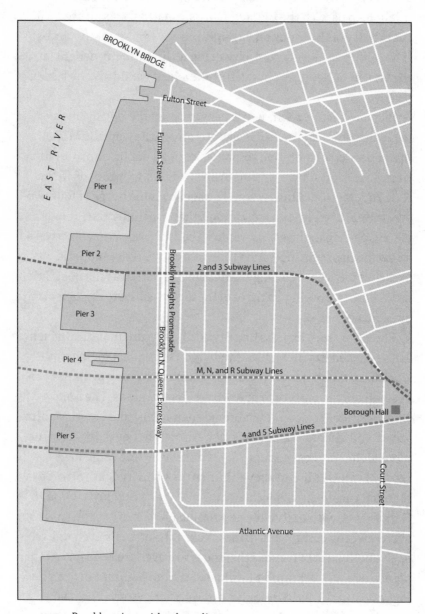

MAP 4. Brooklyn piers, with subway lines

tightly together that there was no room left. Trains were late, canceled, and backed up on the tracks like cars in a traffic jam.

A third tunnel, for the BMT R line, running from South Ferry in Manhattan (under Pier 4) to Court Street (opposite Brooklyn's Borough Hall), is important to explain the glitch the MTA barges were causing in the *Floating Pool Lady*'s moving schedule. On September 11, 2001, the R line was damaged by the attack on the World Trade Center, and the subway, crucial to the functioning of Brooklyn's central business district, shut down. Now the MTA, under the mandate of the Department of Homeland Security, had crews in the East River hard at work reinforcing the tunnels to protect badly overcrowded subways against a repeat of the attacks. The barges carrying these crews happened to be in the precise spot where the *Floating Pool Lady* was going to anchor. In a complex project, small surprises can be a nuisance. This was an obstacle I could not have predicted.

To deal with this stumbling block, we hired a new member for the team: Shea Thorvaldsen. Shea was a tall, handsome, and young maritime engineer ten years out of Tulane. In addition to his job managing city waterfront projects for D'Onofrio Contractors, he, like our insurance guru John Keenan, was a passionate sailboat racer and could handle offbeat projects. He had just three weeks to oversee the move to the summer site; the underwater and land connections including anchors, electricity, waste, and water; and the delivery and installation of the gangways. For now, because he had professional connections to Spearin, Preston & Borrows, Inc., the engineering contractor for the tunnel, Shea entered the MTA scene.

On June 6 a new Harry Potter movie titled *MTA and the Floating Pool* was on the imaginary screen in my head. MTA's higher-ups went to the pool with the project executive from Spearin to see how the contractor could accommodate the *Lady*'s move. These visitors were, as could be expected, focused on their own concerns, and they were not at all up to speed on what the BB Park Conservancy and Neptune were trying to accomplish with the *Lady*. Their questions to Shea post-visit confirmed their lack of understanding. One observer asked whether the barge could stay where it was (between

Piers 2 and 3) or be moved to the end of one of those piers to capture the view of the city skyline? Yes, it was a lovely view, but I could argue that access was poor for the public at both its current location, where there would be no room for a beach, and at the end of one of the piers. Furthermore, anything berthed at the end of a pier would be beyond the pierhead line and therefore in federal waters and subject to congressional approval, a decades-long process. Pressing further, the Spearin representative asked Shea if the barge could be opened to the public while staying in place, *then* once his tunnel workers were out of the way moved to the new location? Or, he guessed correctly, "can the barge not be moved once it's open for business?" We needed Jennifer Rimmer to make a call, but until she knew for sure that the pool was a go, she would demur.

A BEWILDERING ARRAY of agencies and parties will have their say in a public project initiated and run by a private individual. Frustration over the stalled construction, uncertainty over the date of the move, and MTA's obstruction were about to be superseded by yet one more major problem: grave uncertainty over the US Coast Guard's classification of the barge. Were we a recreational facility (sure, a venue where kids could swim), an attraction (yes, swimmers would have a fabulous view of the Brooklyn Bridge and the Statue of Liberty), or a coastwise vessel (not quite; we weren't going anywhere)? The agency's involvement had been a given from the start, but its level of participation had always been in question. In January 2005 Kent Merrill, aided by maritime lawyer Brian Starer and his Washington, DC, associates, had worked with the Coast Guard's Marine Safety Center in DC to secure a certificate of documentation for a "recreational vessel." We were content. If the agency officials saw the barge as more of a permanently moored structure than a fully operational vessel, we believed that the Coast Guard's involvement would come to an end.

However, at 9:00 a.m. on May 31, 2007, just before the Neptune team began to work overtime, we were nearly swallowed into the belly of the whale. At the request of the Coast Guard's Staten Island office, Kent and Jonathan met with Commander Eric J. Bernholz, chief of the Coast Guard Inspections Division, to present the floating swimming pool and its proposed operations. The meeting was cordial, but the commander's position spelled trouble. He asserted that the *Floating Pool Lady* should be considered a "passenger barge." Why the sudden change? The new mooring system. The switch from spuds to anchors made the facility less a permanent structure under the jurisdiction of a city agency and more of a vessel. More important, the risk to the barge was greater than before she left Louisiana when Kent had secured the recreational vessel designation. The barge was now in New York, an area that had suffered terrorist attacks, and there would be a risk of drowning once the pool was operational. One-sided negotiations ensued. Kent tried valiantly to introduce a new solution. He suggested the classification "Attraction Vessel," which was the documentation applied to the Science Barge that had opened at Pier 84 in Manhattan on May 4, 2007.

Similar to the Waterfront Museum barge in Brooklyn, the New York Sun Works, a nonprofit organization, had leased a 1940s steel deck barge from Hughes Marine at Erie Basin in Red Hook. Like the *Floating Pool Lady* but closer to home, the barge had been used for cargo work in New York Harbor. In the summer of 2006, in record time, and on a local pier in Red Hook, the founders built an urban farm on the barge. Their objective was to teach students and educators about the science of sustainability through hydroponic farming. Since its opening, to avoid having to secure permits from the DEC, the Science Barge had been docking, for two months at a time, at six stops along the Manhattan waterfront. Visitors who boarded saw tomatoes, cucumbers, bell peppers, herbs, and lettuce growing in recirculated water, as well as a mix of waste products. At the opening ceremony, scientists spoke about the need to feed over a million people in the city in the next quarter century and that New York Sun Works studies indicated this could be accomplished with similar gardens on rooftops in the five boroughs. Parks commissioner Adrian Benepe, who had his own floating venture on the books, spoke eloquently about this facility: "This barge is a metaphor for us and for the future of this planet. We can float together, or we'll surely sink together."

However, an attraction classification was not on Commander Bernholz's list. He rejoined with the term "Coastwise Vessel." This designation indicated full passenger status for the barge, more costs for Neptune, and changes to the vessel. The Coast Guard was going to require inspections and vessel security plans to protect the *Lady* and the individuals aboard. Instead of using wristbands to control swimming groups and their time allowed in the pool, Marianna and American Leisure would have to check all bags, possibly with electric scanners, before patrons entered the gangway. To deal with the risk of drowning, the Coast Guard would mandate lifesaving training and equipment, including a rescue boat and a witnessed man overboard drill, as well as random tests for drugs and alcohol. Also, even though the barge was not plying the waterways, one licensed mariner would have to be on board twenty-four seven, thus requiring extra accommodations on the barge.

And there was one more restriction. Unsure as to whether funds coming from the state to the BB Park Conservancy would be sufficient to cover operations until Labor Day, Marianna and I had discussed charging admission to early morning and evening swims. If we shared the results, they might even give Neptune a temporary boost. The not-for-profit awaited several large donations, but they would not come due for nearly a decade. Meanwhile, once I had received the bills from the loyal team and various vendors, Neptune would be $1 million in arrears, a staggering amount of debt. However, pay-to-play, according to Bernholz, would not be possible. It would simply confirm what we wanted to avoid: that the *Lady* was a coastwise vessel. In short, the Coast Guard wanted regulatory control of all ongoing and some financial operations.

On June 9, when Jonathan should have been concentrating on finishing the construction, he and Kent were instead assembling the required paperwork for the coastwise vessel designation: architectural plans by Jonathan and Kent's plans well beyond what he had long ago submitted for a recreational vessel. As he described it, we were sliding into a "bureaucratic quagmire." Two days later, Kent was even less sanguine. "I'll work all this week," he wrote, "to submit everything called for. After that, I'll keep on them to get us the necessary certificates as fast as possible, and perhaps even reduce their requirements." His closer was grim: "It's doubtful this Coast Guard process will be completed by the July 3 deadline."

In addition to the paperwork, construction in the pool continued. Neptune's attorney, Steve Crainer, was partly occupied with reviewing contracts for our painter. The company, Ahern, had to sandblast the pool, review the paint with the manufacturer, and paint the pool in time for it to dry before filling it with a three-inch hose line. On June 11 Ahern began painting the pool in an elegant marine blue chosen by the perfectionist, Jonathan. As soon as Ahern's paint roller touched the side of the pool, Jonathan received an urgent message from the unsinkable Marianna: "Don't paint the bottom yet!" She was negotiating with a major retailer for a sponsorship, and the deal included an assurance that the company's brand would appear on the bottom of the pool. She had hoped that swimmers looking through goggles, viewers on the promenade looking through sunglasses, and passengers on flights looking out of airplane windows would see a large red bull's-eye with two rings: one white, the second red—the familiar Target logo. About to lose his temper, Jonathan responded testily to Marianna: "We are painting it now. Do you really want us to stop?" But the deal fell through, and the painting continued uneventfully.

On June 10 Marianna gave me the first happy news I'd received in almost two weeks. Jennifer Rimmer had sent the BB Park Conservancy permission to start work on the beach. Two days later, there was additional good news from Shea Thorvaldsen. His message, broadcast to everyone, was that the first gangway would arrive at the summer site in six days. When installed, it would attach the barge to the beach. But I had "miles to go" before that happened. First, I had to resolve the Coast Guard dilemma.

After wracking my brains, I made a snap judgment. If I intervened, I could possibly convince Commander Bernholz that the *Lady* had a public purpose worth supporting and, to that end, to quickly return to the recreational designation. If memory serves, I realized that I knew Eric Bernholz personally from my waterfront work in city agencies and the Downtown Alliance. Aware that I had made an inexcusable mistake in not attending the May 30 meeting, on June 12 I picked up my landline and called him. My pitch was similar to my earlier fundraising letters. I told him that Neptune was a not-for-profit and that my only goal was to create a prototype floating swimming pool to be used in recreationally underserved communities in the New York/New Jersey region. I told him that from July 3 to Labor Day, another not-for-profit, the BB Park Conservancy, would manage the operation of the *Floating Pool Lady* on a trial basis, as an interim-use facility in Brooklyn Bridge Park. Then I added one significant element not heretofore discussed: in the fall of 2007 Neptune would donate the *Floating Pool Lady* to the New York City Parks Department.

Commander Bernholz's response was a complete reversal. He quickly became an official trying his best to be accommodating. Within hours after I put down the receiver, a note popped up on my computer. He had been thinking and doing some research. *If* we did not receive remuneration and *if* the Neptune Foundation were a not-for-profit and were donating the barge to another not-for-profit entity (like the city or the state), *maybe* the Coast Guard could consider designating the *Floating Pool Lady* a "Recreational Vessel" (Indeed! Wasn't that the documentation certificate that we already had?) The plan review and security plan that Kent and others had already spent hours working on would no longer be needed. If there were other issues such as safety or the allowable number of swimmers in the pool, the Coast Guard could deal with city agencies already in the loop. Bernholz asked me to forward to him a synopsis of our conversation, including a description of the "chain" of custody from the barge owner, to the operator, to government entities. Once he had that, he wrote, "I'll share it with my bosses."

I was elated that Bernholz had listened and reassessed his position. This Jonah-like adventure into the bureaucratic whale's belly was about to end. I wrote to Bernholz as he had asked and, with persistence, included a line about the possibility of charging admission for off-hour use. Then I concluded with the following: "I hope this clearly describes what the *Lady* is about and that the appropriate Coast Guard rules can apply so that we can open on July 3." I pushed "send" on my computer and held my breath.

At 2:00 p.m. on the afternoon of June 13, Commander Bernholz, having spoken to his superiors about the "risk" of our operation as well as the safety of bringing people aboard the vessel, had come to a conclusion in our favor. Since I was just letting people swim out of the goodness of my heart and not receiving anything for it, it was not a commercial enterprise and therefore could keep its recreational vessel designation. Kent, who had kept us afloat during those trying days, clarified this sentiment: "When a citizen who's really just trying to do the right thing makes an impassioned plea, and there are no hard and fast rules for how to classify it, then the decision is more likely swayed in the supplicant's favor."

In response, I wrote a letter on official stationery repeating the contents of my latest electronic message. Since Neptune's deficit would be covered by pledges and bridged by loans, I included this crucial line: "No fees will be collected at any time, by anyone in the process (Neptune Foundation, Brooklyn Bridge Park Conservancy, or the City of New York)." I told Kent to stand down on his work on the coastwise vessel designation papers. At least our uncertainty with the Coast Guard was no longer in our way.

I have in my archives one last message from Eric Bernholz. At 3:30 p.m. he wrote that believe it or not, he had a solution that was within the regulations and not considered remuneration. We could place a container "labeled 'voluntary donations' to collect just that." Marianna's team tried this method of collecting monetary donations but ultimately found that checking the end-of-the-day accounts to make sure there was no pilferage was too onerous to make it worthwhile. Another attempt to raise additional funds (i.e., a membership program), also approved by the Coast Guard, failed. The aborted program would have allowed the Conservancy to charge members to have after-hour parties on the beach. A section of the pool would open to the public, and the remaining section would be reserved for members and their guests. Because it was too complicated or too late to introduce the program, or due to a lack of interest, no such events took place.

NOW IT WAS TIME to enjoy the final details of the pool's completion. However, more obstacles, real and potential, remained. I would spend the next two weeks holed up at my desk—computer keys clicking under my fingers and telephone to my ear—jousting over the DEC consent order that had been shown to me, unaccompanied by legal counsel, on May 21.

Thankfully, Steve was now on the case, and we began the word-by-word review of the drafts that wafted over our desks. One version showed that September 15 was still the season-end removal date from the site in Brooklyn. But a caveat had been added: if we wanted the *Lady* to winter anywhere in New York State, Neptune must obtain a DEC permit. Was a permit also needed for the summer at Piers 4–5? Given prior discussions with the regional staff, their expeditious approval of either document was unlikely. We needed to move the *Lady* to less exigent waters.

Perhaps we could return to New Orleans and offer hurricane-devastated residents an oasis? Otherwise, I could follow up on a call from Mayor Charles Burkett in Surfside, Florida, who inquired if the pool would be available for the winter season. As the tables turned, officials in New Orleans had lost interest (out of sight, out of mind?), and the costs of insurance and towage to either of those southern states made those solutions cost-prohibitive. Shea Thorvaldsen came to the rescue. He found a permanent home for the barge right across the Hudson River in New Jersey beginning on the required move-out date. I crossed that worry off my list.

With the postseason site out of the way, the DEC $50,000 civil penalty remained my greatest concern, causing many sleepless nights. It was not in Neptune's budget, and even worse, the pool would never open if I declined to pay it. Proposed word changes about the fines and who pays were circulated for the next week between Steve Crainer and me, as well as between Steve and the DEC's assistant regional attorney, Udo Drescher. Then, once again to my astonishment, on Thursday, June 14 I received another draft of the consent order accompanied by the following directive from Drescher, in a legalese I barely understood, or perhaps my disbelief precluded full comprehension: "The use of the Floating Pool during this season in the absence of a DEC permit will require that the parties consent to the attached consent order by close of business tomorrow, June 15, 2007. . . . Mrs. Buttenwieser, you or another person authorized by the Neptune Foundation must return the executed order to my attention by c.o.b. tomorrow. . . . During the next week, I must obtain . . . the penalty." Aghast, I saw the penalty numbers: $50,000 to be paid by Neptune and the BB Park Corporation, plus an additional $11,000, a fine to be suspended for timely compliance. Who chose this outrageous amount? It came top-down from DEC commissioner Grannis's office: $1,000 a day as penalty for Neptune's work at Pier 2 without prior approval. Though unstated, the purpose of the fine was to send a strong message to any future happy-hour barges and the like who were waiting for DEC to set a legal precedent. Was it not also retribution from the Region 2 office for daring to bring the *Lady* to New York?

The penalty was a given. If we shared the fine equally—clearly the mooring of the pool at Piers 4–5 would benefit the park as well as Neptune—each portion would be $25,000. A relief? No. On speaking with Jennifer Rimmer, we were advised that the BB Park Corporation would not pay any portion of the penalty. Steve, who had my back, then took charge, and the next week resembled a fast-forwarded movie. At 5:14 p.m. that afternoon, he wrote to Drescher that BB Park Corporation was out of the penalty game. For this reason, and because the board of directors of the foundation had to approve the terms of the consent order, Neptune would not respond as requested by the end of the next day (June 15). I forwarded Steve's comments to Jennifer Rimmer and prepared myself for the board meeting.

This group, with Larry also in attendance, met for an emergency conference call on Friday, June 15, which was Drescher's original deadline. It was a democratic process, so the six members presented six different perceptions. Bob Douglass was my white knight. His belief in my work and his political contacts in Albany were crucial to opening the floating pool. Bob was irate. He would not let the DEC push us around. He stated that whatever the cost, we should not cave in to DEC's demands to make the pool operational for the summer. I disagreed. If we did not open on July 4, the *Floating Pool Lady* would be dead on arrival because there would be no constituency to fight for it. Someone blamed the governor for not keeping the DEC commissioner in line. Another suggested that we go to the press. Ever accommodating, Kent Barwick said he would work with us to get the permit. Carl Weisbrod offered to call Jennifer Rimmer's boss, Pat Foye, regarding the BB Park Corporation's refusal to share in the fine. Bob Douglass, despite his fury, but with an obvious desire to stand up to the powers that be for Neptune's cause, offered to call Foye's boss, Avi Schick. Bob's goal was to convince Schick (a man unlikely to compromise) to either reduce or remove the penalty altogether. My head was spinning. We adjourned the meeting until the following Monday at 1:30 p.m.

Drescher responded to Steve's latest comments on the order after the board meeting had ended, and it was a lengthy list. Some of the items, such as an error in a legal citation, were acceptable to him, whereas others were not. And the pressure from the state remained high. Rimmer thanked me for forwarding Steve's correspondence with Drescher, commenting, "Please be aware that I am receiving concerned calls re your need to sign and the repercussions of not doing so." *Repercussions?* That vague threat sent me into another tailspin, and I made a mental list of what more could possibly happen. On Monday, June 18, as promised, Steve sent Udo Drescher Neptune's last revisions to the consent order.

In preparation for the second conference call with the board, Steve Crainer and I discussed the meeting's endgame—namely, should I sign the order or not? This decision, which was another very difficult one for me, showed how interdependent the issue had become. Marianna Koval needed me to sign because, until I did, the state—under the auspices of Avi Schick, who was assuming increased control over the entire process of getting the pool open on his own terms—held tight to the funds that Marianna needed to pay for setting up the park and operating the pool. Steve Kass, the pool operator, could not hire lifeguards in time for the opening until he received funds from Marianna. Jennifer Rimmer reminded me of the repercussions if I did not sign. Though unstated, I knew the fallout would be the loss of her willingness to call the MTA to get three barges off the site so that we could immediately lay anchors for the *Lady*'s arrival. Jonathan Kirschenfeld's work was at risk as the DOH would not sign its permit until all other agreements were concluded. That consent signature was at the bottom of this house of cards. Without it, we'd all fall down. Still, moving the signature to the top of the pack would require a last-minute inspection of the pool, all of its machinery, and its water supply.

All of the Neptune board members except Carl Weisbrod called in at 1:30 p.m. on Monday the 18th. As promised, he had sent a note to Pat Foye that touched on all the bases. He mentioned the inequitable $50,000 burden DEC was placing on a charitable operation in an attempt to provide a sorely needed recreational resource to the Brooklyn community. He asked if the ESDC or the BB Park Corporation could share the cost with Neptune. Foye responded to Carl that he was aware of the problem, he had spoken to DEC commissioner Grannis, and he politely noted that he was familiar with "Ann and Neptune's good work." He did add that he would inquire and get back to Carl. By 10:00 p.m. on the night before I would have to sign the consent order and wire a check for $50,000, there was no word from Foye.

Bob Douglass, who was on the line, had spoken with Avi Schick but had a similar experience: no follow-up. Bob reiterated that I must not pay the fine and that he would resign if I did pay. Why he stood firm in his position, I can only guess. Perhaps it was because he was so incensed by Foye and Schick's behavior and took it personally. Certainly, knowing Bob, he believed that I shouldn't be punished for doing something decent. Either way, his stance would penalize me: I would either ensure the opening by paying the fine or I would lose my most respected board member.

We were at a standstill, made worse by what Steve Crainer called "the parable of horrors." We had to assume that we would hear nothing good from Foye and Schick. If we paid the fine, it might jeopardize our not-for-profit status and affect donations. The choices were four, as Steve indicated: I could sign the consent order and send no money (the pool wouldn't open). I could sign and also send $50,000 (Neptune would lose Bob Douglass). I could sign, send $50,000, and seek reimbursement (a ridiculous notion). Or I could walk away, and my baby would be lost forever. At the close of the meeting, I took a deep breath and made an executive decision. I would pay the full amount personally, all the while thinking how fortunate I was to even have this option available to me.

AT 2:30 P.M., shortly after the board meeting had ended, Steve Crainer received a message from Udo Drescher indicating that Neptune could stay in Brooklyn until September 15, without a separate DEC permit. Then, in a description of closed-door, political maneuvering, Drescher revealed the history of the penalty numbers. DEC had entered the discussions of the settlement for Neptune's bad behavior at Pier 2 with a fixed fine. None of the parties had been allowed to negotiate a change in the amount. There was no recourse. We had to sign and pay the fine.

"Transparency in government" is a much-talked-about phrase. Would it have helped if the DEC had shared more information with me from the beginning? Instead of brushing me aside when I asked questions about the ongoing negotiations, perhaps they could have invited me to attend Jennifer Rimmer and Richard Dorado's meetings with DEC staff or offered a more open response to my questions than just "leave it to us." If the process had been transparent, all of the participants would have known from the start that a fine was nonnegotiable. What would I have done with that information? Get someone connected at the top to call? I tried that. It didn't work. Would I have walked away? Definitely not—I had too much to lose and too much responsibility to my board, my team, and my donors.

The next morning, June 19, I waited for a FedEx package from Drescher with the signatory page, went to the bank to wire $50,000, and returned home. As soon as I stepped inside, the phone rang.

Drescher was on the line, telling me to cancel the wire and await further directions. The bank attendant with whom I spoke moments later must have thought I had lost my mind, which I was probably in the process of doing.

It was quiet until late in the afternoon the following day when an absurd event happened. I received a call from the top: Avi Schick. This verbally forceful, physically imposing, black-bearded man shouted at me disrespectfully. I was so stressed out that I neither heard nor remembered a word of what he was saying. I, the ferocious little lady, was knocked down by my own exhaustion and his fury. I handed the phone to my unshakable, logical, and calm attorney husband, Larry, and sat nearby while Schick continued his tirade. When Larry asked why the BB Park Corporation refused to pay its share, Schick brusquely explained that he believed DEC had no authority. The pool was on ESDC property, and one state agency, DEC, cannot penalize another. Why hadn't the state officials thought of this at the outset? Furious, Schick shot back negative responses to each question.

Then, all of a sudden, discussion of reducing the fine was off the table. Still discourteously blunt in his manner, Schick announced that the matter had moved up to the highest levels in Albany: Judith Enck, whom Governor Spitzer had appointed deputy secretary for the environment. A lifelong environmentalist, Enck, unless otherwise instructed by the governor, might rule that shadows and water dependency came before a recreational opportunity for the less advantaged. Nonetheless, Schick said not to sign anything or do anything about the fine. Suddenly, perhaps in an attempt to make up for his explosion and to play the savior, while still taking the credit, he advised us to be patient and said that he was trying to eliminate the problem. The call ended with an order to hold off on any announcement of a July 3 press opening, plans for which were already in the works. Larry put down the phone, and we looked at each other in amazement at the storm that had just transpired. Then I hugged Larry and thanked him for being there for me and for the pool.

Following the call with Schick, things moved quickly, and the good news was back on my radar, forcing me to rush from one thing to another as if I were running a premarathon race. The word that Shea Thorvaldsen circulated rose from *good* to *fantastic*. Workers were placing the anchors between Piers 4 and 5. The final anchor would be ready for attachment to the *Lady* the following morning. Jennifer Rimmer had made the call, and the MTA was out of the way; field supervisor Chris Sedita, hired by Sciame Construction to complete the work on the *Lady*, had started to fill the pool. I did not travel to Brooklyn to observe, but Jonathan Kirschenfeld, ever the artist, described the results: "I was at the *Lady* this morning, and the filled pool is indeed exciting. It has a lovely greenish tint, a cross between the East River and the Mediterranean."

However, unfinished business caused anxiety. The consent order and insurance were unresolved; the DOH needed to test the water chemistry; Rimmer had to give permission to move the barge; Shea and his team needed to move it; Commodore Construction had to complete the paver installation; and the barge required a bow-to-stern cleaning before welcoming the public. Was there time—or was it already too late? Much to Jonathan's annoyance, with her intensity and take-charge character, Marianna was dogging him with questions. Why was no one working on Saturday? Was it correct that the pool had failed DOH inspection? Jonathan liked Marianna and respected her sense of responsibility, but he was irritated that she seemed to have such a lack of faith in the team's collective abilities.

I, on the other hand, had total faith in my team: the fines, insurance, and permits were now in the hands of others. My immediate job was to ask Jennifer Rimmer politely if we could move the barge. It was a question of semantics: Was the barge now a workplace or a pool? We had insurance coverage to do work while attached to BB Park Corporation property. However, liability coverage was missing for the barge's "use" as a pool. "Since we will only be doing work until opening day," I asked, "would it be acceptable to move the barge to the new BB Park Corporation site?" Rimmer's correspondence was always polite and friendly. A very formal response (unlike her) arrived three hours later. Its language was reminiscent of the "state operative's" message eight months earlier informing us that the pool could not be brought to Piers 2–3 until Neptune's $5 million liability insurance was in place. Now we could not leave that site until we had new insurance coverage (increased, for the use of the pool, to $10 million), signed the consent order, and paid the fine.

At 4:22 p.m. on Sunday, June 24, in an attempt to explain how dire the situation was, I sent Shea's schedule for moving the pool to Rimmer. Unless the move took place in three days (Wednesday, June 27), Shea could not guarantee a July 3 opening. Two hours later, Rimmer replied that she hoped to have a resolution on the consent order the next day. "Terrific!" I replied, my enthusiasm betraying a belief that my request to allow us to move the barge to finish the work would be accepted. Henceforth, we were no longer in day-to-day communication; it was minute-to-minute.

Monday, June 25 was a day for great news. At 3:24 p.m. Rimmer wrote, "Not quite done with the Consent Order, but ok to move the pool into place today." Twenty-three minutes later I wrote Shea that the barge could be moved anytime he was ready. On Tuesday he informed everyone that the move would begin at 7:30 a.m. Wednesday morning. A heads-up went out to all: no one would be able to access the barge that day.

Archives show that on Tuesday evening Rimmer sent me two emails. The first, at 6:26 p.m., asked me to please call her due to a change of plans. At 10:00 p.m. another very formal note appeared: "We appreciate your patience as we work through the insurance prior to moving the pool." Had Rimmer been chastised by someone who reminded her that this was business, not friendship? Somehow, I wasn't worried. In preparation for watching the *Lady* move to her new berth in Brooklyn at dawn, I had eaten an early dinner and gone to bed. I had not seen either message.

At 7:00 a.m. the next morning, I sweet-talked my way onto the supposedly inaccessible barge. I descended the ramp to see that the pool was filled to its four-foot height with 140,000 gallons of pristine, clear water. The water began to shimmer as a pair of Miller's tugboats eased her away from Piers 2 and 3. As I looked out across the East River, sun streaming down, I wished I had my sun hat on—and what's more, how could I have forgotten my camera?

The day was clear, and many of the team members were on land watching the pool being towed to its new location. My view of the Lower Manhattan skyline without the Twin Towers was stunning in both a positive and negative way. It was amazing and shocking. For Marianna and Jonathan Kirschenfeld, the sight of the *Lady* coming into her new home was spectacular. Both were watching from atop One Brooklyn Bridge Park—the warehouse still being reconstructed into condominiums. For Jonathan, it was one of the most satisfying moments of his life. Marianna too allowed herself a brief moment of pleasure before returning her focus to the tasks that still required completion. On the *Lady* I grabbed the white railing to steady myself as we rounded Pier 4. Ahead, several large buoys were located in the basin that marked the heavy mooring cables that would attach the *Lady* to her anchors. I was elated. My Kafkaesque journey was over.

Or was it? At 10:04 a.m. I was driving Jonathan back to Manhattan. My cell phone rang insistently, and I asked him to answer for me. It was Marianna. She read the message that she had just received from Rimmer: "Please be advised that barge cannot be moved to the mooring site between Piers 4 and 5 until [all] insurance policies are in place. . . . Thank you." Eight minutes later, Marianna responded, "The barge was already moved as scheduled." At 10:54 a.m. I returned home, my elation from the morning's events blunted by Rimmer's notification, only to receive a letter that amplified Jennifer's call. It came as a fax from a higher-up: Anita Laremont, senior vice president/legal and general counsel to ESDC. She confirmed that all access and use of the barge had been cut off until the state had proof of adequate insurance coverage.

The next day, June 28, the consent order was resolved. Udo Drescher advised Steve Crainer and me that he had been instructed to revise DEC's previous order on consent and that he had enclosed a new document for me to sign that confirmed Schick's call. The civil penalty had been reduced. I signed the consent form, ran again to the bank to procure a certified check for $20,000 to be paid to the DEC Marine Resources Account, and messengered the packet to Drescher in Long Island City. Then I waited with bated breath for the executed consent order. The signature of the regional director for NYSDEC Region 2, Suzanne Mattei, was on my desk the following morning. She had signed under duress from the higher-up mentioned in Avi Schick's call the day before. This contretemps was over.

I had totally lost contact with events on the *Lady* since she had arrived in her summer spot. Fortunately, Marianna and I had a team, and when I checked, I was happy to learn at a distance that they were hard at work readying the facility for its opening. Marianna had hired a private cleaning crew and, assisted by volunteers, worked into the night scrubbing, vacuuming, cleaning toilets, and hauling trash away from our incredibly filthy barge. American Leisure's hip lifeguards, dressed fashionably in bright red shorts, T-shirts, and visor caps emblazoned with "American Leisure Lifeguard" on the front and "The Floating Pool, Brooklyn, New York" on the back, strolled from one place to another or performed yoga moves. Others, including American Leisure's Lyn Parker, the take-charge and exceedingly capable pool and staff manager, were becoming accustomed to the roll and pitch of the pool. Lyn, wearing crisp khaki shorts and a white shirt, her hair tied up in a ponytail, chewed on ginger to calm her stomach. Team Neptune's construction manager, Steven Sivak, supervised last-minute concrete work, including the cutting and fitting of concrete pavers into the remaining empty squares around the pool.

Architect Jonathan Kirschenfeld was also there. For him, a mere bystander role was insufficient. He picked up several large grills and started carrying them across the deck for others to install into the railings. Enter a photographer for the *New York Times* to shoot the construction progress. On seeing Jonathan, she stopped and motioned for him to proceed across her frame. Two days later, the *Times* would publish that shot of our internationally renowned architect toting the grill in an article titled "Brooklyn, Your New Floating Swimming Pool Is Almost Ready Now."

WITH THE UNPLEASANT dispute with the DEC finally over, all I wanted was to hop into my car and drive to the *Lady* to check on her progress for myself. But there was more. The issue of insurance that had plagued the project from day one in Brooklyn reappeared. A draft of a license with the BB Park Corporation, sent to Neptune, the BB Park Conservancy, American Leisure, and others involved, certifying each participant's summer relationship, had arrived on my desk back on May 15. Given Neptune's exasperating history of document signing, I had turned first to section F, that is, the insurance section. The usual items, including personal injury, were listed, but the dollar amount required for coverage was missing. Would that be the same as we had negotiated for the *Floating Pool Lady*'s berth between Piers 2 and 3—or not?

Not until June 5, when I was dealing with the potential conflict between the *Lady*'s berthing and the MTA, did I learn that the requirements included, besides the irksome (and senseless) automobile liability insurance that had kept the *Lady* from landing on Halloween Eve, an expense listed solely for Neptune. We needed to buy protection and indemnity (P&I) insurance. And because this applied to a barge and pool, where people might drown (or fall on or off the boat and die) and where the vessel might get loose and hit a pier or moving ferry (or even crash and sink), the coverage required was a whopping $10 million. In addition to a dollar amount that was inconceivable in Neptune's budget, where were we going to find a company that would underwrite this crazy risk? In the ensuing weeks, our insurance guru, John Keenan, put out requests for this coverage on the street, but no firm would touch this hybrid project. The maritime insurers refused to cover a pool on a vessel where people might drown or jump overboard. The land-based companies didn't insure boats. In the underwriter's terms, so many companies had refused coverage that Keenan's request became contaminated through too many denials.

Six weeks later, at 4:30 p.m. on June 27, with only six days to go, ESDC stepped in. Their attorney, Richard Dorado, chaired a conference call to start addressing the liability insurance requirements. Obviously, this had become the last sticking point, not only for Neptune but for the state official who had told Jennifer Rimmer to make it happen. I had only one peek at the discussions. Curiously, two days before, perhaps in an attempt to show me that she was an ally, Jennifer had asked Dorado to send me the latest in-house draft of the license agreement for review. My eyes popped. The P&I coverage had been halved to $5 million.

Thirteen respondents were on the call with Dorado that afternoon, including Neptune's Steven Crainer and insurance guru John Keenan; Nezam Nasroodin, one of the ESDC insurance operatives who had delayed the *Floating Pool Lady*'s October 2006 arrival in Brooklyn; Jennifer Rimmer from American Leisure; and Marianna Koval, along with her attorneys. There was also a new name. Rose Keville was listed as a consultant for ESDC and the BB Park Corporation. Who is this? I thought suspiciously. And why is she on the case?

Avi Schick, now the puppeteer for the insurance act, had asked Rose to participate. She was eminently well qualified to do so. President of an eponymous insurance agency that specialized in risk management, Rose had spent seven years as the director of New York State's Bureau of Risk and Insurance Management. Her job now was twofold: convince ESDC, which had not publicly confirmed Rimmer's draft of the license agreement with the lowered P&I insurance, to do so, and to find a broker willing to provide Neptune with that coverage at a reasonable price.

It took only a few hours for Rose to accomplish the first task. By the end of the conference call, the ESDC had formally accepted the reduction of the P&I to $5 million. Next, since Neptune's insurance guru, John Keenan, had been unable to find a viable carrier in New York State, ESDC waived a requirement that the carrier had to be within the state, thus opening the market nationwide. Rose enlarged the search. She hoped to have an answer by July 1, two days before the event that had finally been scheduled to introduce the press and elected officials to the pool. Rose told Keenan, who was leaving for a previously scheduled yacht race, that if she could not secure the required coverage, she would get the state to waive it. On hearing this, I decided I would wait and see.

Much to my surprise and relief, on Monday, July 1 I received a call from Vice President Mark Bernstein at Willis, a brokerage firm that specialized in marine protection and indemnity insurance. He could procure the required $5 million policy for the *Floating Pool Lady*, but the premium was $100,000, which is high for Neptune's budget. I thought for a moment and, assuming this would be the only offer we got, I looked at my watch—we had less than twenty-four hours to the pool's opening—and told Mark to buy it. Ten minutes later, he called again. Another vendor had made an offer: coverage of the same policy for $40,000. "You are my savior," I shouted into the telephone. "Bag the other and buy this one!" I notified Dorado that I had the insurance. I signed the license agreement to moor the *Floating Pool Lady* between Piers 4 and 5 in Brooklyn Bridge Park and to allow the BB Park Conservancy, as well as its pool operator, contractors, and invitees, to access and use the *Lady*.

But what was the hidden truth of the chain of events that led to the metaphor that I will call "the insurance spaghetti making"? I had always assumed that Dorado had filled in the numbers in section F of the license agreement. How had he decided on the dollar amount he should enter for the P&I that would be sufficient enough to cover such tragedies as deaths by drowning or a sinking barge? When no carrier would underwrite John Keenan's request for coverage, what powers and what contacts did Rose Keville bring to the table? Who was Mark Bernstein, and, in the end, was there a hero? On June 4, 2007, when Dorado began to compose Neptune's license agreement with the BB Park Corporation, he had to fill in six monetary blanks on the page titled "Neptune Foundation Pool Insurance Requirements." Most of the items requiring coverage were boilerplate and common to licenses the state was preparing for Marianna Koval's conservancy and others. Since the *Lady* posed additional risks, the ESDC decided that the P&I coverage must be greater . . . but by how much?

The State Risk Management office was the place to contact for answers, and thus began the chain of events The go-to person for marine insurance, Mark Bernstein, was the first strand in the spaghetti making because he had history with the state. He had arranged marine liability insurance for Governors Island before it opened to the public. The Governors Island Preservation and Education Corporation had to protect itself from lawsuits if visitors were injured in a ferry accident en route. Closer to home, the state had also asked Mark to set up marine liability insurance for the piers in Brooklyn Bridge Park and Hudson River Park. Mark's first reaction to the state risk officer's query about Neptune's P&I was to recommend a whopping $25 million. However, after reflecting on the fact that Neptune was a not-for-profit entity, he had lowered the suggested amount to $10 million, which is where it stayed, until it didn't. Mark was both a hero for ultimately securing the coverage and a villain related to the cost thereof.

Rose Keville was the next strand of spaghetti to be added to the pot. Seeking coverage as promised for the reduced P&I, Rose sought a marine insurance broker. On July 1 she called her friend, the same Mark Bernstein, and asked for his help. The two had worked together to set up the insurance for Governors Island. Mark agreed to take on the job to find a vendor if he had an exclusive. His objective, given Neptune's history, was to weed out underwriters without the capacity to complete the transaction.

Then two more strands of spaghetti were added, and the pot was about to boil. Mark had two contacts at companies in Louisiana who had not been approached by Neptune's broker, John Keenan. Both companies were top-rated, and even better, they knew and had provided coverage for the Bollinger shipyard and its customers. Neptune would fit right in. Mark did not attempt to negotiate the first offer: Neptune would pay that company $100,000 for coverage. When the second contact asked, "What's the price?" Mark was ready to play poker. He responded, "$50,000," or half the first offer. Mark thought, after all, it was low risk (i.e., only two months). Then he took a chance. It was June 30, the end of the month, and his friend needed to show some new premiums on the company's books. For Mark, the company was like "a policeman [who] needed to give out more tickets to meet a quota." Mark lowered the ask to $40,000—a $60,000 savings to Neptune from the original price—and his friend agreed. The spaghetti was cooking.

Ultimately, who deserves credit for the positive outcome? Was it the first in, the last out, no one, or everyone? Rimmer and Dorado had the BB Park Corporation in line two weeks before the final decision to lower the P&I was confirmed. It was to everyone's benefit that the pool would open on time. Days before the ESDC press office issued its detailed "immediate" release, three newspapers—the *New York Sun*, on June 27 (the day Rose Keville appeared on a conference call); and the *New York Times* and *Post* on June 30—all contained articles with details about a floating pool set to open in Brooklyn. In another time, this might have been labeled "fake news." However, the articles did add pressure on the state for the pool to open. There was someone higher up who probably wanted the credit for the opening. Enter Schick, who passed the job on to Rose; with her contact Mark and his insurance broker connection, all of them had parochial interest in solving a piece of the problem.

ON JULY 2, the day before the planned press conference, I drove to the pool to do a final check, blithely assuming that Jonathan had the DOH permit under control. However, a final sign-off from the DOH was a nail-biter. Although Jonathan Kirschenfeld and the pool architect, Joel Trace, had been working with DOH engineers James Luke and Chris Boyd since mid-June, final approval could not be given until the last minute. DOH needed proof that water on the barge complied with federal and state drinking water standards. Initially, Luke and Boyd had to approve the plumbing and sewage lines that Neptune's marine engineer, Shea Thorvaldsen, had connected from upland outlets to the barge. However, not until the last minute, when everything was up and running, could they test the chemistry of the drinking water to make sure it was potable and evaluate the pool water for cleanliness and chlorine levels.

For a DOH representative to sign the permit also required proof that the public would be safe. Work on the pool had to be completed, and there should have been no chance of anyone tripping over left-over pallets or construction materials. To avoid drowning accidents, warnings such as "No Diving" and "4 Feet Deep" were etched in large letters on parts of the pavers. However, compliance meant that their placement around the pool had to make sense. A paver with the letters "NOD" had to lie adjacent to the paver with the rest of the letters, "IVING." "DEEP" could not appear to the left of "4 Feet." DOH had to approve more wording on a large sign that swimmers passed on their way to the pool. Unlike the multilingual signs in some of the nineteenth-century floating baths, the 2007 sign, required at the time in English only, read, "BY ORDER OF THE DEPARTMENT OF HEALTH: urinating, discharge of fecal matter, spitting, blowing the nose in the swimming pool [and the list went on] is prohibited . . ." Thanks to Jonathan, who had figured out how many square feet each person could legally and safely occupy in the pool at a time, the following words were added to the bottom of the sign: "Maximum Pool Capacity: 174." One more item on the DOH checklist was American Leisure's onboard and entry-and-evacuation safety plan; its operator's certificate; and proof that all of the lifeguards were certified to meet city safety standards.

In the end it was easier for Jonathan to deal with the final, anxiety-provoking sign-off from DOH than it was to face the challenges of finishing the pool. On July 3, hours before the on-site press conference, and twenty-four hours before we were to open to the public, Jonathan met with Chris Boyd, head of the Public Pool Department of DOH, to get the thumbs-up. But there was still unfinished work. Jonathan had a solid relationship with Boyd, who had helped shepherd the project through its long and difficult regulatory review and was a big fan. They walked the full facility, below and above deck, and in Jonathan's words, there were still a few fixes that he wanted done that stood in the way of a sign-off. I assured him these would be completed by the time the pool opened the next day. One and a half hours before the press and public officials arrived, Boyd signed off on the permit, and a huge disappointment and multilevel disgrace were averted. Jonathan was giddy with relief that he'd passed the inspection. We had come a long way from that early June evening: a workerless barge; a grubby, waterless pool; a fine; a brokerless insurance policy; and no idea as to where the *Lady* would open.

CHAPTER 10

The Big Jump

JULY 3 DAWNED WARM and sunny. I made my way out to the pool early, leaving Larry to follow with our two daughters and several teenage grandchildren. Separately, our son Peter was on his way with a second grader carrying green swimming goggles. The plan, according to the ESDC press office, was to orchestrate a symbolic jump into the pool for the cameras to record . . . without me. At my age I had no intention of donning a swimsuit, much less getting wet in public. I arrived at the *Lady* dressed as a lady: all in blue, with a matching straw hat, medium-heeled, open-toed shoes, and Greta Garbo sunglasses.

When I arrived at the *Lady*, I encountered Jonathan Kirschenfeld who, when the signal was given, was watching the first of many parents and children board the gangways and make their way onto the barge. One of his dearest friends was at the front of the line with her two young girls. Jonathan, in one of the highlights of his adult career, saw the excitement in the girls' eyes as they rushed toward the water and heard them say to their mom, "Did Uncle Jonny really make this from an old barge?"

I had encountered the *Lady* in many guises: as an architect's model and in photos of her as the C500 barge—the enormous rectangular cavity that bared her original inner workings—and as a floating pool in formation. I had also experienced the *Lady* in person: on her arrival in New York City with storm water from the Atlantic sloshing around in her pool, in visits to check out the work in progress, and on my trip from Brooklyn Piers 2–3 to her summer home between Piers 4 and 5.

Today was different. I held my breath as I walked up the picture-perfect gangway and into the spacious entry and gathering space, Jonathan's "sun court." The light-gray pavilions with their multicolored roofs shared a space in the middle of which was a shallow spray pool and an elegant semicircular bench. On a level below, the pool now glimmered a blue that matched the nearby Port Authority sheds. In the foreground the Statue of Liberty and the Manhattan skyline stood in silhouette. The *Lady's* architecture, now complete, shone in the sunlight, pristine and coherent; in Jonathan's words, "She sang!" Twenty-seven years before, I had seen a Jacob Riis photograph of children in homemade outfits swimming in a rickety wood structure. In a moment I would walk down the ramp from the ladies' dressing room to the pool and see children in store-bought swimsuits jumping into the water in a re-creation of that complex.

But wait, on arrival at the pool, someone from the media jammed a microphone into my face. He wanted a comment from me: the human Floating Pool Lady. Usually shy, I was surprised to find myself comfortable talking about this project I knew so well. Without a moment's forethought, I answered, "Normally it takes nine months to gestate and give birth. This baby took twenty-seven years, and here she is!" A broad smile crossed my face, and I added, "Hooray!"

With the interview out of the way, it was time for the big first splash. With the Brooklyn Bridge behind them, Brooklyn borough president Marty Markowitz and parks commissioner Adrian Benepe were ready to leap into the pool. Waiting anxiously in a row with a bunch of children from the neighborhood and local day camps were Steve Crainer's son, William, and my seven-year-old granddaughter, Annabelle, wearing her green goggles. The commissioner called out, "Are you ready, kids?" Then he laughed and blew a whistle, and everyone jumped. Cameras flashed, capturing the event. I sought out Annabelle hidden in the water behind several overweight boys, met her at the edge of the pool, pulled her out, and received a dripping-wet hug. Once dressed, she sat outside the pool next to her aunt Carol, in her usual pose, reading a book.

I watched Adrian, chest deep in the water, talk about his hopes for the *Lady*'s future to the reporters on land, who were leaning forward in a dangerous tilt. Perhaps she will float somewhere in the Bronx. Making my way through the crowds alongside the pool, I thoroughly enjoyed the smiles and high fives of well-wishers, friends, former government associates, and politicians who were not there to swim but had come to be at the opening of a unique and newsworthy event.

Larry and I were finally in a taxi on our way home. I leaned over to hug him in appreciation for his advice, encouragement, and multiple types of support ever since the day I announced: "I'm going to build a floating pool!" Exhausted, elated, and in disbelief that we had crossed the finish line, I watched in amazement as the *Floating Pool Lady* appeared on the yellow cab's TV screen. This evening, the local elected officials, the ESDC's Pat Foye, and Avi Schick, Annabelle, and all the children would see themselves on the news.

The next day, the weather for the opening to the general public was cloudy and cold, not exactly conducive to swimming. Nonetheless, David K. Bromwich, age twenty-eight, arrived at the pool at 5:30 a.m. He wanted to be the first in line and was willing to wait until the 11:00 a.m. opening to be the first "to swim in water on water." I stayed home that day and, as a nod to her persistence and companionship throughout the process, left Marianna Koval to enjoy the pool's public debut. Marianna tucked her hair behind her ear, and with a gleam in her eye and a warm smile on her face, she and the BB Park Conservancy staff got down to business. Her mother described watching her daughter at the scene: "Taking a deep breath, Marianna lifted the chain across the entrance to the barge, releasing the impatient crowd, which then, shouting and laughing, tore up the gangplank. She walked up with them. . . . It was thrilling down to her toes, to watch their excitement."

Over four thousand people came to the barge that day, and about a thousand of them entered the pool. An observer on Marianna's team sent congratulations to Jonathan and me, describing everything as going "swimmingly." That evening, 1010 WINS posed a riddle that echoed my description: "How do you swim in a pool and a river at the same time?"

A few days later, I decided to visit the pool unannounced to see my creation in action. I parked in the space reserved for AB; crossed the beach in my flip-flops, hat, and camera, which I had remembered to take this time; said hello to the rainbow of New Yorkers patiently waiting in line for their turn to swim; and headed up the gangway and onto the barge. I was bowled over, thrilled, and embarrassed by what I experienced. Without my knowledge, Lyn Parker had decided to introduce the Floating Pool Lady. After putting my eye to the camera's viewfinder in preparation for a shoot, I was shedding tears of joy. Dozens of happy, wet faces had turned toward me, clapping and yelling, "Thank you!" I had realized my dream.

THE REST OF THE summer passed quickly. In July I made visits to the pool at odd hours to meet the press and to see my creation in action as it served the public. No longer shy, I enjoyed speaking with individuals at the pool. One day, a little boy standing in line cried out, "I know who you are, you're the Floating Pool Lady." Another time, a Muslim woman, covered from head to toe in a hijab, approached me while her husband and kids stood nearby in bathing suits. She hugged me and said, "Bless you."

I will also never forget one hot summer day when I visited the pool and introduced myself to a group of eight-year-old girls. One of them looked me straight in the eye and asked, "Why did you make the pool free for us?" Why, indeed? Thinking of the ups and downs of my journey, the title for a future book flashed through my mind:

No Good Deed Goes Unpunished. But the girl's question also returned me to that first, simple inspiration that had ignited these long years of difficult, fascinating, and often frustrating work: the desire to provide a beautiful New York City waterfront experience to children just like her. The punishment was over; my good deed had been received.

In August we were faced with the reality that, to conform to the DEC agreement, we had to be out of New York State by September 13. At 8:30 a.m. on September 12, I would be leaving my apartment to take a seat in the front cabin of the *Gabby L Miller* as she towed the *Lady* to Bayonne, New Jersey. On the way, I might have the chance to scan the Brooklyn waterfront and see what public access/park developments had occurred or were occurring. Environmental protections were on order for Grand Ferry Park. New trees and a line of boulders would be placed by the East River to protect the upland neighborhood from flooding in heavy rains, such as the storm that had occurred in April.

However, from there, largely due to the 2007–9 Great Recession, the Brooklyn waterfront was dead. The Domino sugar factory, to the north of Grand Ferry, sat empty and awaited purchase by a residential developer, who eventually had financial problems and in 2012 sold the property to the Brooklyn-based Jed Walentas of Two Trees. A waterfront esplanade from Grand Ferry connecting to Domino's new twenty-first-century park was still almost a decade away. Greenpoint's Transmitter Park, in a process similar to Mayor Russo's support for the *Floating Pool Lady* to open in Hoboken, also remained stagnant. A blueprint for the city's entire waterfront had to become a priority for the two top city officials, Mayor Bloomberg and city council chair Christine Quinn, in order for Transmitter Park to open. In New York City's case, both officials were still in office when the park, a part of that blueprint, opened in December 2012.

Team Neptune returned to work one last time. Shea Thorvaldsen and Steve Crainer prepared a winter storage contract with Bayonne shipyard. Kent Merrill made a list of needed marine repairs, and

Jonathan Kirschenfeld did the same for the on-deck structures. When the time came to donate the *Lady* to the Parks Department, she had to be in tip-top condition.

Much to the distress of Mona Bregman, aka "Princess Mona," who had visited the pool daily to exercise her back and legs and had provided a bagel breakfast for the pool staff on her birthday, the *Floating Pool Lady* closed for the season on Labor Day. Attendance for the six weeks that she was open was amazing: 49,494.

The team from Neptune, BB Park Conservancy, and American Leisure; Jennifer Rimmer; and several elected officials (among them then councilmember Bill de Blasio) came together at the pool for one last celebration on September 9. Larry and I brought Julia, our fifth-grade granddaughter who had been at camp on opening day, to join the festivities. After watching or participating in tugs-of-war and limbo dancing, Lyn stopped the party to present me with a light-blue bound book inscribed with tributes and thank-you messages that she had collected from workers and visitors to the pool.

The consistently positive thoughts in this book summarize the pool's accomplishments in the summer of 2007. The *Lady* wasn't just another cookie-cutter pool; she evoked an appreciation of the care and artistic sensibility that had gone into her architecture. Rachel wrote about "the efforts to create the many details." Kevin wrote about the "FLAWLESS" design; others used the words "beautiful" and "beautifully executed." Many of the comments reflected the diversity captured in the final attendance report. The pool was a community resource that brought families and neighbors, Brooklynites and New Yorkers, and even the global community together. Remembering my long-ago suggestion to New Orleans mayor Ray Nagin, I found the plea of a nameless visitor from his city ironic. "I wish you could help us out," this person wrote, hinting that a floating pool in the Big Easy would be most welcome.

"Bring her back!" were three constantly repeated words. This sentiment confirmed that the *Lady* had done what Marianna Koval had for years been trying to accomplish: getting the community involved and pushing for the park to be built. My dream had taken hold in the hearts of the community members, and its realization had become a viable interim use. Those Brooklynites who came to the *Lady* by foot, by shuttle from local subway stops, and by car formed the preliminary constituency for finally getting a park started and the realization of Marianna's dream.

The party ended with a quick dog-and-pony show performed by the principals for the assembled:

JONATHAN: "I enjoy doing projects that are too difficult to do and too unrealistic."
ANN: "We are going to do it!"
JONATHAN, JENNIFER, MARIANNA, AND LYN: "We did it!"

ON SEPTEMBER 9 I was driving home alone from Brooklyn after discussing the pool's departure with Shea Thorvaldsen and members of Marianna Koval's staff. My cell phone rang, and thus began a comical episode that in less than an hour reflected the many chaotic moments during the twenty-seven years of bringing the floating pool project to completion. On hearing the classic ringtone, I relived the anxiety I had felt when Jennifer Rimmer called me to say that the *Floating Pool Lady* could not be moved. However, this time, Jonathan Kirschenfeld was not sitting next to me to answer. In those days before hands-free phone use was common, I had to keep my eyes on the road and wait to call back until I arrived home in Manhattan. I parked the car, picked up the phone, pressed "call," and was told by a receptionist, "Mrs. Buttenwieser, come over to Gracie Mansion immediately. The mayor is about to start the awards ceremony." "What ceremony?" I asked. "The New York City Neighborhood Achievement Award. Didn't you get the invitation?" No, I had not.

In just twenty minutes, I ran home, changed from a T-shirt and shorts to a blouse and skirt, put on a hat to cover my unwashed hair, and slipped into a pair of turquoise stiletto sandals. I folded myself into a taxi, and in another fifteen minutes I arrived at Gracie Mansion's East End Avenue entrance, where I was met by the receptionist who had called. She picked up her walkie-talkie and notified someone close by that I had arrived. As I had been doing for years, I ran and met resistance, catching my heels in the sidewalk cracks and nearly taking a tumble. I entered the mansion's garden where a crowd sat patiently waiting for me, filling all the available folding chairs. They turned to watch me stagger up the railless steps to a prefabricated stage. To my surprise, Mayor Bloomberg, Brooklyn borough president Marty Markowitz, NYC Small Business Services commissioner Rob Walsh, and Marianna Koval were all waiting for me there.

Before I had time to catch my breath, Markowitz began to speak. Then the mayor, with a handshake and a hug, gave me a large framed document that bore the words, "In tribute to Ann Buttenwieser, founder and president of the Neptune Foundation who turned her dream into reality in Brooklyn this summer . . ." Just as when Lyn Parker introduced me to the pool full of happy swimmers, I found myself speechless. This time, I did not cry. Instead, I gazed out at the audience, where I saw such familiar faces as Shea and his group of engineers, as well as my good friend, former parks commissioner Henry Stern, all smiling and applauding, and I thought that many of them should have been up on the stage with me. Then I turned to the mayor, thanked him, and smiled.

YES, I HAD TURNED my dream into reality. But what I did was not about me. What about the *Lady*'s social/recreational, equity, and urban planning benefits? She opened up a portion of the heretofore closed waterfront for recreation, fully meeting one of the expectations on which she was founded. Patrons, mainly Brooklyn residents, along with others from the Bronx, Manhattan, and Staten Island, came to the edge of the East River to swim. Parents brought kids from Brooklyn Heights for a dip. A Russian couple came from Brighton Beach. A Japanese neurosurgeon and his wife visited from the Upper West Side, and a mother who had not been in a pool in eight years because of an accident traveled from Harlem to try the *Lady*'s water.

As an intriguing new facility, located in an easily accessible, upscale neighborhood, the pool quickly became the city's newest tourist attraction. Visitors from Europe, the Caribbean, and the Far East gazed at the swimmers, took pictures, ate in the nearby pizza restaurant, and contributed to the local economy.

The recreationally underserved population in this location was small. However, unlike the early sex-segregated floating baths where patrons preferred to swim with people of similar backgrounds, in this floating pool the diversity of age, race, income, and ethnicity that is New York City today swam together. Congressional representative Nydia Velasquez had secured federal money to run buses that brought patrons from some outlying areas to the pool. Teenagers came from the Farragut Houses public housing project to let off steam. And, unlike the boys at the floating baths who stole their friend's clothes, thanks to their respect for Lyn Parker—who greeted the older kids and told them, "Look, you want to be part of this? You behave. If you don't, you're off"—they behaved.

Locating the floating pool in the former Port Authority piers proved that such an interim use could activate a community to want more, and in 2009 construction began on Pier 1, the area to the north of where work on the *Floating Pool Lady* had taken place, and for which the New York State Department of Environmental Conservation had fined the Neptune Foundation. The access to the waterfront in the resulting Brooklyn Bridge Park would become an example for planning and community participation to the north and south of the park.

The *Floating Pool Lady* had proven that she could equitably serve a diverse population but that a new venue would be needed to increase opportunities for the recreationally underserved. She had proven that she could draw crowds to a once-closed-off waterfront and, most important for planning the city's future, that a park could grow in Brooklyn.

CHAPTER 11

The *Lady* Moves to the Bronx

NOW IT WAS TIME to transfer the *Floating Pool Lady* from Neptune to Parks, Ann to Adrian. The Parks Department chief engineer John Natoli, "the Fixer," who among others in the Parks Department had questioned Commissioner Benepe's wisdom in signing on to this project, was now in charge of moving the barge from the Bayonne shipyard to the Bronx. On May 29, 2008, eight months after the closing party in Brooklyn, Natoli announced that his men were loading the work barge with the anchors, gangways, platforms, chains, and so on in order to accompany the *Lady* to the Bronx. Two days later, workers on flat-top barges and men and women walking along the East River could see the *Lady* in transit to Barretto Point Park in the Bronx.

Similar to the concrete plant at Stuyvesant Cove Park in Manhattan, this park, located at the south end of Tiffany Street in the Bronx, prior to 1950 was the site of an asphalt plant, which probably provided road-surfacing material. A visitor in 1978 would have found the property abandoned and the leftover sand and gravel from the factory taken over by weeds and illegal dumping. By 2001, when the Parks Department acquired the land from the neighboring Department of Environmental Protection (DEP), the area had been designated a brownfield. Five years later, after decontamination and a redesign of the landscape with native plantings, green lawns, an open-air amphitheater, and riverside vista points, Barretto opened to the public. Two additional elements of this park are evidence of the current status of the East River waterway in the Bronx. A small beach where visitors can sunbathe and kayakers can land hosts the message, "No Swimming." On the other hand, a fishing pier invites neighbors to scrape crabs from the pilings and, with their rods, catch snappers. Eating one's catch is not recommended but is done nonetheless.

Because this was a new facility for the Parks Department, Commissioner Benepe questioned whether anyone would come and whether the event would be incident-free. To be safe, he decided on a soft opening (i.e., without an announcement to the press). But that was not to be. Shortly before June 27, Mayor Michael Bloomberg informed the Parks Department that he wanted to preside at the ribbon-cutting event. Politically, this would give evidence to the public of Bloomberg's commitment to opening up the waterfront.

Nine months after the *Lady* had moved from Brooklyn to New Jersey, she opened at Barretto Point Park in the South Bronx, one of the city's most recreationally deprived neighborhoods. On that day, and for ten summers thereafter, children and their parents from this low- and lower-middle-income community, with the city's highest rates of asthma, obesity, and diabetes, had a new destination, as did curious people from other parts of the city and indeed the world. In their bathing suits and flip-flops, towels slung over their shoulders, they walked past a closed juvenile detention center, a fish-processing plant, parked eight-wheeler trucks, and boarded-up industrial plants. Also, amid the stink from the New York Organic Fertilizer Company plant and the city's wastewater treatment facility, they prepared to jump into a pool floating in the East River.

As I stood there on opening day, I was accompanied by three city officials who had a part in the floating pool: Mayor Michael Bloomberg, who brought excitement to the pool's opening; parks commissioner Adrian Benepe, who, when the pool was only a dream, had accepted it for his domain; and Emily Lloyd, commissioner of the DEP, who, as mitigation for the expansion of the adjacent waste treatment facility, had worked with Adrian to bring the pool to the Bronx and had arranged for the upland connections of the barge's electric, water, and waste lines. But I had eyes only for the children who, like they had in Brooklyn a year before, and as seen in Jacob Riis's nineteenth-century photographs, were piled up at the edge of the pool as they waited for the dignitaries to join them in the jump.

But they had to wait. Following the required opening remarks, the mayor, in a black Parks Department T-shirt and bathing shorts, his arms wrapped around the shoulders of a let's-get-on-with-it, smiling young boy, remained in place. Two teenage girls sporting white T-shirts emblazoned in black letters with the words "The Point" approached the speaker's platform. Together, as a gift to me, they held out a framed photograph of the Hunts Point Floating Bath, which was located, before a landfill obliterated it, in Barretto Bay at the height of the floating baths, circa 1888 to 1915. These two teenagers, who, like me, had educated themselves by researching floating baths, were visible proof that the *Floating Pool Lady* was indeed a historic legacy. History aside, shortly thereafter Adrian blew the whistle, and a new community of children from the Bronx jumped into the twenty-first-century version of a nineteenth-century bath.

THE TRIP TO ARRIVE at this opening in the Bronx is an example of public policy at work. Step back to a Parks Department meeting on October 26, 2007. For Department of Environmental Conservation (DEC) commissioner Pete Grannis, the purpose of the gathering was to meet with Commissioner Benepe to begin the discussion about getting a permit for the Parks Department to return the *Floating Pool Lady* from exile in New Jersey to New York in the summer of 2008. Governor Eliot Spitzer had appointed Grannis, a former state legislator representing the Upper East Side, nine months before. After he was settled in office, I had invited Grannis to visit the pool in hopes of getting a favorable reaction and political support from the top DEC official. Grannis did not visit the pool in Brooklyn until just before its closing. Unable to reach me, he had called my husband Larry and told him that he found the pool "impressive." One of his officials had a different opinion. Suzanne Mattei, an uncompromising environmentalist in her role as director of the NYC field office of the Sierra Club, now DEC's regional director, hated the pool categorically.

Seated at the head of the Arsenal's familiar conference-room table was Commissioner Benepe surrounded by his floating pool team. On one side of the table sat DEC commissioner Grannis and Executive Deputy Stuart Gruskin, whose comments had been helpful when meeting with me and Parks Department representatives in his former position in the DEC regional office. Suzanne Mattei sat next to me on my right, and to my left was Stephen Kass, an environmental attorney at Carter Ledyard & Milburn who was working for me pro bono and had my back. Commissioner Benepe opened the meeting with a welcome to Grannis. He called on me next to show a presentation that I had prepared on the history of the floating pools, from the early baths to the *Floating Pool Lady* in Brooklyn.

Next came Mattei, the official who had signed Neptune's permit in June under duress, and would now have to pass on the DEC permit application that the Parks Department required. The woman rose to her full, very tall height and began her pitch. She made a few polite preliminaries and then lit into me, the lady on her left. In a strident voice, she indicated that the barge should have never been brought to New York. Furthermore, without giving a reason, the pool should not have opened in the first place.

I sat rigid in my seat, out of not fear but discomfort at Mattei's performance in front of officials who were there to support the pool. Then Stephen Kass whispered to me words that reminded me of my encounter with the redhead at CB1 in 2004: "Shall I tell her how much you are getting out of this venture?" The meeting ended with everyone in shock. The two commissioners exited first, but as I waited for the elevator, Adrian reappeared to tell me that Mattei had been allowed to let off steam and that Grannis was on board.

The first stage of implementing the DEC's policy (i.e., that facilities floating in the river require a permit) showed that different points of view would have to be accommodated. But, not unlike the fine that the DEC imposed for the floating pool's stay between Piers 2 and 3 in Brooklyn, this time, even though a city agency (not a not-for-profit) was in the lead, the state would remain in control, and there would still be a price to pay. In the fall of 2007, with the help of environmental consultant Fred Jacobs, the Parks Department began eight months of negotiations to acquire the DEC permit for the *Floating Pool Lady* to land at Barretto Point Park.

When negotiations were complete and the multipage application had been submitted, the DEC issued to the Parks Department a three-year "temporary" permit, renewable up to four times, with conditions. Again, the objective was to discourage others who might follow with similar propositions from trying to throw shade on the river with projects that were not water-dependent. Some constraints were sensible. For example, one required a three-year study of the impacts of the shade cast by the barge on the marine habitat below. Perhaps, I thought, if it were determined that the fish actually felt safe and thrived in the shadow, that argument against the barge could be eliminated. Indeed, evidence of prospering aquatic life might argue for even more floating barges in the river. However, this study was not about saving fish in a recreational environment but was designed to further city policy to increase waterborne transportation. Ferry routes would open to serve new waterfront high-rise housing developments in Greenpoint and Williamsburg and public recreation areas such as Soundview Park in the Bronx heretofore unreachable except by car or bus. Passenger access to these ferry landings is made via floating barges. The DEC was using the floating pool as a template to determine just how much these structures, allowable by law, might harm the marine environment.

Another condition in the DEC permit for Barretto Point Park required a study of the local water quality with remedial recommendations. Because it was accessible on hot days, with no pool nearby, dozens of teenagers dove into the dark and dirty Bronx River. Here, like in Greenpoint, the combined sewer outfalls dumped sewage into the river after heavy rainfalls. Adding to the pollution, a crane on a barge heavy with garbage spilled debris into the river as it lifted it into a recycling container. I had often suggested that the *Lady* could garner a constituency for river cleanup projects. At some point in the future, a pool enclosed in a barge would be redundant, and city dwellers could swim unencumbered, directly in the rivers, which might be possible soon.

In 1989, while working for the Parks Department, I curated an exhibit of photographs of the contemporary waterfront. One of the images was of a woman in a bathing suit walking out into the East River at the foot of East Twentieth Street. In front of her were dozens of pilings that had once upheld a pier where cement from a cement plant had been loaded onto barges. In the water under the woman's feet was a small beach made of the remains from cement truck pours. Today, this is the location of Stuyvesant Cove Park, and the area where cement once overflowed is now filled with native plants. One can fish here but not swim.

The need for more pools is evident. According to an editorial in the *New York Times* in the summer of 2019, only fifty-one outdoor pools were open. Fifty-one pools divided among a population of 8.4 million equals "150,000 people per pool."

More swimmers are entering New York City's rivers each year. Under the governance of New York Open Water, one can race around Manhattan. In 2017 nearly seventy entrants swam around Governors Island. Also, according to the DEP, the waters they are swimming in are cleaner than they have been since the early 1860s. The only thing keeping New Yorkers from swimming any time they want in the foreseeable future is climate change. With warming weather comes more rain, and with more rain come overflowing sewers and polluted waters.

The most absurd penalty that the DEC imposed on the Parks

Department was the one that had also been imposed on Neptune. It required the barge to be stored off-season "outside New York State coastal waters." This set the agency up for a large recurring expense for both moving and berthing the pool elsewhere during the fall-to-spring period when the pool was not in use. The Parks Department paid for her roundtrip voyage from New York State to New Jersey through 2017. However, her time had become finite. The following summer, in accordance with the Parks Department's agreement with the DEC that the barge would be permitted to berth in the Bronx for only ten years, she would not be allowed to return. But the policy debate would continue, and the outcome would not change much.

In June 2017 I ran into Adrian Benepe's successor, parks commissioner Mitchell Silver, at a fundraiser for the Battery Conservancy. He greeted me, introduced me to some bystanders as the Floating Pool Lady, and then added, "You know, Ann, this will be the pool's last summer. The State Department of Environmental Conservation ten-year permit is going to expire." I sat through the speeches at the gala, but my mind was elsewhere. How was I going to light a fire under the powers that be at the Parks Department to apply for a totally new permit? And, even if I did, would the new leadership at the DEC regional office be willing to start over and grant one? Then I wondered how the governor's office might react if I leaked news about the pool's closure to the press with an upcoming election in November 2018.

The next morning, I asked for advice from Adrian Benepe, the *Floating Pool Lady*'s godfather. When he told me that the environmental staff in the governor's office were already in conversation with the DEC about the *Lady*'s future, my relief was palpable. As in prior years, the process to secure a DEC permit moved at a snail's pace, but the race to the finish was not quite as tight as it was in Brooklyn ten years before.

Stephen A. Watts III, the DEC's regional permit administrator, on May 21, 2017, forwarded to the Parks Department the signed DEC permit allowing "long term, but temporary mooring of a floating freshwater swimming pool . . . off Barretto Point Park in The Bronx." Once again, there were trade-offs, some positive, others negative. What did "long term" mean? Three years renewable had been changed to five years renewable once. And "temporary"? This indicated that the water-dependency policy was still in place, until the area's water quality was safe for swimming, something that would only be possible if the city continued to finance the removal of combined sewer outfalls. "Temporary" now had an additional meaning: until the agency "has achieved an alternative, publicly accessible upland swimming facility that would serve the same community." As had been said at every meeting with the DEC regional staff, this would require available inland property and a higher cost to build than a pool on the waterfront. On paper, the life granted to the *Lady* in the Bronx, beginning in 2018, was another ten years. The Parks Department was able to show the savings in towing and shipyard rental costs if the requirements for the barge to leave the state at the end of each season were removed. Officials at the DEC acquiesced. This economy was now available for maintenance to prolong the shelf life of the pool.

As shown in the current DEC permit for this water-based recreational facility, the overall policy outcome is that the DEC policy is unchanged. No filling in waters is allowed unless the underlying project is "water-dependent." For the DEC, acceptance of a floating pool means that the agency's way of doing business would have to be different. Effecting change is not easily accepted, even if it is for the public good. However, is preservation of the marine environment not also a public good? Is the DEC wrong? Is the fear realistic that the floating pool will set a legal precedent, leading other less desirable and beneficent enterprises to fight for space and clog the environmentally fragile waterways? Can the agency predict the future? Perhaps no change to the status quo means they can at least feel content that no *new* bad things will happen and that the marine environment can be preserved. The solution was a ten-year permit that lets prospective applicants know that the *Floating Pool Lady* has not changed the rules. That door is still closed.

In a decade, if the DEC policy holds, the *Floating Pool Lady* may sit in disuse at the mouth of Pugsley Creek in the Bronx. Perhaps the rivers in the South Bronx will be clean enough for swimming by then; if so, the project will have accomplished one of its central goals. However, what if the rivers are still not swimmable and no land and financial resources are available to build an in-ground pool? Hasn't the *Floating Pool Lady* enhanced the public enjoyment of the water? And isn't that enough?

Epilogue

SWIM, NEW YORK CITY'S CHILDREN, SWIM!

ON JUNE 27, 2018 (with state elections five months off), the State Department of Environmental Conservation's permit allowed the Parks Department to open the *Floating Pool Lady* at Barretto Point Park in the Bronx, in the first year of an additional decade stated in the permit. My husband Larry accompanied me on my annual opening day visit, and we walked up the gangway behind a group of laughing, swimsuit-clad children.

On the wall to the left of the entryway hung signs similar to those of the nineteenth-century floating baths, but the words reflected Caribbean immigrant populations and changing times. In English, Spanish, and Creole, some twenty-first-century rules were posted: "Prohibited: smoking and electronic equipment on deck, including . . . cell phones." Here women, men, and children swim together in clean water without having to pay a cent.

Every year since the *Lady* began her career in these waters, I have been flatteringly greeted with hugs and handshakes by the pool's managerial staff, her lifeguards, and a police officer. This cop knows most of the kids from his winter shifts at the local high school, so he greets the teenagers by name and sets a high bar for behavior. Standing before me at the pool's overlook were two small girls with heads full of colorful plastic barrettes, their backs covered with sunscreen. In the pool below, children of all colors, shapes, and sizes enjoyed their first day of summer vacation. A mother held her baby, a father watched spunky young boys dunking their heads under water, a teenager adjusted his goggles, and another swam laps. At one end of the pool, a young couple held hands. At the other end, a grandmother dangled her feet in the pool and watched a small child. Much like Jacob Riis's nineteenth-century monochrome photographs, everyone was enjoying themselves and bobbing in the clean, aqua water of the pool on a warm, sunny day—in living color.

I surveyed this scene with such pleasure, for here was proof that creating this facility yielded many accomplishments. Regarding physical indicators, when the *Floating Pool Lady* closed in Brooklyn Bridge Park in September 2007, her construction and finishes such as painting the pool had been completed on time. She was successfully connected to electric, waste, and water lines. MTA no longer interfered, and she did not roam from her attached anchoring system. She opened at the appointed hour with all required permits and, except for drinking fountains not always meeting Department of Health standards, operated without incident. No one had jumped overboard. Jonathan Kirschenfeld, who kept the truth of the unsigned DOH permit to himself, delivered on his statements to me on the day I first met him in 1998. He also delivered on his statements to Jennifer Rimmer and to the entire working group seated around a conference table at ESDC headquarters in May 2007. He had designed a floating pool and had orchestrated it to completion. The Neptune Foundation had functioned well. In 2008, as president of Neptune, I donated the pool to the New York City Parks and Recreation Department. On June 28, 2017, the New York Department of State confirmed that the Neptune Foundation had been dissolved.

The *Floating Pool Lady* had also weathered two hurricanes and a formidable rainstorm. When superstorm Sandy hit New York City on October 29, 2012, damage to the facility was minimal. Sandy hit the Bronx at a very low tide. This caused the barge's landside entry and exit ramps to be tipped sideways. One of the options the Army Corps of Engineers studied to protect the city from further floods is a six-mile-long wall with gates that open and close. According to environmental critics, that scenario poses a major problem to Barretto Point Park, as well as all of the communities along the East River. When the gates at the base of that area are closed, rising high tides, and higher sea levels due to climate change, will erode the edges of the park to which the floating pool barge is attached. In addition, sewers will overflow and add waste to runoff from street debris to pollute the waterways, just when New Yorkers look forward to swimming in the rivers.

Successful social and environmental indicators also show accomplishments. For Marianna Koval and the Brooklyn Bridge Park Development Corporation, the pool needed to create a constituency to finally start the park. Indeed, Marianna helped form a vocal propark group from over forty-nine thousand persons who used the pool for swimming or relaxing. Demolition of existing maritime structures began in 2008, and, with funding from the city, shovels were in the ground a year later.

In the Bronx the children in a recreationally underserved neighborhood no longer have to swim in putrid waters. The neighborhood had already been introduced to the East River waterfront via Barretto Point Park's landscape design, but until that estuary is swimmable, Hunts Point residents can swim in water *on* water. And that is also a significant recreational addition to the Parks Department's Bronx portfolio. In 2019, despite over twelve inches of rainfall in July and August, but aided by temperatures in July that sat between 90 and 93, the pool had a seasonal record of nearly fifty thousand swimmers. This number was higher than all of the intermediate-size pools in the borough.

When I founded the *Lady*, I argued that she could become a catalyst for cleaning New York City's rivers. The current DEC permit requiring a study of the local water quality with remedial recommendations may help achieve that. Meanwhile, the pool had an additional environmental success. Shortly after the *Lady* opened at Barretto Point Park, a constituency formed to cleanse the air. The pool sat between two odor-producing facilities, the DEP's waste treatment plant and the New York Organic Fertilizer plant. The Natural Resources Defense Council, prompted by local citizens and swimmers using the pool, started a nuisance lawsuit against both. Within a year the fertilizer company closed, and the city treatment plant abated its odors.

Public access has been a goal in all the Department of City Planning waterfront reports since the early 1990s. The agency's first Comprehensive Waterfront Plan title says it all: "Reclaiming the City's Edge." In this first document, presented publicly in 1992, the planners discussed two types of access: linear and point. The floating pool increased point access to two locations on the East River—the first between Brooklyn's Piers 3 and 4 when the floating pool opened in 2007, and the second a year later at the foot of Tiffany Street in the Bronx. The planners' approach also evolved with the changing attitudes toward public access to the working waterfront. During the Progressive Era, pier space was granted first to paying users, such as regional shipping lines. In 1992 planners concerned about a decline in New York's shipping dared not rock the boat. Public access to the working waterfront might conflict with operations and was assumed to be unsafe. However, the following words left the door open: "Modest public access improvements near certain working waterfront uses can benefit workers and residents in nearby areas."

An attitudinal change among planners and New York City's Percent for Art law (which requires 1 percent of the budgets of certain city-funded construction projects to be used for public artwork) resulted in public access amenities at the Newtown Creek Wastewater Treatment Plant. In 1998 the DEP began to enlarge the thirty-one-year-old facility. The agency worked with members of the local Greenpoint community that opposed the expansion to mitigate the opposition. The treatment plant now has inviting public amenities, including a visitors' center with a man-made waterfall, a nature walk along Newtown Creek, and its eight metallic "digester eggs" lit at night with blue light.

As an urban planner who believes that the public learns about a city's operations when recreational and industrial uses are mixed, I accept that residents must traverse an industrial area to reach the *Floating Pool Lady* at Barretto Point Park, Hunts Point. In 2019, in their six- to seven-minute walk, residents from the private Carnes McKinny apartments and from the New York City Housing Authority's Hunts Point Avenue Rehab passed a trucking company, a recycling plant, a salvage yard (all with eighteen-wheelers parked outside), a produce market, and a steel distributor. These businesses, like the asphalt plant that long ago preceded Barretto Point Park, keep the city working.

JUST AS MY RESEARCH into New York City's nineteenth-century floating baths resulted in creating the country's only contemporary floating pool, so has this facility influenced others to replicate and improve the prototype that floats at Barretto Point Park in the Bronx. Two such projects are in New York, one is in Chicago, and perhaps someday one will be in Hoboken.

In 2009, less than two years after the *Floating Pool Lady* had left Brooklyn, I heard from Joshua Laird, then the assistant commissioner for planning and parklands at the Parks Department. He said the city was interested in creating a replacement pool for Brooklyn Bridge Park. Some of the elements for success were already in place, including a constituency led by local state senator and swimming advocate Daniel Squadron and joined by residents (and potential voters) who had enjoyed the *Floating Pool Lady* in 2007. Nancy Webster (Marianna Koval's replacement as executive director of the Brooklyn Bridge Park Conservancy) agreed to fund a feasibility study with lead author Jonathan Kirschenfeld, the *Floating Pool Lady*'s architect. Joshua suggested that a floating pool rather than an in-ground one would be economical without detracting from the park's green space. Missing was even a glimmer of capital funding from Squadron or the city.

The design for *Pool II*, which Jonathan hoped would be approved for construction by city hall before Mayor Bloomberg left office, showed an Olympic-sized "river-friendly" floating pool in the East River between Brooklyn Bridge Park's Piers 2 and 3. The plan proposed an all-season recreation complex built from scratch, with sky-lighted below-deck changing rooms and a pool with a translucent bottom to minimize marine shading. Its multiple purposes would also include acting as a pedestrian walking bridge between the outer ends of the two piers and as a wave attenuator and boat tie-up on the East River's edge. The estimated cost was between $14 and $17 million.

However, that project was not to be. The mayor's office and the DEC suddenly hesitated to jump on board with *Pool II*—perhaps because a second unique swimming facility, + POOL, also sought a home in the East River outside the park. As we have seen, political offices eventually pass on to others, and priorities change. Mayor Bloomberg's three terms were over, and the de Blasio administration would not give public money to *Pool II* without soliciting a competitive bid. Jonathan's team was the only one specifically qualified and experienced in New York City's floating pool facilities to respond, but city hall never issued the required request for proposals.

I learned years ago from Justin Murphy at the Downtown–Lower Manhattan Association (when I wanted to issue an RFP for a developer to place a floating pool at the Battery) that once a community has a facility, the city cannot take it away without repercussions. By 2012 the Brooklyn Bridge Park community had experienced a summer with the *Lady* in their front yard and would wait no more. They wanted to swim *now*. Under pressure from park users and local politicians, the BB Park Corporation established and ran a small above-ground pop-up pool on the Pier 2 upland for six years. But construction to complete this portion of the park eventually forced the pop-up's permanent closure. At the beginning of its last season in June 2018, Eric Landau, the president of the BB Park Corporation, held a press conference. A plethora of appointed and elected officials, members of Love Our Pool, and the BB Park Conservancy's Nancy Webster joined him as he announced future construction of a permanent in-ground pool in Squibb Park, between the Brooklyn Heights promenade and Brooklyn Bridge Park. The estimated cost at the time was $10 to $15 million dollars. As of 2019 the pool had been placed on hold while a Brooklyn Queens Expressway review panel selected a plan for reconstruction of 1.5 miles of the roadway. Had Mayor de Blasio's administration paid attention to *Pool II*, it would be open now, and neither the new costs nor the debate over Squibb Park Pool would have been necessary.

The idea for + POOL, a river water–filtering, floating, plus sign–shaped pool designed as four pools structured together, was conceived in 2010 by four friends: artists Archie Lee Coates IV and Jeff Franklin and architect-designers Dong-Ping Wong and Oana Stanescu. When I asked whether the barge-based *Floating Pool Lady* influenced their desire to take on such a project, Coates told me that our project set the precedent. The + POOL team formed a nonprofit and decided to take a great technological leap forward that was also a return to the past. Their pool would be submerged in the river like the historical floating baths, but its walls would comprise a permeable filtration system. Think of a big strainer removing contaminants and odors from urban waterways. A combination of materials would filter over a million gallons of river water daily to provide a chemical-free, clean, and safe Olympic-size pool. At the end of the day, the cleansed water would return to the river. Although + POOL's proposed water-cleaning efforts could hardly make a dent in the East River's filthy water, it aspired toward a river that might one day be swimmable.

Initially, two Kickstarter campaigns funded + POOL's test of the filtration concept in the harbor for five months. According to Coates, this provided the design and engineering team with necessary data to develop a filtration system that fully filters bacteria and other pathogens from the river. As of 2020, ten years into the project, + POOL has traversed paths similar to those traveled by the *Floating Pool Lady*. A DEC permit may be less important given that the project's ambition to restore river water makes it a water-dependent project, so the DOH's permit is a challenge. The agency currently has no rules to ensure the safety of such an innovative and quirky project that, if it doesn't work as promised, could sicken swimmers. The city is on board, as evidenced by the Economic Development Corporation's September 2019 release of a request for expressions of interest (RFEI) for a "floating, self-filtering pool" in the

Two Bridges neighborhood in Lower Manhattan. No city or EDC funds are promised, however, so the winning team assumes the costs. The team at + POOL responded to the RFEI with their vision and hopefully await designation to open the river for swimming just north of the Manhattan Bridge.

The *Floating Pool Lady* sparked interest among cities and private individuals worldwide. The emails and phone calls have poured in from Newark, New Jersey, to the Dublin Docklands, and from Queens to Hong Kong. Some, with no idea of the towing and insurance costs, wanted to borrow the *Lady* off-season. Others doing preliminary research on pool barges wanted advice. Still others wanted to know the required permits or how to set up a nonprofit foundation; of course, there were always questions about the costs as well. I responded politely to all of these inquiries, and equally politely offered the professional services of Jonathan Kirschenfeld and myself should they actually want to start acting. Often, I hung up the phone annoyed that my brain had been picked for an hour or so for no apparent benefit. The only person who followed up their initial email and has stayed in touch with me was Beau D'Arcy.

Starting small, Breakwater Chicago grew into a much larger project than the *Floating Pool Lady* did and, though it is a commercial enterprise, has benefited from lessons I learned creating the *Lady*. Starting Breakwater Chicago in 2012, D'Arcy was later joined by co-founders Ashvin Lad and Elizabeth Bell. They aimed to create a destination for boaters and nonboaters on Lake Michigan, just off Chicago's shoreline. Breakwater Chicago's design evolved through its early years, starting as a permanent structure and becoming a semisubmersible and semipermanent structure. Later, it evolved into a 300-by-100-foot commercial passenger vessel. Among the amenities occupying the eighty thousand square feet of this floating island will be several restaurants, a spa, a private club, and eight swimming pools with entry fees. As of 2020, construction on Breakwater Chicago has not begun. When it happens, I hope to attend the opening.

My Hoboken friend and floating pool advocate Michael Krieger (who continues to monitor waterfront use controversies in that city) notified me in the summer of 2019 about a huge conflict over the future use of the former Union Dry Dock property located on the Hudson River north of Stevens Institute. The controversy involved entities familiar to me. On one side, New York Waterway, founded by Arthur Imperatore, Sr., in 1986, intended to use the property for industry: maintaining, repairing, and refueling its ferry fleet. Opposed to Imperatore's plan were the City of Hoboken, its citizens, and civic groups. One such group was the Fund for a Better Waterfront, which in 1990 won the City of Hoboken's acceptance of a continuous waterfront park. Their objective was to include the dry-dock site in this park. Thinking creatively reveals another approach. The *Floating Pool Lady* sits successfully in an industrial area of the South Bronx. In Hoboken, why not combine a floating pool with a ferry maintenance site? According to Michael, if the economic, political, and institutional capacities and the land-use changes met public expectations, an opportunity for a floating pool in Hoboken could be reconsidered. Would I attempt to navigate the political waters in New Jersey to launch a new floating pool across the Hudson? Now that I learned my lessons, I just might.

AT THE POOL ON June 27, 2018, I walked through the women's dressing room and past the translucent mural with images of the fish that once populated the East River, and may again one day. I high-fived the attendant, removed my flip-flops, and walked down to the pool. The day was clear and, across the river to the left, I could see the Vernon C. Bain prison ship floating in the East River outside of Rikers Island. Downriver on the right, the supertall 432 Park Avenue punctuated the skyline, dwarfing the Empire State Building farther downtown.

When I reached the pool's far end, I was invited to sit among a group of swimmers for a photo op. Unlike the little girl who fell into the South River decades before, I felt like a happy adult on the shore. I looked at the dream I accomplished with my team, and I asked myself, "If I knew everything I was going to go through before I started this project, would I do it again?" I saw the smiles on the faces about to be photographed, and my answer was "Yes!" Memory can fade quickly, but the satisfaction and joyful moments always remain. The *Floating Pool Lady* is more than a floating pool and more than the realization of a personal dream. She reflects New York's storied past, inspires future waterfronts in New York City, and more. In this part of my life, I had bobbed along and fought the currents just to keep my head above water until I reached the safety of a boat called the *Floating Pool Lady*. I managed with a talented team who came aboard, worked hard, stayed the course, and encouraged me to keep going until a vision had come true. In the process I learned many survival lessons. Some takeaways can be described in few words: have passion and patience, persevere, roll with the punches, stay focused, laugh at absurdities, and—most importantly—follow your dream.

I bid the swimmers goodbye, and as I stood and walked away, I smiled and thought, "Ann, you and the *Lady* are lucky this was an election year!"

Acknowledgments

I WOULD LIKE TO thank the following for helping make this book possible: Team Neptune, without whom the story would not exist; Dorothy Potter Snyder, editora sin par; Ed Vesneske Jr., whose indexing revealed a "floating fool"; Annabelle Buttenwieser, Regina Myer, and Suzanne O' Keefe, for their insightful feedback; Michael Walsh, for endless photographic somersaults and for the Centerfold; Three Hills editor Michael McGandy, who kept my feet to the fire; Cornell University Press acquisitions assistant, the orderly Clare Jones; copyeditor Lori Rider, whose fine-tuning pointed out a zero missing in a footnote; Jennifer Savran Kelly, supportive production editor; and others in the CUP production and marketing departments who brought the book to press.

A Note from the Author

WHEN I WAS WRITING THIS BOOK in the summer of 2020, the COVID-19 pandemic was very much in evidence. The New York City economy and parks system were in a state of flux. The Department of Parks and Recreation needed to provide outdoor activities for as many residents as possible—residents who had been sequestered for months. Funds and lifeguards were available to open portions of beaches and a few large pools where social distancing was possible. It was inefficient for the agency, with its reduced budget, to hire staff for smaller pools where only a limited crowd could be allowed. For the first time in thirteen years the *Floating Pool Lady* did not open.

Notes

PROLOGUE

2   *Yet I was compulsively engaged*: Paraphrased from David Brooks, "Does Decision-Making Matter?" *New York Times*, November 25, 2016, https://www.nytimes.com/2016/11/25/opinion/does-decision-making-matter.html.

3   *We knew from the beginning*: Regina Myer, comment to author, ca. May 2019.

5   *You gotta fight*: Comment to editors from reader Marta Gutman, date unknown.

1. FIRE AND WATER

8   *In the fall of 2001*: The Waterfront Center, a nonprofit educational organization, was formed in 1981 in the belief that waterfronts—where the land meets the ocean, bay, lake, river, or canal—are unique, finite resources. The vital characteristic that separates waterfronts from other areas in a community is the relationship to water. The chief goal of the center is to assist communities and

the professions in making the wisest and best long-term uses of waterfront resources for maximum public benefit. Waterfront Center (website), accessed October 16, 2017, http://www.waterfrontcenter.org/index.html.

8 *Adam was a Greenpoint resident*: Telephone interview of Adam Perlmutter as recalled by author, August 10, 2017.

9 *Lesson learned*: Jane Jacobs, *The Death and Life of Great American Cities* (New York: Vintage Books, 1961), 360–62; Alice Sparberg Alexiou, *Jane Jacobs: Urban Visionary* (New Brunswick: Rutgers University Press, 2006), 55; Anthony Flint, *Wrestling with Moses: How Jane Jacobs Took on New York's Master Builder and Transformed the American City* (New York: Random House, 2011), 84–88; New York Preservation Archive Project, accessed August 9, 2017, http://www.nypap.org/preservation-history/shirley-hayes/.

9 *The layers of bureaucracy*: Jacobs, *Death and Life*, 406.

9 *Their efforts were for naught*: Ibid.

10 *These boards gave*: Gotham Gazette, accessed March 21, 2016, http://www.gothamgazette.com/lessons/boards.shtml.

10 *The boards have strictly*: Official NYC website, accessed July 1, 2016, http://www.nyc.gov/html/cau/html/cb/about.shtml.

11 *Waste fumes were*: Niles Eldredge and Sidney Horenstein, "A Case Study in Pollution: Newtown Creek," in *Concrete Jungle: New York City and Our Last Best Hope for a Sustainable Future* (Oakland: University of California Press, 2014), 165.

11 *Between 1940 and 1950*: Ibid., 167; Peter Andrey Smith, "Liquid Cow and Black Mayo," December 6, 2013, http://nymag.com/news/intelligencer/newtown-creek-2013-12/.

11 *According to*: Newton Creek Alliance (website), accessed November 17, 2018, http://www.newtowncreekalliance.org/greenpoint-oil-spill/; Riverkeeper (website), accessed November 17, 2018, https://www.riverkeeper.org/.

12 *This is what happened*: City Department of Environmental Protection (website), accessed August 11, 2017, http://www.dec.ny.gov/chemical/48595.html.

12 *The defense for*: Ann L. Buttenwieser, *Manhattan Water-Bound: Planning and Developing Manhattan's Waterfront from the Seven-*

teenth Century to the Present (New York: New York University Press, 1987), 103–4.

12   *Sulphur dioxide*: "Air Polluted along East River," *New York Times*, September 1, 1974, http://www.nbrienvis.nic.in/Database/1_2463.aspx.

13   *This goal can be realized*: David N. Dinkins, Mayor, Richard L. Schaffer, Director Department of City Planning, *New York City Comprehensive Waterfront Plan Reclaiming the City's Edge*, 1992, I, 51, 65, https://www1.nyc.gov/assets/planning/download/pdf/about/publications/cwp.pdf.

13   *In 1997*: DOT Grand Ferry Park, NYC Parks, accessed August 11, 2017, https://www.nycgovparks.org/parks/grand-ferry-park/history.

14   *The estuaries around*: Riverkeeper, Spring 2005, https://www.riverkeeper.org/wp-content/uploads/2009/06/RKSpring2005.pdf.

14   *Despite the objective conditions*: NYC Swim (website), accessed August 11, 2017, http://www.nycswim.org/.

15   *Traditionally, the residents*: Jim Yardley, "Garbage In and In . . . and In: Greenpoint Residents Unite to Fight Influx of Trash," *New York Times*, April 4, 1998, http://www.nytimes.com/1998/04/18/nyregion/garbage-in-and-in-and-in-greenpoint-residents-unite-to-fight-influx-of-trash.html.

15   *In 1997 a more diverse*: Community Board 1, Greenpoint 197-a Plan, Spring 2002, https://www1.nyc.gov/assets/planning/download/pdf/community/197a-plans/bk1_greenpoint_197a.pdf; MAS study.

15   *In this 1997 document*: North Brooklyn Neighbors (website), accessed August 14, 2017, http://gwapp.org/about/archive/solid-waste/; http://gwapp.org/about/history/.

15   *When Michael Bloomberg*: "Letter from the Commissioner of Parks and Recreation"; Greenpoint-Williamsburg Open Space Master Plan, undated, iii.

15   *The EDC is*: "Wikipedia: New York City Economic Development Corporation," last updated June 9, 2020, https://en.wikipedia.org/wiki/New_York_City_Economic_Development_Corporation#cite_note-6.

17   *Development of the site itself*: Greenpoint 197A Plan, Recommenda-

tions, 17–18. The WNYC Brooklyn transmitter site was decommissioned in 1990, and the AM transmitter was moved to Belleville Turnpike in Kearny, New Jersey.

17 *Adrian liked the idea*: Author interview with Adrian Benepe, January 2, 2016.

18 *In September 2003 I arranged*: Author's email to Donna Walcavage, September 22, 2003.

19 *He had procured*: David Yassky, in conversation as recalled by author, January 17, 2018.

19 *I immediately sent*: Author's email to Joshua Laird (Director of Planning, New York City Parks Department) and Jeannette Rausch, June 23, 2004.

2. THE EUREKA MOMENT

24 *I knew at this moment*: Ann L. Buttenwieser, *Manhattan Water-Bound: Planning and Developing Manhattan's Waterfront from the Seventeenth Century to the Present* (New York: New York University Press, 1987).

25 *These numbers would*: Official NYC website, accessed July 28, 2017, nyc.gov/html/dcp/html/census/1790_2000_hist_data.shtml; Ira Rosenwaike, *Population History of New York City* (Syracuse: Syracuse University Press, 1972), 63.

26 *In the report*: John H. Griscom, *The Sanitary Condition of the Laboring Population of New York with Suggestions for Its Improvement* (New York: Harper & Brothers, 1845), 5, 3.

26 *In other words*: Association for Improving the Condition of the Poor, *First Report of a Committee on the Sanitary Condition of the Laboring Classes in the City of New-York with Remedial Suggestions* (New York: John Trow, 1853), 101; Kate Holladay Claghorn, "Foreign Immigration and the Tenement House in New York City," in *The Tenement House Problem*, vol. 2, ed. Robert W. Deforest and Lawrence Veiller (New York: Macmillan, 1908), 73–87; Jacob Riis, *The Battle with the Slum* (New York: Macmillan, 1902), 176–82; Ida Van Etten, "Russian Jews as Desirable Immigrants," *Forum* 15

(1893): 172–82, http://tenant.net/Community/LES
/vanetten.html.html.

26 *Once in New York*: Claghorn, "Foreign Immigration," 86.

26 *The sanitarian reformers*: Jacob Riis, *How the Other Half Lives: Stud-
ies among the Tenements of New York* (New York: Dover, 1971), 122–
30; Daniel Eli Burnstein, *Next to Godliness* (Urbana: University of
Illinois Press, 2006), 65, 264, 267–88; Jacob Riis, "The Jews of New
York," *Review of Reviews* 13 (1896): 58–62, http://tenant.net
/Community/LES/jacob4.html.

28 *A policeman accosted*: Riis, *Battle*, 265–67. The park, located between Baxter, Worth, Bayard, and Mulberry Streets, was renamed Columbus Park in 1911.

28 *In 1868*: "Public Baths," *New York Times*, July 12, 1868.

28 *Among the rationalizations*: The Mayor's Committee of New York
City, *Report on Public Baths and Comfort Stations* (1897), 26–27.

29 *But there remained*: Ibid., 27.

29 *It took two more*: Ibid.; Laws of the State of New York, 1868, chapter
879.

29 *If my plan worked*: Joanne Witty and Henrik Krogius, *Brooklyn
Bridge Park: A Dying Waterfront Transformed* (New York: Empire
State Editions/Fordham University Press, 2016), 125.

30 *The openings between*: Metropolitan Sewerage Commission of
New York, "Sewerage and Sewage Disposal in the Metropolitan
District of New York and New Jersey, Report 486" (1910), 486;
"Public Baths under the Supervision of the Borough President of
Manhattan, 1914"; Charles F. Bolduan, "Public Baths in New York
City," *Monthly Bulletin of the Department of Health of the City of New
York* 4, no. 5 (1914): SPI v47:24–27.

31 *To allow their use*: The inhabitants of the apartment are unclear.
Some reports describe a residence for the superintendent and his
family. In the 1800s, as paved streets and electricity reached
waterfront areas, many of the lines to the baths were switched
away from gas.

32 *One might also conjecture*: City of New York, Department of Public
Works (DPW), Annual Reports (1870–1938); City of New York, Office of the Manhattan Borough President (MBP), Annual Reports

(1870–1938); City of New York, Department of Docks (DD), Annual Reports and Correspondence (1870–1938). The correspondence shows that Krack's East River Bathing Company was located at East Third Street from 1874 to 1877; at Grand Street from 1877 to 1888; at East Fifty-First Street in 1881; and at East Twenty-Eighth Street from 1885 to 1888. Frank Hines, "Up-to-Date Floating Baths," *American Physical Education Review* 22, no. 2 (1917): 80.

32 *The city was allowed*: All numbers in parentheses indicate 2020 dollars; DD Correspondence (1870–1935); DPW and MBP Annual Reports (1870–1938).

32 *The DD*: The DPW awarded a construction company in Greenpoint $27,500 ($592,000) to build four new baths. However, there were complaints about the work, and it is unclear if the company completed the job. "The Swimming Baths," *New York Times*, June 25, 1876; DPW Annual Report, 1876.

33 *The construction cost*: Aerial photo of Lower Manhattan, ca. 1922; Brooklyn had three baths built under separate legislation.

33 *Pay for employees*: DPW Annual Report (1884), 8; MBP Annual Report (1902), 56; MBP Annual Report (1898), 67–69. The floating baths were operated under the jurisdiction of DPW until consolidation. Beginning in 1900 the baths were run by each borough. Under Manhattan's borough presidents the baths were first under the jurisdiction of the Office of Commissioner of Public Works, and subsequently of the superintendent of public buildings and offices. The Parks Department under Robert Moses did not take charge of the baths that remained until 1938.

33 *To achieve the public goals*: "Free Baths," *New York Times*, June 24, 1870. In a communication to the common council, the DPW commissioner gave the following list of his recommended locations: on the West Side, near the Battery, Washington Market, Canal Street, Fourteenth Street, Twentieth Street, Thirtieth Street, and Fiftieth Street; on the East Side, near Peck Slip, Catherine Street, Twentieth Street, and Fiftieth Street.

34 *Finally, in 1890*: Opening dates of each pool depended on space availability and heat waves. For example, in a hot early June in

1895, the DPW commissioner opened the free baths a week early. They were often closed early due to insufficient funds to pay the attendants. "Free Baths for the Public," *New York Times*, June 4, 1895. Information on placement of the baths was found in DD Annual Reports; DPW Annual Reports; MBP Annual Reports; and newspaper articles.

34 *Nevertheless, within*: The Brooklyn borough president ran five baths located near the Bridge Street pier (moved to Dock Street) and at Fifty-Second Street, North First Street, Noble Street, and Conover Street. One bath, run by the borough president of the Bronx, was located in Port Morris.

34 *The attendant is sitting*: *Opening of the Free Baths in New York*, June 16, 1883, engraving, in author's collection.

35 *They boarded*: "The Public Baths," *New York Times*, July 4, 1870.

35 *Working-class men*: "The Baths on Sunday," *New York Times*, July 11, 1870.

35 *To improve order*: MBP Annual Report (1910), 130; Stanley Fox, "A Public Bath," *Harper's Weekly*, August 20, 1870, reprinted in John Grafton, *New York in the Nineteenth Century* (New York: Dover, 1877), 94.

35 *One day, Katz wrote*: Norman N. Katz, letter to author, May 23, 1981.

36 *When the pools*: "Costumes at the Public Baths," *New York Times*, June 15, 1889; attendance was 2.1 million in 1888 and 1.7 million in 1889 (DPW Annual Reports 1888 and 1889).

36 *Those who could not*: Marilyn Thornton Williams, *Washing the Great Unwashed: Public Baths in Urban America, 1840–1920* (Columbus: Ohio State University Press, 1991), 136.

36 *Description of attendees*: "Ladies Day at the Baths," *New York Times*, June 29, 1895.

36 *Although the original*: "Free Baths."

37 *Their one-piece*: "Ladies Day at the Baths."

37 *Perhaps a minute*: "Teaching the Girls to Swim: Part of the Public-School Course," photograph, in author's collection. The board of education discontinued its classes in 1905. Yet because the poor lived in a city of water, there was a need to continue to teach

swimming to preserve lives. The US Volunteer Lifesaving Corps stepped in the following year to provide swimming lessons at all of the floating baths.

38 *Other articles provide*: "Where a Modern Paris Might Award the Golden Apple Real Summer Girl Haunts Free Summer Baths—Fat Women and Babies There, Too," *New York Times*, July 17, 1904; "Public Baths."

38 *This hatred resulted*: "Ladies' Day and How the Girls and Children Enjoy the Sport," *New York Times*, August 28, 1872; J.R. Logan, W. Zhang, and M.D. Chunyu, "Emergent Ghettos: Black Neighborhoods in New York and Chicago, 1880–1940," *American Journal of Sociology* 120, no. 4 (January 2013): 1055–94; Gilbert Osofsky, "Race Riot, 1900: A Study of Ethnic Violence," *Journal of Negro Education* 32, no. 1 (1963): 16–24.

39 *The article goes on*: "The East Side in Bathing," *New York Tribune*, July 11, 1897; "How Poor People Bathe: Scenes in the Baths and at the Piers . . . ," *New York Tribune*, August 14, 1881.

39 *Their heads turned*: "The Battery Bath," *New York Daily Herald*, August 14, 1881, 14; Grafton, *New York*.

41 *Patrons who paid*: DD Correspondence (1870–1935); "Opening of the Bathing Season," *New York Times*, June 12, 1874; "Free Baths," *New York Times*, June 28, 1871; "New York's Free Baths," *New York Sun*, October 25, 1878. Over time, the city opened playgrounds and recreation piers that, when they adjoined the existing floating baths, gave residents a variety of facilities to keep them out of trouble—and out of the way—in their free time. In 1902 the borough president of Manhattan placed a floating bath on the East Side at Corlears Hook, adjacent to a city park that opened three years later. A floating bath moored at West Fiftieth Street adjacent to a recreation pier looked like a makeshift image of a seaside resort. Additionally, the city purchased private property upland to create De Witt Clinton Park. Originally a children's playground, by 1906 grass, trees, and an urban garden extended the compound along the West Side waterfront from Fifty-Second to Fifty-Fourth Streets.

41 *One solution*: In 1902, out of the fifteen public baths, two each

were moored at East Third Street, East Twenty-Fourth Street, the Battery, West Twenty-Fifth Street, and West Thirty-Fifth Street.

42 *Ironically, the article*: "Public Baths."

42 *As the sewers*: Riis, *Battle*, 282; Frank Tucker, "Public Baths," in Deforest and Veiller, *Tenement House Problem*, 2:55.

43 *In 1902*: MBP, Annual Report (1902), 12, 68.

3. WATERFRONT IN DESPAIR

45 *After an intensive*: Daniel D. Jackson, *The Merchants Association of New York, Report to the Committee on Pollution*, December 1907.

46 *There was no scientific*: Ibid., 12.

47 *However, there were*: Jeff Wiltze, *Contested Waters: A Social History of Swimming Pools in America* (Chapel Hill: University of North Carolina Press, 2007), 66.

47 *Bath reformers*: City of New York, BOE, "Minutes" (1915), 3348, 3595, 3869, 3989, 3990–99. The minutes do not include breakdowns of the numbers who use tubs, showers or pools. Marilyn Thornton Williams, *Washing the Great Unwashed: Public Baths in Urban America, 1840–1920* (Columbus: Ohio State University Press, 1991), 64.

47 *However, admitting that*: "Influence of the Polluted Waters on Public Health through Bathing, in Sewerage and Sewage Disposal in the Metropolitan District of New York and New Jersey" (1910), Section 111, 486–96; MBP Annual Report (1910), 131; "To the Editor of the New York Times," *New York Times*, May 27, 1911.

47 *A court in England*: Mark Kurlansky, *The Big Oyster History on the Half Shell* (New York: Random House, 2007), 261.

49 *There was still*: New enclosed wood tanks were added to the remaining five pools the following year.

49 *This was an approximate*: MBP Annual Report (1913), 175; "Public Baths in New York City," *Monthly Bulletin of the Department of Health* (1914), 118; Frank V. Hines, "Up-to-Date Floating Baths," *American Physical Education Review* 22, no. 2 (1917): 81–82. The baths in Brooklyn and the Bronx were permanently closed at this time due to lack of space.

50 *It is likely that*: "Wikipedia: Characteristics of New York City Mayoral Elections," last updated June 7, 2020, https://en.wikipedia.org/wiki/Characteristics_of_New_York _City_mayoral_elections.

50 *Despite cries*: The forerunner to the present-day city council, the Board of Estimate and Apportionment was composed of eight ex-officio members: the mayor of New York City, the New York City comptroller, and the president of the New York City Council—each of whom was elected citywide and had two votes—and the five borough presidents, each having one vote. "Oust Controller, Cry Children: Opposition to Floating Baths Stirs 300 at Board of Estimate," *New York Tribune*, May 29, 1915.

51 *All new or renovated*: Landmarks Preservation Commission, "First Houses" Landmark Designation, November 12, 1974, 5.

52 *In the fall of 1935*: "Public Baths Here Will Be Renovated: City Expects to Get $1,500,000" *New York Times*, September 1, 1935.

52 *By Labor Day*: Hillary Ballon and Kenneth T. Jackson, *Robert Moses and the Modern City: The Transformation of New York* (New York: W. W. Norton, 2007), 135.

53 *A letter to me*: Letter from Robert Moses to author, September 15, 1980; "Journal of the Proceedings of the Board of Estimate of the City of New York," 1936, 1938.

53 *Fearing that pieces*: Letter from Harold Libby, Principal Engineer, War Department, New York District, to Hon. John McKenzie, Commissioner of Docks, City of New York, May 27, 1942.

54 *The public has been*: Ann L. Buttenwieser, *Manhattan Water-Bound* (New York: New York University Press, 1987), 203.

54 *In view of the riots*: Lindsay often visited Harlem and was credited with averting riots after the assassination of Martin Luther King, Jr.

54 *In addition*: "Whatever Happened to Rochester's Swimmobiles," June 30, 2018, https://www.democratandchronicle.com/story /news/local/rocroots/places/2018/06/30/whatever-happened-rochesters-swimmobile/747281002/; "The Swimmobiles That Cooled Off a Hot City," *Ephemeral New York* (blog), accessed

November 17, 2018, https://ephemeralnewyork.wordpress.
com/2014/06/05/the-swimmobiles-that-cooled-off-a-hot-city/.

55 *Access to the river*: Susan Saunders, "Lower East Side, Early '70s,"
http://2.bp.blogspot.com/-dRWSERT_OSw/VPAHisy2CKI
/AAAAAAABT_U/fL6E67KiTSc/s1600
/New%2BYork%2BCity%2Bin%2Bthe%2B1970s%2B(21).jpg.

55 *Shelley Seccombe's*: Shelley Seccombe, *Lost Waterfront: The Decline
and Rebirth of Manhattan's Western Shore* (New York: Fordham
University Press, 2007), 11.

55 *On January 18*: Buttenwieser, *Manhattan Water-Bound*, 204–6.

56 *In it, I asked*: Ann L. Buttenwieser, "Floating an Old Idea," *New
York Times*, May 23, 1981; DD Correspondence (1870–1935); DPW
and MBP Annual Reports (1870–1938).

56 *I had just secured*: Governor Mario Cuomo and Mayor Edward
Koch formed this group after the failure of Westway to recommend scenarios for the future of the West Side Highway.

56 *That decade's events*: Thomas J. Lueck, "New York Port Changes
with Shifting Economy," *New York Times*, June 1, 1986. https://
www.nytimes.com/1986/06/01/nyregion
/new-york-port-changes-with-shifting-economy.html.

56 *As I wrote*: Ann L. Buttenwieser, *Manhattan Water-Bound*, 2nd ed.
(Syracuse: Syracuse University Press, 1987), 207.

57 *But the nineteenth-century*: Phillip Lopate, "Her New York," *New
York Times*, November 7, 2008, www.nytimes.com/2008/11/09
/nyregion/thecity/09huxt.html.

58 *This was the synchrony*: Bargemusic (website), http://www.
bargemusic.org/about.html; Daniel J. Walkin, "Olga Bloom, Violinist, and Violist Who Created Bargemusic, Dies at 92," *New York
Times*, November 25, 2011, http://www.nytimes.com/2011/11/26/
arts/music/olga-bloom-violinist-and-violist-who-created-barge-
music-dies-at-92.html.

58 *The barge sits*: Buttenwieser, *Manhattan Water-Bound*, 2nd ed., 238;
Bryan Miller, "View from the River Café: 40 Years of Feasts and
Firsts," *New York Times*, July 31, 2017, https://www.nytimes.com
/2017/07/31/dining/the-river-cafe-brooklyn.html.

58 *A spate of high-handed*: Buttenwieser, *Manhattan Water-Bound*, 2nd ed., 205.

59 *Developers submitted*: Ibid., 225–36, 250.

59 *It would be*: Ibid., 206; Timothy L. O'Brien, "How Trump Bungled the Deal of a Lifetime," January 27, 2016, https://www. bloomberg.com /opinion/articles/2016-01-27/donald-trump-s-track-record-on-deals. Television City died in a recession, a fight with Mayor Koch over abatement, and community opposition. In 1994 a group of Hong Kong investors purchased and then developed the site with input from the community. It is known as Riverside South.

60 *Local community boards*: William W. Buzbee, *Fighting Westway: Environmental Law, Citizen Activism, and the Regulatory War That Transformed New York City* (Ithaca: Cornell University Press, 2014), 1. See also Buzbee's introduction, 1–4; Buttenwieser, *Manhattan Water-Bound*, 2nd ed., 209–19; Robert Hanley, "Transitway to Follow the Hudson," *New York Times*, October 29, 1986, http://www.nytimes.com/1986/10/29/nyregion/ transitway-to-follow-the-hudson.html; Buttenwieser, *Manhattan Water-Bound*, 213–14.

61 *I had also brought*: Buttenwieser, *Manhattan Water-Bound*, 2nd ed., 220–22; Rem Koolhaus, *delirious new york* (New York: Monacelli Press, 1994), 307–10.

61 *But that formidable*: Buttenwieser, *Manhattan Water-Bound*, 2nd ed., 214; Buzbee, *Fighting Westway*, 2.

62 *Their causes*: *Protection of Waters Program*, Article 15, Environmental Conservation Law Implementing Regulations 6NYCRR Part 608.

62 *As described by*: Buzbee, *Fighting Westway*, 81.

62 *On the basis*: Ibid., 201.

62 *So, in September*: Buttenwieser, *Manhattan Water-Bound*, 2nd ed., 219–25.

63 *Having changed little*: NYC Population Census, accessed July 25, 2018, https://www1.nyc.gov/assets/planning/download/pdf /data-maps/nyc-population/census2000/nyc20001.pdf.

63 *With spaces and*: Nina S. Roberts and T. Rao, "The Modern Urban

Park: Access and Programming: Where Have We Been, Where
Shall We Go?" (Unpublished manuscript, San Francisco State
University, 2014), 5, http://userwww.sfsu.edu/nroberts/
documents/UrbanParksWhitePaper_Roberts_032514.pdf; City of
Fort Collins Parks and Recreation, "Environmental Best Management Practices Manual 2011," 41, https://www.fcgov.com/parks/
pdf/bmp.pdf.

64 *Transforming the Battery*: Warrie Price, correspondence with author, May 14, 2019.

4. HOBOKEN HO

66 *I met Michael*: The Waterfront Center was the first nonprofit organization to look at waterfronts from the community's perspective.

66 *In 1986*: Robert Hanley, "Transitway to Follow the Hudson," *New
York Times*, October 29, 1986, http://www.nytimes.com
/1986/10/29/nyregion/transitway-to-follow-the-hudson.html.

67 *"You were a godsend"*: Jonathan Kirschenfeld, interview with author, February 23, 2018.

67 *"I remember"*: Ibid. Jonathan Kirschenfeld, AIA, is the founder of
Jonathan Kirschenfeld Architect PC. He has been in private practice in this firm since 1998. He has been internationally recognized for design excellence on his socially sustainable projects,
such as day care centers and supportive housing for tenants who
had been homeless. In 2017 he and his firm were recognized as a
Social Design Circle Honoree by the prestigious Curry Stone
Prize. Kirschenfeld is the founder of the Institute for Public Architecture (IPA), a not-for-profit organization that promotes socially engaged architecture through research, exhibitions, and a
residency program for young design practitioners. "About the
Firm," accessed February 21, 2020, http://kirscharch.com
/about/.

68 *Jonathan immediately*: Others involved in these early meetings
were Linette Widder (architect and floating pool researcher),
Richard Amper (publicity), Joe Tortorella (professional engineer

and principal in firm of Robert Sillman Associates Structural Engineers), Johann Mordhorst (Jonathan Kirschenfeld Architects), and David Plotkin (marine engineer at Steelstyle).

68   *One of our first*: James Sanders and Associates, American Leisure Corporation, and Sidney Johnson and Associates, "Floating Recreation Center" (presentation, February 1987). The Parks Council was the forerunner to New Yorkers for Parks.

70   *And then his professional*: Jonathan Kirschenfeld interview.

72   *A floating pool*: Joshua Laird, discussion on city pools, prior to the meeting, 1998.

73   *One might assume*: In 1902 the Hoboken bath served 45,000 bathers, compared to an average of 130,000 men and women per bath in Manhattan.

73   *In the 1950s*: Hoboken History, accessed June 11, 2019, https://www.thirteen.org/hoboken/history_post.html.

73   *Meanwhile, local*: Stuart James, "Living High in Hoboken," *New Jersey Monthly* 1, no. 10 (August 1977): 38–45; Amy Taubin, "Delivered Vacant," *Village Voice*, June 1, 1993, 56; Vincent Canby, "Recording Eight Years of Change in Hoboken," *New York Times*, October 10, 1992; *Delivered Vacant*, directed by Nora Jacobson (1993; Nora Jacobson/Island Pictures).

74   *Speculators bought*: Hoboken Historical Museum, accessed October 16, 2007, https://www.hobokenmuseum.org/explore-hoboken/historic-highlights/hoboken-in-wwi/; Christine A. Ziegler, *Immigrants in Hoboken: One Way Ticket, 1845–1985* (Charleston: History Press, 2011), 125.

74   *That year, Congress*: "Hoboken, New Jersey," Wikipedia, accessed February 13, 2020, https://en.wikipedia.org/wiki/Hoboken,_New_Jersey#Post-World_War_II.

75   *He also helped*: Michael Krieger, email to author, April 20, 2016.

75   *In 1982*: Tom Jackman, "Hoboken: The Tide May Be Turning," *New York Times*, July 10, 1983.

75   *Not until 1984*: Edward A. Gargan, "Koch and Cuomo Agree on Waterfront Proposals," *New York Times*, November 19, 1983, https://www.nytimes.com/1983/11/19/nyregion/koch-and-cuomo-agree-on-waterfront-proposals.html; Josh Barbanel, "Assem-

bly Passes Waterfront Projects in Queens and Hoboken," *New York Times*, June 27, 1984; Robert Hanley, "Transitway to Follow the Hudson," *New York Times*, October 29, 1986, http://www.nytimes.com/1986/10/29/nyregion/transitway-to-follow-the-hudson.html.

76 *In the early 1990s*: This group became a nonprofit and changed its name to Fund for a Better Waterfront.

76 *Hoping to get*: Cassandra Wilday, telephone interview as recalled by author, October 30, 2017.

77 *A sign that*: Carter Craft, email to author, October 29, 1999; Jack Silbert, "On the (Better) Waterfront," *hMag*, May 12, 2014; Jay Romano, "How a 'Bunch of Amateurs' Learned to Fight City Hall," *New York Times*, March 29, 1992.

78 *Michael also told*: As noted in author's diary, March 2000.

79 *The meeting went well*: From L. Michael Krieger, Esq., to John M. Carbone, Esq., memorandum draft, "Opportunity to Locate a Floating Pool on Hoboken's Waterfront," April 6, 2000.

79 *Straightening myself up*: As noted in author's diary, March 2000.

82 *He proceeded*: Dean Marchetto and Associates, presentation to author, "Preliminary Pier C Development Plan," 2000.

82 *As I left*: Timothy Calligy, letter to author, August 3, 2000.

84 *They figured*: Neptune Foundation, Inc., Floating Pools Project Financial Projections 2001–2006.

85 *As Merrill recalled*: Jonathan Kirschenfeld, paraphrased response to questions posed by author, February 23, 2018; Kent Merrill, edited response to questions posed by author, December 22, 2017. The team's adjuncts were Robert Sillman Associates (structural engineers), Joel Trace, AIA (swimming pool consultant), Tillett Lighting (lighting consultants), and Truax and Company (translucent murals).

85 *After review*: Anthony Russo, letter to author, September 25, 2000.

86 *The agreement*: Mission Statement, meeting with the City of Hoboken, October 18, 2000.

86 *Now I could*: Certificate of Incorporation of the Neptune Foundation, §402, Not-For-Profit Corporation Law 3.I.a, November 6, 2000.

86   *To promote*: Ibid.

87   *That evening*: David Danzig, "Floating Municipal Pool on Tap,"
     Hoboken Reporter, December 10, 2000.

87   *Paraphrasing some*: Ibid.

88   *She reported*: Joyce Wadler, "Across the Hudson, a Dream Drops
     Anchor," *New York Times*, December 14, 2000.

5. FINDING THE *C500*

90   *On April 9*: Meeting minutes as recorded in author's notebook,
     April 9, 2001.

90   *In addition*: Michael continued practicing law first on his own,
     and since 2004 as counsel for Dunn Lambert LLC, in Paramus,
     New Jersey, and New York City. He continues to speak both do-
     mestically and internationally on balanced waterfront develop-
     ment worldwide, including quality public access.

91   *I wondered*: Jonathan Kirschenfeld, email to author, June 17,
     2002.

92   *I had expended*: Thanks to Michael Krieger for helping me under-
     stand that my work, though commendable, would inevitably
     meet resistance.

92   *Together*: Jonathan Kirschenfeld Architect, PC (website), accessed
     December 12, 2017, http://www.kirscharch.com/about.

93   *Then I recalled*: "Today, NY4P is the citywide independent organi-
     zation championing quality parks and open spaces for all New
     Yorkers in all neighborhoods." Offshoot of the Parks Council, ac-
     cessed November 18, 2017, http://www.ny4p.org/about.

94   *In my case*: The pro forma showed $1,931,500 for the first pool lo-
     cated in Hoboken, New Jersey.

94   *A "naming" was*: The Neptune Foundation, Inc. Naming opportu-
     nities: barge, $2,000,000; pool, $500,000; children's spray pool,
     $100,000; decorative curved bench (surrounding spray pool),
     $25,000; pool lights, $25,000; pavers (four sets), $50,000/set; in-
     dividual benches (20), $5,000/bench.

95   *At Reebok*: Edward Meyer, conversation as recalled by author, No-
     vember 20, 2017; Jarod Moses, email to author, April 9, 2001.

96　*I enclosed*: Author's letter to David Rockefeller Sr., January 20, 2002.

96　*Still waiting*: Letter to author from the Executor of the Estate of Edith K. Ehrman regarding the Estate of Edith K. Ehrman, January 17, 2002.

96　*My Parks Department*: Riverside South Park; Riverside Park; 125th Street/Harlem Piers; Harlem River Park; East River Piers 42 or 36; Tiffany Street Pier, Bronx; Gantry State Park, Queens; Fort Totten/Bayside Marina, Queens; India/Java Street, Brooklyn; Pier 1 Brooklyn; Louis Valentino Park, Brooklyn. In conducting my search, I ruled out sites that had nearby pools, problems with water depth or river width, possible negative community reaction, or no access for a needy community.

97　*The demise of Westway*: Chapter 592S, 7845 Hudson River Park Act.

97　*In Brooklyn*: The official name is WNYC Transmitter Park.

98　*Although many people*: Meeting with Emily Lloyd as recalled by author, February 20, 2002.

98　*Lane had more*: Meeting with Terry Lane as recalled by author, March 5, 2002.

98　*For Jeannette*: Conversation with Jeannette Rausch as recalled by author, March 2002.

99　*National historic resources*: Meeting with Connie Fishman as recalled by author, October 24, 2002.

99　*He handed me*: "Construction of a Floating Pool at the WNYC Transmitter Site in Green Point," *Price List 2003*, September 22, 2003.

100　*In the McLaren*: Greenpoint–Williamsburg Waterfront Open Space Plan, 8.

100　*With newly elected*: Elizabeth Hawes, "What's New York the Capital of Now? Public Space; The Waterfront: 2004," *New York Times Magazine*, November 20, 1994, https://www.nytimes.com /1994/11/20/magazine/whats-new-york-the-capital-of-now-public-space-the-waterfront-2004.html.

100　*Its principal*: "History," New York Harbor School, accessed February 13, 2020, https://newyorkharborschool.org/history.html.

100　*In Manhattan's*: "Meet the River Project," River Project, accessed

February 13, 2020, https://river-project.squarespace.com/what-we-do.

100 *Brooklyn's Community Board 1*: The City of New York, planyc, a greener, greater new york, 2011, http://www.nyc.gov/html /planyc/downloads/pdf/publications/planyc_2011_planyc_full_ report.pdf.

102 *Believing, as my father*: In 1992, three years after the *Exxon Valdez* oil spill, the International Convention for the Prevention of Pollution from Ships, called the MARPOL Convention, was amended to require all newly built tankers to have double hulls. A double hull is a ship hull design and construction method whereby the bottom and sides of a ship have two complete layers of watertight hull surface: one outer layer forming the normal hull of the ship, and a second inner hull that is some distance inboard, typically by a few feet, forming a redundant barrier to seawater in case the outer hull is damaged and leaks. The space between the two hulls may be used for storage of ballast water.
"Wikipedia: Double-Hull," last updated May 29, 2020, https:// en.wikipedia.org/wiki/Double_hull; "Wikipedia: Double-Hulled Tanker," last updated April 22, 2020, https://en.wikipedia.org /wiki/Double-hulled_tanker.

102 *Roberts twisted*: Author's letter to Mayor David Roberts, March 5, 2004; Maria Zingaro Conte, "Hoboken Plans Two Temporary Pools," *Jersey Journal*, March 8, 2004.

102 *This would give*: Kent Merrill, memorandum to Jonathan Kirschenfeld on project status, February 19, 2004. Meetings with the two lowest bidders, Signal International and Senesco Marine, did not result in lowering the price significantly. Cushing team: Kent Merrill and Ron Williamson.

102 *It would also give*: Ann L. Buttenwieser, *Governors Island: The Jewel of New York Harbor* (Syracuse: Syracuse University Press, 2009).

103 *Waves and swells*: Michael R. Bloomberg and Emily Lloyd, *2005 New York Harbor Water Quality Report*, 24.

103 *The third and major*: Stolt Offshore, Inc., Proposal to the Neptune Foundation, Inc., Floating Swimming Pool Project, April 4, 2004; author's email to Jonathan Kirschenfeld, June 13, 2004.

103 *Kent was searching*: Kent Merrill, responses to questions from author, December 22, 2017.

104 *The other, bearing*: Kent Merrill, email to author, June 21, 2004.

104 *According to Kent*: Ibid.

104 *Four days later*: De Enrique Esparragoza para Tapia Linares y Alfaro, July 22, 2004; Kent Merrill, emails to author, July 14 to July 19, 2004; Ann L. Buttenwieser, emails to Kent Merrill, June 19 to July 15, 2004; Kent Merrill, letter to Don Maggio (broker offering the barge), July 14, 2004.

105 *However, as were*: Kent Merrill, email to author, July 9, 2004.

106 *The extent*: Emails between Kent Merrill and Svein Christoffersen, July 21 and 22, 2004.

106 *Along with the*: Steven Crainer, email to Kent Merrill and Ann L. Buttenwieser, July 26, 2004. Seller accepted the following wording: "#13. Name of Vessel: Seller acknowledges and agrees to transfer, relinquish and grant to Purchaser all of its right, title and interest in and to the name of the Vessel, the C-500, upon the purchase of the Vessel by Purchaser under this Agreement."

107 *I opted*: Kent Merrill, email to Steven Crainer and Ann L. Buttenwieser, July 26, 2004.

107 *"Various types"*: Kent Merrill, email to Steven Crainer and Ann L. Buttenwieser, July 9, 2004; author's email to John Keenan, October 5, 2004; Kent Merrill, email to John Keenan, December 23, 2004.

107 *In the 1990s*: The Metropolitan Waterfront Alliance is described in chapter 3.

107 *In that role*: Carter Craft, interview with author, April 24, 2016.

108 *Unfamiliar with Labor Day*: Author's email to Steven Crainer, September 3, 2004.

109 *An hour later*: Author's email to Steven Crainer, September 13, 2004; Steven Crainer, email to Kent Merrill and Ann L. Buttenwieser, September 13, 2004; Kent Merrill, email to Steven Crainer and Ann L. Buttenwieser, September 13, 2004; Enrique Esparragoza, email to Steven Crainer, September 13, 2004.

6. CONTRACTS AND CRAWFISH

112 *I took a deep breath*: Author's meeting notes, September 13, 2004; author's emails to Steven Crainer, Kent Merrill, and Jonathan Kirschenfeld, September 13, 2004.

112 *A month past*: Kent Merrill, email to Steven Crainer and Ann L. Buttenwieser, January 25, 2005.

113 *The Erie Basin*: Carter Craft, email to author, January 18, 2006.

113 *There would be*: Author's email to Steven Sivak, Steven Crainer, Jonathan Kirschenfeld, and Kent Merrill, October 21, 2004; vendor contracts in author's files; Steven Sivak, interview with author, April 2, 2018.

115 *The facility*: Hilary Ballon and Kenneth T. Jackson, eds., *Robert Moses and the Modern City: The Transformation of New York* (New York: W. W. Norton, 2007), 148.

115 *Allegedly*: Ibid., 149.

116 *Without local support*: Mayor Michael Bloomberg and parks commissioner Adrian Benepe broke ground for the pool's renovation on December 7, 2009, and it reopened three years later. Aaron Short, "The Politics of McCarren Park Pool," *The Awl*, July 9, 2012, https://www.nycgovparks.org/parks/mccarren-park /dailyplant/23037.

116 *Only three people*: NYC EDC Planning Workshop Meeting Minutes, January 5, 2005; Donna Walcavage, email to author, January 10, 2005.

117 *We needed to prove*: New York State Department of Environmental Conservation, 40 CFR 230.10(a): "A permit cannot be issued if a practicable alternative exists that would have less adverse impact on the aquatic ecosystem known as the Least Environmentally Damaging Practicable Alternative."

118 *Ultimately, and thankfully*: Author's notes from meeting with Steve Zahn, Paul Ersboll, Mike Feller, and Jonathan Kirschenfeld, January 12, 2005.

118 *Enter the*: United States Environmental Protection Agency (website), Army Rivers and Harbors Act of 1899, Section 404/Section

10. "The law applies to any . . . excavation . . . or any other modification of a navigable water of the United States. A 404 Permit is required prior to the commencement of construction," accessed July 2, 2020, https://www.epa.gov/cwa-404 /section-10-rivers-and-harbors-appropriation-act-1899.

119 *Steve Crainer*: Floating Swimming Pool graphical comparison of barge types (including outfitting), May 11, 2004.

119 *When Keenan explained*: John Keenan, email to Steven Crainer and Kent Merrill, March 10, 2005.

119 *That was some*: Pool Meeting agenda, December 2, 2004.

120 *"You can count"*: Letter from Peter L. Buttenwieser to author, November 16, 2004.

122 *The words of*: Adrian Benepe, in response to interview question, January 2, 2005; Joyce Purnick, "Maybe a Wish Holds Water, After All," *New York Times*, March 14, 2005, https://www.nytimes.com/2005/03/14/nyregion /maybe-a-wish-holds-water-after-all.html.

122 *We not only had*: Kent Merrill to Jonathan Kirschenfeld, Steven Crainer, and Ann L. Buttenwieser, April 8, 2005.

123 *The Walcavage designs*: Landscape architect Donna Walcavage led the community meetings in Brooklyn at which I introduced the concept of a floating pool for Transmitter Park in January 2005. She worked with local residents and architects from XYZ to design an open-space master plan and ultimately to construct a pier and small waterside park that did not include a floating pool. Transmitter Park opened in 2012. Kent Merrill, email to author, December 17, 2004.

123 *This public entity*: The BB Park Corporation is a subsidiary of the ESDC. In a 2002 memorandum, the city and state outlined a shared commitment to construct the park. The development corporation has its own board with members appointed by the state and the city. Information on the history of Brooklyn Bridge Park has been derived from the following sources: Joanne Witty and Henrik Krogius, *Brooklyn Bridge Park: A Dying Waterfront Transformed* (New York: Fordham University Press, 2016); Nancy Web-

ster and David Shirley, *A History of Brooklyn Bridge Park: How a Community Reclaimed and Transformed New York City's Waterfront* (New York: Columbia University Press, 2016).

125 *Over the phone*: Justin Murphy, in conversation as recalled by author, late 1980s.

126 *On May 27*: Corey Phelps, email to Kent Merrill, May 5, 2005.

127 *According to Kent*: Kent Merrill, email to Jonathan Kirschenfeld, Steven Crainer, Steve Sivak, Stefan Danicich, and Ann L. Buttenwieser, September 26, 2005.

127 *Despite a large*: Kent Merrill, email to Steven Sivak, Jonathan Kirschenfeld, Steven Crainer, and Ann L. Buttenwieser, October 11, 2005.

127 *On January 17*: Author's email to board members Robert Douglass, Steven Crainer, Carl Weisbrod, and Kent Barwick, January 17, 2006.

127 *It was to be*: Gary Rivlin, "Wooing Workers for New Orleans," *New York Times*, November 11, 2005.

128 *The mayor*: Author's email to Jonathan Kirschenfeld, Kent Merrill, Steven Sivak, and Steven Crainer, January 1, 2006; author's email to Boysie Bollinger, January 12, 2006.

128 *Even though*: In author's interview on February 23, 2018, Jonathan Kirschenfeld admitted that even with the help of the Cushing naval architects, they were out of their depth in regard to shipyard techniques and costs, but in the end this challenge did not delay the project at the yard.

129 *Naively*: Boysie Bollinger, email to author, February 15, 2006.

129 *Scan Amelia*: Morgan City and Amelia are only a few miles apart. Bollinger has repair and conversion facilities at both locations. In Neptune's case, the Morgan City office handled contracts and bills, and the conversion took place in open yards and bayous in Amelia.

130 *"Here, anywhere"*: Opening interview, *Just Add Water: The Story of the Floating Pool Lady*, DC Productions, 2008.

132 *But that was the least*: Author's email to Jonathan Kirschenfeld, Malcolm McLaren, and Steven Crainer, March 1, 2006; Joshua Laird, email to author, March 5, 2006.

133 *A report from*: Memorandum from Kent Merrill to Ann L. Buttenwieser and all interested parties, May 24, 2006.

133 *Since this kind*: As noted in author's diary, June 2006.

134 *In my most*: *Brazil* Trailer (1985), https://www.youtube.com/watch?v=4Wh2b1eZFUM.

134 *I was stunned*: Steven Crainer, email to Ann L. Buttenwieser and John Keenan, October 18, 2006. "You will recall that John and I spoke with you about the CGL insurance ('commercial general liability insurance') earlier this week. CGL is an 'umbrella' liability policy that covers liability that occurs onsite or offsite and is required by BBPDC/ESDC in an amount of $5,000,000. . . . The Foundation does need to obtain this policy. The second type of insurance that John mentioned in his email is commercial property insurance, which would cover items that we place onsite (but not on the barge), e.g., equipment storage. BBPDC will not waive the CGL insurance. I am not certain whether they will waive the commercial property insurance."

134 *For now, we*: Email from Jaimee Schwartz to Steven Crainer, September 20, 2006.

135 *"It is unfortunate"*: Adrian Benepe, email to Ann L. Buttenwieser and Joshua Laird, September 29, 2006.

136 *Neptune did not*: Author's letter to Naresh Kapadia, October 24, 2006.

136 *Meanwhile, to the chagrin*: Jonathan Senderstrom, "Swimming Pool Soon May Float near You," *Daily News*, October 2006; Bill Sanderson, "Floating Pool Will Barge In," *New York Post*, October 2006.

136 *My barge*: Eric Dreijer, emails to Ann L. Buttenwieser and Kent Merrill, October 20–30, 2006.

137 *"He still needs"*: Jaimee Schwartz, email to author, October 26, 2006.

137 *Miller's would do*: Kent Merrill, email to author, October 30, 2006; author's emails to the Neptune team, October 30, 2006.

137 *"Please note"*: Jaimee Schwartz, email to author, October 30, 2006.

7. KAFKA ON THE PIER

140 *It was a completely unexpected*: Jonathan Kirschenfeld, interview with author, February 23, 2018.

140 *Under the Brooklyn Bridge*: The *New York Times* published a long, laudatory article by James Barron complete with a photograph by Tyler Hicks. James Barron, "Two More Ladies in the Harbor, a Floating Pool and the Woman Who Had the Idea for It," *New York Times*, October 31, 2006.

141 *At 9:22 p.m.*: Author's email to Robert Douglass, Steven Crainer, Carl Weisbrod, and Kent Barwick, October 30, 2006.

141 *Several months before*: He provided Neptune with public relations services, including TV and radio interviews, at a very much reduced cost until the pool opened in July 2007.

141 *When I awoke*: Barron, "Two More."

141 *We had the approval*: Nazim Nasroodin, email from to John Keenan and Jaimee Schwartz, 5:24 p.m., November 1, 2006; Naresh Kapadia, email to author, BPPS at Web Brooker, Jim Hetherman at DMJM Harris, and Jaimee Schwartz, 5:53 p.m., November 1, 2006.

142 *In speaking with Wendy*: Telephone conversation with Wendy Laventer as recalled by author, November 2, 2006.

142 *But luck was not*: In Kafka's parable "A Message from the Emperor," the protagonist tries hard but never delivers the emperor's important message. See Franz Kafka, *The Metamorphosis and Other Stories*, trans. Willa and Edwin Muir (New York: Schocken Books, 1975), 158. "You hope and work towards success amidst impossible and hopeless odds." From Joe Fassler's interview with Ben Marcus, "What It Really Means to Be 'Kafkaesque,'" *Atlantic*, January 15, 2014, http://www.theatlantic.com/entertainment /archive/2014/01/what-it-really-means-to-be-kafkaesque /283096/.

142 *The barge waited*: Miller's Launch invoice #6608, October 31, 2006. Yokohama is the name of the company that first developed these large, cylindrical, rubberized tubes, also known as pneu-

matic fenders. They are attached to the sides of vessels to protect them during towing or to piers for short-term berthing.

143 *Captain Pat*: Kent Merrill, email to John Keenan, Jonathan Kirschenfeld, Steven Crainer, Steven Sivak, and Ann L. Buttenwieser, November 9, 2006.

143 *The propellers*: Patrick McGeehan, "*Intrepid's* Move Ends Mired in Failure (and Mud)," *New York Times*, November 7, 2006.

144 *Begun in 1876*: "The Floating Hospital: A New York City Romance at Sea 2014–2020," accessed February 3, 2020, https://thefloatinghospital.tumblr.com/.

144 *Around the time*: "Bathing: Hazardous or Healthy?" in "The Floating Hospital: A New York City Romance at Sea."

144 *He appealed to*: "1,601,933 Cared for on Hospital Ships," *New York Times*, June 11, 1916, mentioned in "Wikipedia: Floating Hospital," last modified September 30, 2019, https://en.wikipedia.org /wiki/Floating_Hospital.

144 *The rule*: Email from author to Sven van Batavia, November 10, 2006.

144 *Carter Craft*: "Hero of the Harbor" is a term used by the Metropolitan Waterfront Alliance for its annual fundraising event.

145 *"It was very nice"*: Carter Craft, email from author to Glen Miller and Sven van Batavia, November 10, 2006.

145 *Then Glen Miller*: Email from author to Sven van Batavia, November 10, 2006.

145 *Two teams*: DMJM Harris and Webb-Broker.

145 *"Team"*: Steven Sivak, email to Kent Merrill, Ann L. Buttenwieser, C. Sedita, and Jonathan Kirschenfeld, September 11, 2006.

146 *In those attacks*: "Wikipedia: Casualties of the September 11 Attacks," last modified June 14, 2020, https://en.wikipedia.org /wiki/Casualties_of_the_September_11_attacks.

147 *The Coast Guard came*: List from 2011 PortSide exhibit "Mariners Response to 9/11," PortSide New York, accessed February 10, 2020, https://portsidenewyork.org/911-maritime-response/.

147 *After a month's wait*: Kent Merrill, email to author, December 7, 2006.

148 *Standing in for*: Mizzi is now president/COO of Sciame and treasurer and board member of Friends of + POOL.

149 *The reason was*: US Department of Labor, accessed February 9, 2007, https://webapps.dol.gov/elaws/elg/longshor.htm#who.

150 *On December 5*: "Bump in the Night" was the subject line on emails from Kent Merrill that described the incident.

150 *But it was a no-go*: John Fahlbusch, "The Floating Pool Lady," *Mooring Inspection*, December 10, 2006.

150 *Missing were costlier*: Ibid.

152 *Missing were*: Memo from Kent Merrill to author, Subject: Floating Swimming Pool—Status of BBP Issues, December 18, 2006.

152 *As the instigator*: Steven Crainer, email to author, December 15, 2006.

8. PERSPECTIVE MATTERS

155 *Boysie Bollinger: Just Add Water*, YouTube, Doug Cabot, director, 2008, https://www.youtube.com/watch?v=npqcFWQfVy0.

155 *Commissioner Adrian Benepe*: Adrian Benepe, interview as recalled by author, January 2, 1916.

157 *For him the aesthetics*: Cabot, *Just Add Water*.

158 *The intent*: *New York City's Waterfront: A Plan for Development*, Report to the Mayor by the New York City Public Development Corporation.

158 *The battle that ensued*: Joanne Witty and Henrik Krogius, *Brooklyn Bridge Park: A Dying Waterfront Transformed* (New York: Empire State Editions/Fordham University Press, 2016); Nancy Webster and David Shirley, *A History of Brooklyn Bridge Park: How a Community Reclaimed and Transformed New York City's Waterfront* (New York: Columbia University Press, 2015).

159 *Here on forty-five acres*: Carr Lynch Hack and Sandell, untitled study of alternative scenarios for Brooklyn piers, 1990.

159 *Without mentioning*: City of New York Department of Planning, *Comprehensive Waterfront Plan, Reclaiming the City's Edge*, 70.

159 *While the UDC*: Webster and Shirley, *History*, 149; Meeting minutes, Floating Pool Anchorage, March 6, 2007.

160 *Frustrated by the inaction*: Webster and Shirley, *History*, 130.

160 *Two years later*: "Port Authority Agrees to Let Piers Be Used for Brooklyn Bridge Park," *New York Times*, February 11, 2000.

161 *By 2007*: David Yassky (former Brooklyn city council member, now a professor at Pace Law School), telephone conversation with author, January 17, 2018. Discretionary funds, also known as member items, are granted to council members to support local not-for-profit organizations. Yassky received $500,000, the full amount allowable at the time. The funds were transferred to the Brooklyn Bridge Park Conservancy to pay for connections to land-based water, electric, and waste outlets.

161 *Three years earlier*: Webster and Shirley, *History*, 149.

162 *Unstated, but known*: Comment from reviewer Marta Gutman, ca. May 2019.

162 *For me, the meeting*: Yogi Berra Museum (website), accessed April 4, 2017, https://yogiberramuseum.org/just-for-fun/yogisms/.

162 *Keeping to*: "Adverse impact on the aquatic ecosystem, and riverbed below," Clean Water Act, §40 CFR 230.10a (1977).

162 *But they hoped*: Floating Pool Anchorage minutes, March 6, 2007.

163 *Commissioner Benepe and Mayor Bloomberg*: As told to author by Joshua Laird, March 6, 2007.

163 *Nonetheless, Joshua*: Floating Pool Anchorage minutes, 2007; water dependency is discussed in chapters 4 and 5.

164 *In 2002*: Eric Goldstein, "The Elections and New York's Environment," *Gotham Gazette*, November 1, 2002, https://www.gothamgazette.com/environment/1510-the-elections-and-new-yorks-environment; New York City Community Garden Coalition, "Where We Stand and How We Got Here," https://nyccgc.org/about/history/.

165 *She had hoped*: Floating Pool Anchorage minutes, 2007.

166 *Would he also*: Draft letter to Hon. Dan Doctoroff from author, undated. Marianna Koval also spoke to her classmate, Spitzer.

167 *To my surprise*: I did not know this until I conducted interviews for this book. Jennifer Rimmer, interview as recalled by author, May 25, 2016; Patrick Foye, interview as recalled by author, April 21, 2016.

167 *The BB Park Corporation*: Jennifer Rimmer's projects included enlargement of the Convention Center, a park on Governors Island, and transformation of the Central Post Office Building into the Moynihan railroad station.

167 *Always thinking ahead*: Marianna Koval, email to author, March 16, 2007.

167 *Although Rimmer*: Joanne Witty, interview with author, January 19, 2017.

169 *Besides enjoying*: Jonathan Kirschenfeld, interview with author, February 23, 2018.

169 *I sent Eagle Rubbish*: Christopher Sedita and Steven Sivak, emails to author, April 20, 21, 24, 2007.

169 *During this catch-up time*: Steven Crainer, emails to author, April 14, 2007.

170 *The Floating Pool Lady*: Robert D. McFadden, "East Coast Storm Breaks Rainfall Records," *New York Times*, April 16, 2007, https://www.nytimes.com/2007/04/16/nyregion/16storm.html.

170 *We were both*: Patricia O'Brien, "A Pool Comes to Brooklyn," unpublished manuscript, October 30, 2007.

170 *Patricia O'Brien*: Marianna Koval, email to author, April 14, 2007.

171 *According to Marianna*: Ibid.

171 *An attorney*: Neptune was party to the following agreements: a license agreement with the BB Park Corporation authorizing Neptune to temporarily moor or anchor the *Floating Pool Lady* in the seabed between Brooklyn Piers 4 and 5; a license agreement with the Brooklyn Bridge Park Conservancy granting "Neptune Permitted Persons" access to and use of the site; and a pool operations agreement with the Brooklyn Bridge Park Conservancy to act as pool administrator and with the American Leisure Activities of NYC to act as pool operator.

171 *Their answer*: Curtis Cravins, email to Marianna Koval, March 16, 2007. The DOS Coastal Zone Management office is committed to balancing competing land and water uses in the coastal zone.

172 *While Jonathan respected*: Jonathan Kirschenfeld, interview with author, February 23, 2018.

172 *As Rimmer described*: Jennifer Rimmer, interview with author, May 23, 2016, February 17, 2018.

172 *Observant Jewish*: George Rieder (chairman of the Boro Park Council), email to Joshua Laird, July 9, 2007.

173 *Although his reaction*: Jonathan Kirschenfeld, email to author, February 23, 2007.

173 *Rimmer needed*: Jennifer Rimmer, interview with author, February 17, 2018.

173 *With my having*: Jennifer Rimmer, conversation as recalled by author.

174 *Ten days later*: Asphalt Green, emails to author, April 8, 9, 2007.

174 *Twenty years*: James Sanders and Associates; Steve Kass and Susan Kronich, American Leisure Corporations; John Carel, Sidney Johnson, and Associates, February 1987. I was a member of the Parks Council Waterfront Committee.

174 *Hearing that*: Steve Kass, email to author, April 18, 2007.

175 *Pleased with*: Steven Crainer, email from author, April 13, 2007.

175 *Their assessment*: Karlee Darby, email to author, April 9, 2007.

176 *Mouth agape*: Lewis Carroll, *Through the Looking Glass* (New York: Avenel Books, 1983).

176 *Like the Bandersnatch*: Lewis Carroll, "Jabberwocky," in *The Random House Book of Poetry for Children* (New York: Random House, 1983); Poetry Foundation, accessed April 6, 2018, https://www.poetryfoundation.org/poems/42916/jabberwocky.

176 *We are a "vessel"*: Jennifer Rimmer and Richard Dorado, email from author, May 21, 2007.

176 *I asked Mal McLaren*: Author's email to Mal McLaren, May 21, 2007.

9. THE ORWELLIAN BUREAUCRACY

179 *The Orwellian Bureaucracy*: Title for this chapter taken from Atul Gawande, *The Checklist Manifesto: How to Get Things Right* (New York: Henry Holt, 2009), 75.

180 *Orange netting*: Description from photograph taken by Steven Sivak, June 1, 2007.

180 *Sivak would*: Steven Sivak, interview with author, April 2, 2018.

180 *Besides me obsessing*: Stephen Sondheim, *Finishing the Hat* (New York: Alfred A. Knopf, 2010), title page.

180-81 *The water depth*: Malcolm McLaren, interview with author, April 12, 2018.

181 *In 1915*: "Wikipedia: Demographic History of New York City," last modified April 9, 2020, https://en.wikipedia.org/wiki/Demographic_history_of_New_York_City.

183 *Trains were late*: William Neuman, "Some Subways Found Packed Past Capacity," *New York Times*, June 26, 2007, https://www.nytimes.com/2007/06/26/nyregion/26mta.html.

183 *The barges carrying*: Patricia O'Brien, "A Pool Comes to Brooklyn," unpublished manuscript, October 30, 2007, 11.

183 *On June 6*: Email from Peter Ladouceur to Shea Thorvaldsen, 9:29 a.m., June 6, 2007.

183 *Their questions*: Email from Peter Ladouceur to Shea Thorvaldsen, 11:57 a.m., June 6, 2007.

185 *He suggested*: Email from Kent Merrill to the Neptune team, May 24, 2007.

186 *"This barge"*: "Wikipedia: Science Barge," last modified February 18, 2020, https://en.wikipedia.org/wiki/Science_Barge; Caroline McCarthy, "New York Barges into Sustainable Urban Farming," CNET, May 7, 2007, https://www.cnet.com/news/new-york-barges-into-sustainable-urban-farming/.

186 *Also, even though*: Memorandum from Kent Merrill to author, "Floating Swimming Pool—USCG Meeting Summary," 2.

187 *As he described it*: Email from Kent Merrill to author, June 9, 2007.

187 *His closer*: Email from Kent Merrill to author, June 11, 2007.

187 *As soon as Ahern's*: However, Marianna did secure $1,500 from another photo shoot.

188 *If memory*: In my stints at the Parks Department and the EDC, Eric and I had worked together on finding berthing sites for Op Sail. In 1996, at the Alliance for Downtown NY, when the Coast Guard left Governors Island, I had tried (unsuccessfully) to convince Eric to also give up a building at the tip of Battery Park that blocked the view from the park to the harbor.

188 *Once he had*: Email from Eric Bernholz to author, June 12, 2007.

189 *Then I concluded*: Letter from author to Eric Bernholz, June 12, 2007.

189 *Since I was*: Email from Eric Bernholz to author, May 15, 2018.

189 *Kent, who had*: Email from Kent Merrill to author, May 13, 2018.

189 *Since Neptune's deficit*: Email from Eric Bernholz to author, June 13, 2007.

189 *At 2:00 p.m.*: Email from Eric Bernholz to author, June 13, 2007.

190 *Thankfully, Steve*: DEC v. Brooklyn Bridge Park Dev.: Brooklyn Bridge Park Cons., The Neptune Foundation Corporation. DEC File No. R-2-20070516-213. Order on Consent. Draft: For settlement purposes only.

190 *But a caveat*: Emails to Steven Crainer from author, May 31 and June 4, 2007; email from Jennifer Coghlan to author, June 6, 2007.

191 *"The use of the floating"*: Email from Udo Drescher to Jennifer Rimmer, Jennifer Coghlan, Richard Dorado, and Ann L. Buttenwieser, June 14, 2007.

191 *Though unstated*: Author's diary, June 14, 2007; email to Neptune board from author, June 14, 2007.

192 *Bob Douglass*: President and chief operating officer of the Park Corporation's parent body, the ESDC.

192 *Rimmer thanked*: Email from Jennifer Rimmer to author, June 16, 2007.

192 *Marianna Koval*: According to Marianna Koval, these capital funds (member items) had been given to ESDC by city council members. Marianna was able to convince ESDC to swap these out for expense monies to pay for the pool operations and all related beach expenses. It was a first, having never been done before. Marianna Koval, interview with author, ca. June 15, 2007.

193 *He did add*: Email from Pat Foye to Carl Weisbrod, June 16, 2007; email from author to Carl Weisbrod, June 18, 2007.

195 *It was quiet*: Among those on the line were Nancy Webster from the BB Park Conservancy and Nazim Nasroodin from ESDC.

195 *This verbally*: As described in Eliot Brown, "Meet Avi Schick: New York's New Steamroller," *Observer*, March 25, 2008,

http://observer.com/2008/03/meet-avi-schick-new-yorks-new-steamroller/2018.

195 *A lifelong*: Robin Finn, "From Voice of the Bottle Bill to Keeper of the Green," *New York Times*, May 4, 2007, https://www.nytimes.com/2007/10/01/nyregion/01greenteam.html; Anthony DePalma, "Gov. Spitzer Picks Activists to Make State a Bit Greener," *New York Times*, October 1, 2007, https://www.nytimes.com/2007/10/01/nyregion/01greenteam.html.

195 *The call ended*: Notes in author's diary, June 20, 2007.

196 *Jonathan liked*: Jonathan Kirschenfeld, interview with author, February 23, 2018.

196 *"Since we will"*: Author's email to Jennifer Rimmer, June 21, 2007.

197 *"Terrific!" I replied*: Author's email to Jennifer Rimmer, June 24, 2007.

197 *At 3:24 p.m.*: Jennifer Rimmer, email to author, June 25, 2007.

197 *At 10:00 p.m.*: Jennifer Rimmer, emails to author, June 26, 2007.

198 *Marianna too*: Parts of this description are taken from O'Brien, "Pool," 1–2.

198 *"Please be advised"*: Email from Jennifer Rimmer to Marianna Koval, June 27, 2007; letter from Anita Laremont to author, June 27, 2007.

198 *The civil penalty*: Udo Drescher, email to Steven Crainer, June 28, 2007; DEC v. The Neptune Foundation DEC File No. R2-20070516-213 Order on Consent, 3.

199 *Two days later*: Ethan Wilensky-Lanford, "Brooklyn, Your New Floating Swimming Pool Is Almost Ready Now," *New York Times*, June 30, 2007.

200 *The land-based*: John Keenan, email to Steven Crainer, June 28, 2007; author's email to Steven Crainer and John Keenan, June 28, 2007.

201 *Her job now*: Conversation with Rose Keville as recalled by author, ca. March 2017.

202 *On hearing this*: Author's email to Steven Crainer, June 29, 2007.

203 *The go-to person*: This section is derived from Mark Bernstein, interview with author, March 3, 2008.

203 *The Governors Island Preservation and Education Corporation*: Later renamed Governors Island Trust.

203 *Mark was both*: Bernstein interview, March 3, 2008.

204 *For Mark, the company*: Ibid.

204 *Days before*: "The Floating Pool at Brooklyn Bridge Park Beach Set to Make First Splash This Summer," *Empire State News*, July 5, 2007; Erin Durkin, "Floating Pool to Open on East River," *New York Sun*, June 27, 2007, https://www.nysun.com/new-york/floating-public-pool-to-open-on-east-river/57360; Michael Kane, "Hope Floats," *New York Post*, June 30, 2007, https://nypost.com/2007/06/30/hope-floats-3/; Wilensky-Lanford, "Brooklyn."

204 *However, not until*: Jonathan Kirschenfeld, interview with author, February 23, 2018.

205 *Thanks to Jonathan*: Maximum capacity for the entire facility is 230.

10. THE BIG JUMP

207 *Jonathan, in one*: Jonathan Kirschenfeld, interview with author, February 23, 2018.

208 *The Lady's*: Jonathan Kirschenfeld speaking to an interviewer in *Just Add Water* and interview with author; Patricia O'Brien, "A Pool Comes to Brooklyn," unpublished manuscript, October 30, 2007, 6.

208 *A broad smile*: Captured by videographer in *Just Add Water*.

209 *This evening*: Among the elected officials were the speaker and local representatives of the city council, a local state senator, and a local congresswoman. Pat Foye represented the ESDC. Avi Schick, Foye's superior, came to enjoy his successful intervention and was very pleased with the result.

209 *He wanted to be*: My description of swimming in a pool on top of the East River. Conversation with David Bromwich as recalled by author, May 23, 2018.

209 *Marianna tucked*: Lyn Parker, interview with author, May 20, 2016.

209 *Taking a deep breath*: O'Brien, "Pool," 16.

210 *That evening, 1010 WINS*: Email from Rubina Shafi to Jonathan Kirschenfeld and Ann L. Buttenwieser, July 4, 2007. In the days to come, with a modicum of disbelief, I would cry out excitedly as the *Floating Pool Lady* repeatedly lighted taxi TV screens.

210 *Dozens of happy*: Description of this event in an email to Steven Crainer from author, July 10, 2007.

210 *In July*: These interviews were orchestrated by several young women at Sharp Communications, the PR firm that once again provided Neptune with reduced-rate services.

211 *However, from there*: Mark Page, "Financial Plan Fiscal Years 2008–2012," January 24, 2008, https://www1.nyc.gov/assets /omb/downloads/pdf/tech1_08.pdf.

211 *The Domino sugar*: Mark Santora, "New York's Next Frontier: The Waterfront," *New York Times*, November 5, 2010, https://www.nytimes.com/2010/11/07/realestate/07cov.html.

211 *A blueprint*: Office of New York Mayor, "Mayor Bloomberg Opens WNYC Transmitter Park, New Waterfront Green Space in Greenpoint," September 10, 2012, https://www1.nyc.gov/office-of-the-mayor/news/320-12/mayor-bloomberg-opens-wnyc-transmitter-park-new-waterfront-green-space-greenpoint.

211 *In New York City's case*: Department of City Planning, City of New York, *VISION 2020*, March 2011, 144.

212 *Much to the distress*: Mona Bregman, "How the Floating Pool Lady Lifted My Summer Doldrums," *Brooklyn Heights Press and Cobble Hill News*, August 9, 2007.

212 *The team from Neptune*: Bill de Blasio, a fan, was elected mayor of New York City in 2013.

214 *Then I turned*: Since its opening, the facility and its architects have received many awards. Among them are the 2007 Waterfront Center Honor Award; 2007 Cooper-Hewitt National Design Awards: Runner-Up, People's Design Award; NYC Department of Parks Best Pool for 2008; and the Municipal Art Society of New York Masterwork Award: Best Neighborhood Catalyst 2008.

11. THE *LADY* MOVES TO THE BRONX

217 *Two days later*: John Natoli, email to author, May 29, 2008.

218 *On the other hand*: Sergey Kadinsky, "Barretto Point Park, Bronx," *Hidden Waters* (blog), August 21, 2017, https://hiddenwatersblog. wordpress.com/2017/08/21/barretto/; "NYC Parks, Barretto Point Park," Highlights, NYC Parks, accessed February 17, 2020, https:// www.nycgovparks.org/parks/X307/highlights/19772.

218 *Shortly before June*: Jama Adams, email to the Parks Department pool team and Ann L. Buttenwieser, June 16, 2008.

218 *Nine months after*: New York City Department of City Planning, "NYC Department of City Planning's Community District Pro-files: Bronx Community District 2," Community District Profiles, accessed February 20, 2020, https://communityprofiles.plan-ning.nyc.gov/bronx/2.

218 *Also, amid the stink*: New York City Health, "Community Health Profiles, Hunts Point and Longwood," 2018, NYC Gov. Assets, https://www1./doh/downloads/pdf/data/2018chp-bx2.pdf.

219 *Two teenage girls*: "A Nonprofit Community Development Corpo-ration Dedicated to Youth Development and the Cultural and Economic Revitalization of the Hunts Point Section of the South Bronx," *The Point*, accessed February 15, 2020, https://thepoint.org/.

220 *Unable to reach me*: My memory of the conversation, supported by an email from Stephen Kass to Carl Weisbrod and me (September 5, 2007) stating: "I had occasion to speak with Pete Grannis yes-terday. . . . I mentioned to him that we were working with you on the pool and that Neptune would be applying for a DEC permit for next summer's location. Pete seemed receptive and expected to work closely with Adrian Benepe on this."

220 *Seated at the head*: The park's pool team members who attended were John Natoli, Steve DesNoyer, Joshua Laird, Jane Rudolf, and environmental consultant Fred Jacobs.

220 *Next came Mattei*: Suzanne Mattei was the director of the NYC field office of the Sierra Club when the barge arrived in New York.

221 *The two commissioners*: As recalled by the author.

221 *In the fall*: In 2008 Fred Jacobs, PhD, was senior vice president at AKRF, Inc.

221 *Perhaps, I thought*: Fish sampling revealed that fish preferred the edge habitat of the physical structure and transitional shade created by the floating barge. Forage-size fish may use the floating barge as a daytime refuge. City Environmental Quality Review, Environmental Assessment Statement (EAS) Short Form, Attachment 4 Natural Resources—Supplemental Information, Normandeau Associates, Inc., *A Study of Aquatic Habitat Natural Resources Impacts of the Floating Pool Lady Barge at Barretto Point Park*, January 15, 2016, rev. March 25, 2016, April 13, 2016, xii.

222 *At some point*: David Gonzalez, "Neighborhood without a Swimming Pool Gets an Alternative to the Bronx River," *New York Times*, June 14, 2008, https://www.nytimes.com/2008/06/14 /nyregion/14pool.html.

222 *Fifty-one pools*: Editorial, "Swim Lessons for All," *New York Times*, August 4, 2019, https://www.nytimes.com/2019/08/03/opinion /sunday/swim-lessons-new-york.html.

222 *With warming*: Tim Donnelly, "Swimming in the East River Could Happen Sooner Than You Think," *Curbed*, February 3, 2020, 4, https://ny.curbed.com/2020/2/3/21120114/east-river-swimming- two-trees-.

223 *Stephen A. Watts III*: New York State Department of Environmental Conservation, Permit No. 2-6007-00741/00009, Permit under the New York State Department of Environmental Conservation Law, Issued to NYC Department of Parks and Recreation, May 21, 2018, 1.

EPILOGUE

229 *One of the options*: The federal government shut down this study on February 26, 2011.

229 *In addition*: Anne Barnard, "The $119 Billion Sea Wall That Could Defend New York . . . or Not," *New York Times*, January 17, 2020, https://www.nytimes.com/2020/01/17/nyregion/sea-wall-nyc. html.

229 *Demolition of existing*: Joanne Witty and Henrik Krogius, *Brooklyn Bridge Park: A Dying Waterfront Transformed* (New York: Empire State Editions / Fordham University Press, 2016), 127, 214–15.

229 *This number was higher*: "VNY Weather Rainfall Summary," CNYWeather.com, accessed February 19, 2020, http://www.cnyweather.com/wxrainsummary.php; pool attendance supplied to me annually by Lawrence Scoones, New York City Chief of Operations, Bronx.

230 *Within a year*: Christopher Rizzo, email to author, July 10, 2008.

230 *The agency's first*: David N. Dinkins, Mayor, City of New York, and Richard L. Schaffer, Director Department of City Planning, *New York City Comprehensive Waterfront Plan: Reclaiming the City's Edge* (Gov. Assets Planning, Summer 1992), https://www1.nyc.gov/assets/planning/download/pdf/about/publications/cwp.pdf.

230 *However, the following*: Ibid., 104.

230 *The treatment plant*: "Wikipedia: Newtown Creek Wastewater Treatment Plant," last modified May 22, 2020, https://en.wikipedia.org/wiki/Newtown_Creek_Wastewater_Treatment_Plant.

231 *In 2019*: Distance from Carnes McKinny Apartments Bronx to floating pool calculated via Google Maps.

231 *Joshua suggested*: Joshua Laird, email to author, March 16, 2009.

232 *The estimated cost*: Pool II Presentation Board and VJ Associates, "Order of Magnitude Estimate, Brooklyn Bridge Park—Pool II," August 19, 2016, http://kirscharch.com/projects/ recreation /floatingpool2/.

233 *When I asked*: Archie Coates, phone conversation as recalled by author, October 15, 2018.

233 *Although + POOL's*: A kiddie pool, sports pool, lap pool, and lounge would open completely into a 9,000 sq. ft. pool for play. See https://www.pluspool.org/pool/.

234 *No city or EDC*: New York City Economic Development Corporation, "East River Swim Facility Request for Expressions of Interest," September 18, 2019, https://a856-cityrecord.nyc.gov /RequestDetail/20190911020; https://pluspool.org/timeline /nycedc-releases-request-for-self-filtering-swim-facility/.

234 *The only person*: I am an original "Friend of Breakwater."

234 *When it happens*: Beau D'Arcy, emails to author, October 17, 18, 2018.

234 *My Hoboken friend*: Michael Krieger, email to author, June 19, 2019.

235 *The controversy involved*: "What's Going On with the Union Dry Dock in Hoboken? An Update + Rally Info," March 7, 2019, https://www.hobokengirl.com/union-dry-dock-ron-hine update-2019/.

235 *According to Michael*: Michael Krieger, email to author, June 19, 2019.

Selected Bibliography

The books I consulted in my research and referenced in the notes are listed below. Information on periodicals, websites, and government reports can be found in the notes.

Alexiou Sparberg, Alice. *Jane Jacobs: Urban Visionary.* New Brunswick: Rutgers University Press, 2006.

Ballon, Hillary, and Kenneth T. Jackson, eds. *Robert Moses and the Modern City: The Transformation of New York.* New York: W. W. Norton, 2007.

Burnstein, Daniel Eli. *Next to Godliness: Confronting Dirt and Despair in the Progressive Era.* Urbana: University of Illinois Press, 2006.

Buttenwieser, Ann L. *Governors Island: The Jewel of New York Harbor.* Syracuse: Syracuse University Press, 2009.

——. *Manhattan Water-Bound.* New York University Press, 1987. (Reissued by Syracuse University Press, 1999.)

Buzbee, William W. *Fighting Westway: Environmental Law, Citizen Activism, and the Regulatory War That Transformed New York City.* Ithaca: Cornell University Press, 2014.

Deforest, Robert W., and Lawrence Veiller, eds. *The Tenement House Problem*. Vols. 1 and 2. New York: Arno Press, 1970.

Duffy, John. *The Sanitarians: A History of American Public Health*. Champaign, IL: Illini Books, 1992.

Eldridge, Niles, and Sidney Horenstein. *Concrete Jungle: New York City and Our Last Best Hope for a Sustainable Future*. Oakland: University of California Press, 2014.

Flint, Anthony. *Wrestling with Moses: How Jane Jacobs Took on New York's Master Builder and Transformed the American City*. New York: Random House, 2011.

Grafton, John. *New York in the Nineteenth Century*. New York: Dover, 1877.

Griscom, John H., *The Sanitary Condition of the Laboring Population of New York with Suggestions for Its Improvement*. New York: Harper & Brothers, 1845.

Jacobs, Jane. *The Death and Life of Great American Cities*. New York: Vintage Books, 1961.

Koolhaas, Rem. *delirious new york*. New York: Monacelli Press, 1994.

Kurlansky, Mark. *The Big Oyster History on the Half Shell*. New York: Random House, 2006.

Riis, Jacob A. *The Battle with the Slum*. New York: Macmillan, 1902.

——. *How the Other Half Lives: Studies among the Tenements of New York*. New York: Dover, 1901.

Rosenwaike, Ira. *Population History of New York City*. Syracuse: Syracuse University Press, 1972.

Seccombe, Shelley. *Lost Waterfront: The Decline and Rebirth of Manhattan's Western Shore*. New York: Fordham University Press, 2007.

Thornton Williams, Marilyn. *Washing "the Great Unwashed": Public Baths in Urban America, 1840–1920*. Columbus: Ohio State University Press, 1991.

Webster, Nancy, and David Shirley. *A History of Brooklyn Bridge Park: How a Community Reclaimed and Transformed New York City's Waterfront*. New York: Columbia University Press, 2016.

Wiltze, Jeff. *Contested Waters: A Social History of Swimming Pools in America*. Chapel Hill: University of North Carolina Press, 2007.

Witty, Joanne, and Henrik Krogius. *Brooklyn Bridge Park: A Dying Waterfront Transformed*. New York: Empire State Editions / Fordham University Press, 2016.

Ziegler, Christine A. *Immigrants in Hoboken: One Way Ticket, 1845–1985*. Charleston: The History Press, 2011.

Key to map 2,
the floating
baths,
page 22

1	E 5th St	31	W 79th St
2	Stanton St	32	W 61st St
3	Grand St	33	W 51st St
4	Corlears Hook	34	W 50th St
5	Jackson St	35	W 46th St
6	Gouverneur St	36	W 45th St
7	Jefferson St	37	W 35th St
8	Pier 36 between Jefferson St & Rutgers St	38	Little W 12th St
9	Pier 33 between Rutgers St & Pike St	39	Gansevoort St
10	Pike St	40	Horatio St
11	Market St	41	Bethune St
12	Rutgers St	42	Charles St
13	E 31st St	43	Morton St
14	E 37th St	44	Vestry St
15	E 50th St	45	Laight St
16	E 51st St	46	Duane St.
17	E 61st St	47	The Battery
18	E 62nd St	48	The Battery
19	E 78th St	49	W 13th St (too shallow, moved to Charles St, between W 10th St & W 11th St)
20	E 80th St		
21	E 86th St	50	W 134th St
22	E 90th St	51	W 132nd St
23	E 91st St	52	W 130th St
24	E 94th St	53	W129th St
25	E 96th St	54	W 99th St
26	W 97th St	55	W 29th St
27	W 96th St	56	W 27th St
28	W 90th St	57	W 20th St
29	W 82nd St	58	W 12th St
30	W 80th St		

Index

Note: The acronym *FPL* used here refers to the *Floating Pool Lady*.
Page numbers in italics refer to maps.

hurricanes (continued)
Sandy, 228–29

insurance
and Brooklyn Bridge Park Corporation, 196–203
on *C500*, 119
and Empire State Development Corporation, 134–38, 140–41, 149, 198–204, 261n134
for Sciame Construction Company work, 149, 152
uncertainty regarding, 107
See also Bernstein, Mark; Keenan, John

Jackson, Kenneth, 24
Jacobs, Jane, 8–10, 49
See also reform movements
Jonathan Kirschenfeld Associates. *See* Kirschenfeld, Jonathan
Just Add Water **(video),** 156, 264n155

Kass, Stephen, 220–21
Kass, Steve. *See* American Leisure Corporation
Kavanagh, Liam, 111–12
See also Department of Parks and Recreation
Keenan, John, 107–8, 137, 200
See also insurance
Keville, Rose, 201–3
See also Brooklyn Bridge Park Corporation: and insurance; Empire State Development Corporation: and insurance
Kirschenfeld, Jonathan, 251n67
and *FPL* classification, 186–87
and *FPL* design, 66–70, 84, 92–93
and *FPL* name, 133
in *New York Times* article photo, 199
and *Pool II*, 231–32
Sciame Construction, as liaison with, 148
See also Floating Pool Lady: design
Koch, Edward, 158
and "opening" of waterfront, 55
and private development, 58–59, 158
Koval, Marianna
and beach at Brooklyn Bridge Park, 170–72, 187
and Brooklyn Bridge Park as potential *FPL* site, 100–101, 167–68
and *FPL* operations, 171–72, 174, 198–99, 269n193
and *FPL* site location, 170
See also Brooklyn Bridge Park Coalition; Brooklyn Bridge Park Conservancy
Krieger, L. Michael, 66, 234–35
as Hoboken Special Waterfront Counsel, 77–79, 86, 90–91
at Port Authority, 74–75
See also Hoboken: FPL site proposal

Laird, Joshua, 72, 96, 99, 124, 160–65, 231